THE OXFORD BOOK OF BIRDS

THE OXFORD BOOK OF BIRDS

Illustrations by
DONALD WATSON

Text by
BRUCE CAMPBELL

OXFORD UNIVERSITY PRESS

Oxford University Press, Ely House, London W.1

GLASGOW NEW YORK TORONTO MELBOURNE WELLINGTON
CAPE TOWN IBADAN NAIROBI DAR ES SALAAM LUSAKA ADDIS ABABA
DELHI BOMBAY CALCUTTA MADRAS KARACHI LAHORE DACCA
KUALA LUMPUR SINGAPORE HONG KONG TOKYO

Printed in Great Britain by Jesse Broad Limited, Altrincham, Cheshire

Contents

ACKNOWLEDGEMENTS

No book on the birds of the British Isles can be written without acknow-
ledgement to the great *Handbook of British Birds* which, although its fifth
and last volume appeared 23 years ago, is still the standard reference book
for description and field characters. The classification of birds has, however, changed since it was published, and we have in the main followed the
arrangement and scientific names used in the journal *British Birds*.

We wish also to acknowledge the most generous help of Dr. A. R.
Waterston and the staff of the Natural History Department of the Royal
Scottish Museum in lending the artist many skins to assist him in painting
the plates: and we appreciate the skill and perseverance of the plate-makers
in producing results so strikingly like the originals.

The booklist on p. 204 is partly based on that compiled for the British
Council by Dr. C. M. Perrins, to whom we tender our thanks; details of
the British bird observatories (p. 203) were kindly supplied by the British
Trust for Ornithology, and the map was based on one in *Instructions to
Young Ornithologists, III*, by Robert Spencer, published by the Museum
Press.

INTRODUCTION

This is a companion book to *The Oxford Books of Wild Flowers* and *Garden Flowers*. Its purpose is to show readers of any age the great range of bird life to be found in the British Isles, to help them to recognize more and more of the birds they can see both in town and country, and, having recognized them, to learn more about them by watching how they behave and listening to their songs and calls.

This book describes every bird which has ever been authentically recorded in the British Isles, even if only once or twice. Consequently, most of the birds of western Europe are included in the text and often in the illustrations too, and also the American visitors whose increase in recent years has been so remarkable. All resident British birds, regular winter and summer visitors, and passage migrants are not only described but are illustrated in the plate opposite the relevant text, which covers their distribution, usual habitats, general habits, and details of nesting and eggs if they breed regularly in Britain. About 320 different species are illustrated, and wherever the sexes differ, both male and female are shown. Juvenile or immature plumages and differences in summer and winter plumages are also often shown.

The arrangement of the book follows in general the accepted scientific order, with occasional minor diversions for the sake of putting together on one page birds which need to be compared when making an identification. The pictures of the birds are based on sketches made in the field and are set in appropriate habitat: moorland birds in a moorland setting; sea birds with a background of sea and sea cliffs; waders on the mud flats which they visit in autumn; woodpeckers with their nest-holes in trees; swallows and martins on telegraph wires and eaves of houses; larks and pipits on grassland. The result is that each plate makes in itself an attractive picture.

The classification and nomenclature used in this book differ a good deal from those adopted by the British Ornithologists' Union in *The Status of Birds in Great Britain and Ireland*, published in 1971. This list rejects seven species which were included in the original edition of the *Oxford Book of Birds*, but adds twenty-three more, giving a total of 468 species recognised in publications up to October 1971; the desert warbler (*Sylvia nana*), veery (*Hylocichla fuscescens*), hooded warbler (*Wilfonia citrina*) and scarlet tanager (*see* p. 192) were still under consideration at that date.

We hope that this book may help to build up interest in the wonderful bird life of Britain, not only among those already knowledgeable but also among people to whom bird-watching is a new pursuit. The great number of large pictures and the easy arrangement of the book should help the beginner. A continuing interest in birds must lead to concern for their future at a time when it is threatened by many modern developments, including especially the use of dangerous chemicals on land and in the water. Nor are the man with the gun and the egg-collector figures only of the past. If we enjoy watching and studying birds, it is our duty also to protect them.

B.C.

D.W.

A CLASSIFICATION OF BRITISH BIRDS

Birds belong to the zoological class AVES. Within the class the main divisions are ORDERS, FAMILIES, GENERA (GENUS), and SPECIES. The individual members of a species normally breed with each other and with no other species. Each species has a *generic* and a *specific* name. For example, the blackbird is *Turdus merula*. The genus *Turdus* belongs to the family *Turdidae* (thrushes) in the order *Passeriformes* (perching birds). Modern classification of birds begins with the most primitive orders and ends with the most highly evolved. The classification which follows gives the orders and families in which the 468 species of British birds are arranged, the figure in brackets after the family name being the number of British species recognised up to 1971. A species is regarded as 'British' if it has occurred, without human aid, at least once, but ten species, originally introduced by man, are so well-established in the wild state that they are also accepted. The page references are to the main text.

Orders	Families
GAVIIFORMES	*Gaviidae* (divers) (4), p. 1
PODICIPITIFORMES	*Podicipitidae* (grebes) (6), pp. 2–5
PROCELLARII-FORMES	*Diomedeidae* (albatrosses) (1), p. 6
	Procellariidae (petrels, shearwaters) (13), pp. 6–9
PELECANIFORMES	*Fregatidae* (frigate birds) (1), p. 10
	Sulidae (gannets) (1), pp. 10–11
	Phalacrocoracidae (cormorants) (2), pp. 10–11
ARDEIFORMES	*Ardeidae* (herons, bitterns) (10), pp. 12–15
	Ciconiidae (storks) (2), pp. 14–15
	Plataleidae (spoonbills, ibises) (2), pp. 12–15
ANSERIFORMES	*Anatidae* (ducks, geese, swans) (48), pp. 16–35
FALCONIFORMES	*Aegypiidae* (vultures) (2), p. 36
	Falconidae (other birds of prey) (22), pp. 36–49
GALLIFORMES	*Tetraonidae* (grouse) (4), pp. 50–53
	Phasianidae (other game birds) (6), pp. 54–57
RALLIFORMES	*Balearicidae* (cranes) (1), pp. 14–15
	Rallidae (rails, coots, gallinules) (9), pp. 56–59
	Otididae (bustards) (3), pp. 82–83
CHARADRIIFORMES	*Haematopidae* (oystercatchers) (1), pp. 60–61
	Charadriidae (plovers, turnstones) (12), pp. 60–65, 78–79
	Scolopacidae (typical waders) (41), pp. 66–79
	Phalaropodidae (phalaropes) (3), pp. 78–79
	Recurvirostridae (avocets, stilts) (2), pp. 80–81
	Glareolidae (pratincoles, coursers) (2), pp. 80–83
	Burhinidae (stone curlews) (1), pp. 82–83
	Stercorariidae (skuas) (4), pp. 84–85
	Laridae (gulls, terns) (31), pp. 86–99
	Alcidae (auks) (7, one extinct), pp. 100–101
COLUMBIFORMES	*Columbidae* (pigeons, doves) (6), pp. 102–105
	Pteroclidae (sand grouse) (1), pp. 104–105
STRIGIFORMES	*Strigidae* (owls) (10), pp. 106–111
CORACIIFORMES	*Alcedinidae* (kingfishers) (1), pp. 112–113

Orders	Families
	Meropidae (bee-eaters) (2), pp. 112–113
	Coraciidae (rollers) (1), pp. 112–113
	Upupidae (hoopoes) (1), pp. 112–113
PICIFORMES	*Picidae* (woodpeckers, wrynecks) (4), pp. 114–117
CUCULIFORMES	*Cuculidae* (cuckoos) (4), pp. 116–117
CAPRIMULGI-FORMES	*Caprimulgidae* (nightjars) (4), pp. 118–119
APODIFORMES	*Apodidae* (swifts) (4), pp. 118–119
PASSERIFORMES	*Hirundinidae* (swallows, martins) (4), pp. 120–121
	Alaudidae (larks) (9), pp. 122–123
	Corvidae (crows) (8), pp. 124–127
	Paridae (titmice) (9), pp. 128–131
	Sittidae (nuthatches) (2), pp. 132–133
	Certhiidae (treecreepers) (2), pp. 132–133
	Troglodytidae (wrens) (1), pp. 134–135
	Cinclidae (dippers) (1), pp. 134–135
	Mimidae (mocking birds, thrashers) (1), p. 192
	Turdidae (thrushes) (30), pp. 136–145
	Prunellidae (accentors) (2), pp. 144–145
	Sylviidae (warblers) (41), pp. 146–159
	Regulidae (kinglets) (2), pp. 158–159
	Muscicapidae (flycatchers) (4), pp. 160–161
	Motacillidae (pipits, wagtails) (12), pp. 162–169
	Laniidae (shrikes) (4), pp. 170–171
	Oriolidae (orioles) (1), pp. 172–173
	Sturnidae (starlings) (2), pp. 172–173
	Bombycillidae (waxwings) (1), pp. 174–175
	Vireonidae (vireos) (1), pp. 192–193
	Parulidae (New World warblers) (8), pp. 192–193
	Icteridae (New World orioles, blackbirds, etc.) (2), pp. 192–193
	Thraupidae (tanagers) (1), pp. 192–193
	Fringillidae (finches, buntings) (38), pp. 174–191
	Passeridae (sparrows) (3), pp. 190–191

1 species of ornamental duck (p. 20) and 4 of game birds (pp. 54–56) are also described.

AN INTRODUCTION TO THE MAIN ORDERS
AND FAMILIES OF BRITISH BIRDS

THE DIVERS (*Gaviiformes*) are perhaps the most primitive group of European birds. Under water they use their feet to propel their streamlined bodies after fish; the front three toes are webbed together, and their legs are placed so far back that they cannot walk properly. They have short tails, and their rather small wings are also set far back, but they fly well, with necks stretched and heads held low. Male and female divers look alike, but all have completely different summer and winter plumages. They nest very close to freshwater lakes or pools, laying two dark brown eggs in an open nest, from which they slide into the water when disturbed. In winter divers go to sea, appearing offshore singly or in small parties. (*See* p. 1)

THE GREBES (*Podicipitiformes*) are a world-wide order of diving birds, found on both fresh and salt water and varying considerably in size. They have softer plumage than divers have, and their front toes are lobed, not webbed. They are reluctant to take wing, though they can fly well, and the smaller kinds tend to haunt thick cover. The sexes look alike and make a complete change of plumage in autumn. They build floating nests moored to water plants or branches, and lay chalky white eggs which soon become stained from being covered when the sitting bird leaves the nest. The young have striped heads. In winter, most grebes go to sea and are solitary. (*See* pp. 2–5)

The order *Procellariiformes* (tube-nosed birds) includes PETRELS, FULMARS, SHEARWATERS, and the ALBATROSSES of the southern oceans. These ocean-going birds are distinguished by having nostrils in tubes along the hooked upper mandible of the bill. They do not normally dive but pick their food — plankton, small fish, offal — from the surface, though shearwaters are an exception. Their front toes are webbed, and the back toe is either very small or absent. Most petrels cannot walk well but they are masters of flight, either the albatross-like gliding of the fulmar or the bat-like flitting of the small petrels. The plumage is alike for both sexes and does not change much during the year. Except when breeding, they are comparatively quiet birds. (*See* pp. 6–9)

GANNETS, CORMORANTS, and FRIGATE BIRDS are included with the pelicans in the order *Pelecaniformes*. None of them have an enlarged bill pouch, but they can stretch their gullets widely when swallowing fish or feeding their young. They are all big sea-birds though some live on or visit fresh water. Gannets and cormorants are found all over the world. They have webbed feet and strong legs, and can stand up and walk quite well if necessary. Gannets fly superbly and dive from a height after their principal food, fish; but cormorants appear clumsier and dive from the surface, usually leaping out to get impetus. They all lay chalky white eggs in open nests on cliff ledges, rocky islands, or trees, and their young take a long time to fledge. (*See* pp. 10–11)

The HERONS and their relations (*Ardeidae*) are mostly large, lanky birds able to walk in deep water and hunt fish and frogs by stalking them or by standing still and stabbing them. They also hunt small animals on land. They have broad wings, long necks and bills, light-coloured eyes, and fine plumes on head and neck in the breeding season. Herons and egrets tend to be black, grey, and white, while bitterns are brown to match their surroundings. They have a powerful flapping flight, head and neck tucked in, legs stretched out beyond the tail, and they also soar in suitable air currents. At rest they stand upright with necks hunched, unless on the watch. Most of them are more active in the evening or at night than by day. Herons and egrets breed in colonies, but bitterns are solitary when nesting. They all build rather flat nests and lay about five blue, brown, or white eggs. They do not usually migrate but may disperse after the breeding season. SPOONBILLS and IBISES (*Plataleidae*) have specialised bills for probing in mud. STORKS (*Ciconiidae*) are a diurnal (day-living) family in the same order. Flamingoes (*Phoenicopteriformes*) bridge the gap between heron-like birds and duck-like birds. (*See* pp. 10–15)

All the members of the *Anatidae*, the DUCK family, have broad, rather soft, skin-covered bills with fine toothed edges and a 'nail' at the blunt tip, and large broad tongues. The three front toes are webbed, and the hind toe is raised off the ground. They have stout bodies, with powerful breast muscles to work the pointed wings, which they flap rapidly in flight, gliding only to land (p. 198). They mostly nest on the ground, lay large clutches of whitish eggs, and line the nest with down from the female's breast. The young, covered with camouflaging down, leave the nest at once and feed themselves. During the summer the adults go into heavy moult, losing their flight feathers, after which most European species migrate in parties or flocks to winter quarters.

There are many differences within the family. SWANS trumpet or are silent, GEESE honk and gabble, DUCKS quack and whistle. Swans, geese, and shelducks have more or less the same male and female plumage, and the male stays near the nest and helps look after the young. The plumage of male ducks (drakes), on the other hand, is usually colourful in contrast to their brown females, and the drakes have spectacular displays; but they take little interest in the nest and usually none in the brood. Ducks are divided into 'dabblers' which feed from the surface or graze, as geese do, and 'divers' which may live on fresh or salt water. The 'sawbills' have rather narrow bills with sawtooth edges for catching very slippery fish. (*See* pp. 16–35, 198–199)

BIRDS OF PREY (*Falconiformes*) have hooked bills and curved talons (claws) specially adapted to a diet of meat. They are mostly brown or grey in plumage, mottled or barred with black and white. Some, such as the falcons, make no nests; others, such as the hawks, build large clumsy nests. They all lay round eggs, usually white or white marked with red, at intervals of a day or more; the helpless young take a long time to fledge. Many birds of prey migrate, following a migrating food supply of small birds or large insects; but some of them are resident when adult, and some pair for life, seldom leaving the area of their nesting place or eyrie. They have various hunting methods: the lightning dive of the falcon, the swift chase of the sparrowhawk, the methodical quartering (searching) of the harriers, the quiet watch and sudden pounce or dive of buzzard or osprey. When plucking their prey, they stand over it with wings half raised, continually looking up between pecks. The swift hunters tend to have small males and larger females, with some plumage differences between them, but the biggest species are more or less alike in size and appearance. Most of them take several years to mature. Birds of prey show a curious tenderness to their young, tearing off strips of meat and offering them in turn. The young often fight amongst themselves, and the stronger ones may kill and eat the weaker. Birds of prey throw up pellets containing inedible hair, feathers, and bones. (*See* pp. 36–49)

There are two families of GAME BIRDS (*Galliformes*) in Europe and·Britain: the grouse, and the pheasants, partridges, and quail — domestic poultry, which are derived from Asiatic jungle fowl, belong to the second group, and turkeys form another family. All are stout-bodied, rather round-winged birds, and have thick scaly or feathered legs with four toes, and strong, slightly hooked beaks. Many have wattles (bare areas of pimply skin) on their faces, extensive and brightly-coloured on some males. In some species the females are drab but the males·have distinctive and elaborate adornments of the head and tail; in other species the sexes are more or less alike.

Game birds either stand up prominently or crouch close to the ground; they often walk or run in preference to flying. They take wing noisily, and their powers of flight vary enormously. Their rather 'mechanical' calls, uttered often from cover, have great carrying power. Their food is mainly vegetable: tender shoots and seeds, but some eat insects as well. Display by males of the bright plumage type is most spectacular (*see* Blackcock) and may be accompanied by remarkable 'songs'; but the males take hardly any part in caring for the young and often have several mates. Males of the duller plumage type help the female. Game-birds lay large clutches of whitish or mottled, often rather pointed eggs. The young, which have beautifully patterned down, are active almost at once, feed themselves, and fly relatively quicker than other British birds. Some species stay in coveys (family parties), which later join into packs (*see* pp. 50–57).

The RAILS (*Rallidae*) are slim, long-legged, long-toed, medium-sized or small birds, with short tails and rather rounded wings. They usually live in thick cover near or over water, except for coots which spend much of their time on open water and dive for their food. The sexes look alike.

Most British rails are reluctant to fly and do so heavily with legs dangling, though they can travel long distances, and some migrate. Some of their relatives, such as the Takahe of New Zealand, have lost the power of flight altogether because they have no natural enemies. Their food is various, both vegetable and small invertebrate animals. Their calls are mostly harsh, repeated croaking noises, often uttered at night. The displays, except of the moorhen and coot, have seldom been watched. They build saucer-like nests, usually well-hidden, and lay large clutches of speckled eggs. The young, covered with dark down and sometimes with bright patches on their heads, are active at once. The CRANES (Balearicidae) and BUSTARDS (Otididae) are both included in the same order (Ralliformes) as the rails. (See pp. 56–59, 14–15, 82–83)

The WADERS or shore-birds are a group of families in the order Charadriiformes related to the gulls and auks but with rather long legs, plump bodies, usually pointed wings, and long bills. Their plumage is generally speckled brown or grey above and light underneath, but there are black and white species. Many have colourful spring plumage on head and breast. Males and females usually look alike, with some striking exceptions, such as the ruff (p. 75). They are nearly all birds of open country, moorlands, marshes, and sea-shores, their long legs and bills enabling them to feed on small animals in mud, earth, or shallow water. Waders breed in single pairs or small groups, but most of them form into flocks in autumn and carry out long migrations. They are the typical breeding birds of the tundras of the far north and migrate to spend the winter round coasts and lakes throughout the rest of the world. Many have complicated spring displays with lively song-flights. They make simple nests on the ground, the female lining a scrape hollowed out by the male with whatever is near at hand. Most waders lay four pear-shaped eggs and incubate them with the points together. The male of some species incubates the eggs and looks after the young, but usually these duties are shared, the female doing the larger part. The colour of the eggs and the down of the chicks match their surroundings, giving them protective camouflage. The young can run and feed themselves soon after hatching. (See pp. 60–83, 198)

SKUAS (Stercorariidae) TERNS, and GULLS (Laridae) are sea-birds related to the waders and with some resemblances: they have pointed and angled wings, longish legs (gulls and skuas), and well-camouflaged downy nestlings. But, except for the skuas, their adult plumages tend to be white or grey; the front three toes are webbed, the hind toe being small or absent. The legs and strong bills are red, yellow, or black, and many species have a projection of the lower mandible called the gonys. The sexes are alike. Most species stay near the coast, except when migrating, and some spend all or part of their lives on or near fresh water. They feed on fish, insects, and carrion, and gulls particularly make use of human refuse. Most of them live in flocks or groups and nest in colonies, often in huge numbers. Consequently their displays, which tend to take place in a confined space on the ground, consist mainly of special calls and movements of the head. They make simple open nests and lay two or three brownish eggs, which are rounder and have darker markings than waders' eggs. Their young, less active than waders, are fed by the parents in or close to the nest for a time. (See pp. 84–99)

AUKS (Alcidae) are all sea-birds with stout bodies, upright stance, and a general plumage pattern of dark upperparts and white underparts. They fly with rapid beats of their short-pointed wings, and legs often spread; they swim and dive expertly, using their wings underwater to hunt fish. They spend all the year in flocks and breed in colonies, sometimes of huge size, laying one or two eggs on exposed ledges or in crevices and holes. The chicks, though covered with dark down from the egg, are helpless at first and have to be fed for several weeks. Like other social birds, auks have various group displays. After breeding, most auks spend the winter out at sea, but may be blown inland by storms. (See pp. 100–101)

PIGEONS and DOVES (Columbidae) are stout-bodied land birds with close, soft plumage, similar in both sexes, and often grey ('dove-grey'), light brown, and pink, with an attractive powdery bloom. They have soft swollen bases to their upper mandibles, two-lobed crops, and strong gizzards. Their legs are often red, their wings broad, pointed, and angled at the wrist for fast flapping flight. Wing clapping often plays a part in their displays. Their calls are coos or purrs. They eat almost entirely vegetable matter: seeds, fruits, stems, and leaves. They lay two white eggs in a very simple nest on a branch or in a hole, and both parents incubate them. At first they feed their young (squabs) on pigeon's milk, made from the lining of the crop and taken from the parent's throat. (*See* pp. 102–105)

OWLS (*Strigiformes*) have sharp claws, a hooked bill, and a bare patch (cere) at its base. They are a very distinctive group of birds owing to their large round heads and big eyes, brown or yellow, gazing forwards from a 'facial disk' of stiff feathers which grows from a fold of skin round their cheeks. The position of the eyes is fixed, but to compensate, owls can twist their long necks right round. Their ears are large and hearing acute. Their legs are feathered, and their plumage, usually mottled brown, grey, and white, and the same in both sexes, is soft and loose, and they fly silently. Their calls are a variety of hoots and shrieks, carrying a long way, and they have menacing threat postures. They display in the air and on perches. Though typically nocturnal, owls do not mind daylight, and some regularly hunt by day. They pounce on their prey — mainly small mammals and birds, insects and worms — and swallow it whole, throwing up the indigestible parts as pellets. They lay their round white eggs in holes, old nests of other birds, or on the ground, at intervals of two or more days; so the young hatch separately and are blind and helpless at first. The female usually incubates, and the male brings in food. (*See* pp. 106–111)

The WOODPECKERS (*Piciformes*) are specialised perchers, adapted to climb trees, with two toes pointing each way and stiff tail feathers to support them against the trunk. They are colourful, with slight differences between male, female, and juvenile, and their flight is undulating or wave-like. They have loud, ringing calls, and some have 'drumming' displays, tapping a chosen dead branch rapidly to produce a carrying sound. They feed typically by chipping away dead wood and 'winkling out' insect grubs with their very long tongues. (*See* pp. 114–115)

The CUCKOOS (*Cuculiformes*) are a world-wide order of perching land birds with long tails, usually shaped like a graduated fan, and thin skins. The sexes are more or less alike, with grey or brown upperparts, often spotted or mottled, and pale underparts. Some of them lay their eggs in other birds' nests and are called 'parasitic'; others build simple nests of their own. (*See* pp. 116–117)

NIGHTJARS (*Caprimulgiformes*) have tiny bills but very wide mouths fringed with stiff bristles adapted for hunting moths and other insects. They hunt at dusk and remain hidden during the day. They have beautifully mottled 'blending' plumage. SWIFTS (*Apodiformes*) have the same feeding habits but hunt by day. They spend more time on the wing than any other birds, except perhaps albatrosses. Their very small feet do not allow them to walk properly or to perch, but they can cling to walls. (*See* pp. 118–119)

The great order of passerines or perching birds (*Passeriformes*) includes the sub-order *Oscines* or song-birds to which all the British species belong. They show a range of adaptation from the comparatively 'unspecialised' but intelligent crows to the swallows, which resemble the aerial swifts; the shrikes, which are like birds of prey; the TREECREEPERS and NUTHATCHES, which have some of the habits of woodpeckers; and the DIPPERS, which can swim and dive. But basically their structure is similar, and they almost all have recognisable, usually musical, songs, they build complicated nests, and their young are helpless when hatched. (*See* pp. 120–191)

SWALLOWS (*Hirundinidae*) have pointed, rather curved wings, forked tails, short legs, flat bills, and wide mouths, which adapt them for a life mainly in the air; but, unlike swifts which they resemble superficially, they can all perch and walk. Their plumages are dark above and light below, and the sexes are alike. They feed on the wing on flying or floating insects and collect the lining for their nests in flight; they gather mud for the foundations off the ground. They have twittering calls and songs. Most species live in parties or flocks and nest in colonies. They are summer visitors to Britain and undertake long migrations. (*See* pp. 120–121)

LARKS (*Alaudidae*) superficially resemble the pipits and, like them, are birds of open country, living on the ground or in the air, though they can perch on trees and posts. They usually have pale underparts and light-brown upperparts with darker markings, shortish tails, often with white outer feathers, and often a small crest. The sexes are generally alike. They have long feet and claws and run fast, feeding on small invertebrate animals and seeds. They usually have fine songs which they utter in flight. Their nests are on the ground, and the eggs and downy young blend with their surroundings. The young may leave the nest before they can fly. (*See* pp. 122–123)

The CROWS (*Corvidae*) are the largest and among the most intelligent passerines; there are very large numbers of several species in Britain. They are typical land birds with strong legs, feet, and claws, and powerful bills with bristles lying along the upper mandible. The sexes are alike, juveniles resemble the adults, and plumages tend to be glossy black. They all may form flocks or parties, the rook and jackdaw having highly developed 'societies'. Their broad wings are suitable for flapping flight and soaring, but they are equally at home on the ground where they walk or take big hops. Their calls are harsh croaks and caws, though some have quite musical songs, and some are good mimics. They eat fruit, seeds, small animals, and carrion. Their nests in rocks or trees are strongly built of sticks and mud, wool, and plant material, and the eggs are greenish-blue with brown markings. Both parents carry food to the naked young in their throat pouches. (*See* pp. 124–127)

The TITS or TITMICE (*Paridae*) are all small or very small, stout-bodied, and usually brightly coloured. They move actively from twig to twig, clinging to trunks and walls and hopping on the ground. They have rather long legs, feet, and claws, and short, straight, powerful bills. They often have a distinctive cap, and the sexes look more or less alike; juveniles, though like adults, usually have a yellowish tinge. Tits feed on small insects and other creatures in trees and bushes, and on nuts and seeds; but most of them also take human food scraps. They usually have simple songs and a variety of call notes. Males display to females by fluttering their wings and offering them food. Members of the genus *Parus* build mossy nests in holes and lay large clutches of white eggs with red spots, which the female alone incubates. After nesting, mixed parties roam the woodland, often joined by other small birds. The long-tailed tit differs from the *Parus* tits in building an elaborate domed nest in the open. The bearded tit is considered by some authorities not to be closely related. (*See* pp. 128–131)

The family *Turdidae* ranges from the THRUSHES to WHEATEARS, CHATS, REDSTARTS, NIGHTINGALES, BLUETHROATS, and ROBIN. They are all rather plump-looking, with long legs and straight bills, and spend much time on the ground. The sexes may be alike or quite distinct; and the juvenile plumage usually looks scaly. They eat mainly small invertebrate animals, worms, and fruits. The thrushes include some of the best song-birds. They build substantial nests, and the five or six eggs usually have a bluish ground colour with red-brown markings. They rear two or even three broods a season. The males of most species do not help in building or incubation but do feed the young. (*See* pp. 136–145)

Some authorities consider the ACCENTORS (*Prunellidae*) to be closely related to the thrushes; others to the warblers. They have rather short legs, but long feet and claws, strong bills, wide at the base and tapering, and generally streaked or spotted brown plumage — male and female being more or less alike, and juveniles slightly different. They feed both on small invertebrate animals and seeds. (*See* pp. 144–145)

The WARBLERS (*Sylviidae*) are a large family of rather small song-birds, fairly closely related to the thrushes. They are slim and thin-billed, usually brownish or greenish, with males, females, and juveniles looking more or less alike. They have rather long tails and feet adapted for perching rather than for running. They live mainly in thick cover, only showing themselves to display or to sing. Their food is insects and other small creatures, with some berries and seeds. They are nearly all summer visitors to northern Europe and Britain, where four main groups are represented. The genus *Sylvia* includes some of the larger species. The males tend to have black or grey caps and a tufted appearance. They inhabit low scrub both in woodland and on bushy heaths, and build slight but strong open nests, laying about five well-marked eggs. The grasshopper warblers (*Locustella*) are brown-backed, with long, rounded tails and 'reeling' songs. They live in thick vegetation usually near water, and are generally shy. They build well-hidden nests on or near the ground and lay about six white eggs, usually spotted with red or brown. The 'reed' warblers (*Acrocephalus*) are also brown-backed and round-tailed, but tend to live in the taller vegetation near water. They have loud, sustained songs, with repetitions of notes and phrases, and mimicry. Their nests are usually slung or woven round stems of reeds and other tall plants, and they lay about five eggs well-marked with green or brown. The 'leaf' warblers (*Phylloscopus*) get their name from their greenish plumages and habit of feeding in trees and bushes; they also catch flies in the air. They are all small or very small and have a variety of songs, with plaintive call notes. They build domed nests on or near the ground and lay five to seven roundish white eggs with red or brown markings. (*See* pp. 146–159)

The FLYCATCHERS (*Muscicapidae*) are related to the warblers and thrushes, and all are sometimes included in one large family. They are specialised for catching insects on the wing or amongst foliage, having flat bills with strong bristles at the base, short legs, and rather weak feet compared to the thrushes; they seldom move about on the ground. They nest in cavities or on ledges, and their young are usually spotted like young thrushes. They are summer visitors to northern Europe. (*See* pp. 160–161)

The SHRIKES (*Laniidae*) are large or medium-sized passerines, with strong slightly-hooked bills and notches on the cutting edges of the upper mandible. They have short strong legs, long, rounded tails, and broad wings with variegated plumage. Juveniles and some females are barred brown. They catch flying insects, small birds, lizards, and small mammals, impaling them on thorns in 'larders'. Their songs are not often heard but may be quite musical, though their call notes are harsh. They build substantial, rather untidy nests in bushes, and their eggs have characteristic zones of markings. (*See* pp. 170–171)

PIPITS and WAGTAILS (*Motacillidae*) have long legs with long hind claws, fitting them for life mainly on the ground, where they run like larks. They have long tails, thin, straight bills, and rather broad wings. Apart from some of the wagtails, they tend to have brown, sandy, or yellowish plumages streaked with black on the upperparts. They all have white or whitish outer tail-feathers. Their flight is distinctly undulating. They feed principally on insects and other small invertebrates, seizing them on the ground or in the air. The pipits have well-developed songs, delivered in the air; the wagtails make more use of their plumage in display. They all nest in hollows or recesses, laying five or six eggs, generally with dense brown or grey markings. Young pipits often leave the nest before they can fly. Most species are summer visitors to northern Europe or at least local migrants. (*See* pp. 162–163)

The large family *Fringillidae* includes both FINCHES and BUNTINGS, seed-eating song-birds, the former being mainly tree-living and the latter ground-living. Finches, especially hawfinches (p. 175), have stout bills, and those of crossbills (p. 181) are specially adapted. Males, females, and juveniles usually have distinct plumages, the males often being very colourful. They tend to live in parties outside the breeding season, and also may nest in groups. The nests, built by the females, with the male often in attendance, are solid cups of twigs, grasses, moss, and lichens, lined with finer materials. The five or six eggs are often blue with scrawled dark markings. The young are at first covered with light down. The parents carry away their droppings, but towards the end they cease to do so, and the nest becomes very dirty. (*See* pp. 174–185). Buntings have sparrow-like plumages, except for the heads of the males. Most species have white outer tail-feathers, like larks and pipits. Their open nests are on or near the ground, and the eggs have thin or thick dark scrawly markings. Buntings are both resident and migratory. (*See* pp. 186–191)

The two SPARROWS (*Passeridae*) are closely related to the tropical weaver-birds, and it is possible that they may at one time have moved north from much further south. They differ from finches in small points of anatomy, and they are noted for their large flocks and breeding colonies. (*See* pp. 190–191)

THE MAIN PARTS OF A BIRD

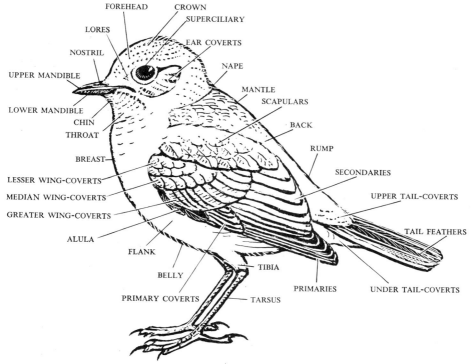

FOREHEAD CROWN
SUPERCILIARY
LORES
EAR COVERTS
NOSTRIL
NAPE
UPPER MANDIBLE
MANTLE
SCAPULARS
LOWER MANDIBLE
CHIN
BACK
THROAT
RUMP
BREAST
SECONDARIES
LESSER WING-COVERTS
MEDIAN WING-COVERTS
UPPER TAIL-COVERTS
GREATER WING-COVERTS
TAIL FEATHERS
ALULA
FLANK
TIBIA
BELLY
UNDER TAIL-COVERTS
PRIMARIES
PRIMARY COVERTS
TARSUS

ABBREVIATIONS AND CAPTIONS TO PLATES

At the end of the text (on pp. xvi–193) for all the commoner species a simple device has been used to show (a) in which months of the year the bird can be seen in Britain, (b) in which months eggs or young in the nest may be expected, (c) the months when song can be heard. Only certain families of birds have songs which can be readily recognised as such.

The annual cycle of a typical resident bird might be this:

1 2 3 **4 5 6** *7 8 9 10 11 12*

The bird is to be seen in every month. The figures **4 5 6** in bold type show the nesting period, and the figures underlined are the months of song.

The chart for a typical summer visitor might be this:

. . *(3)* *4* **5 6 7** *8 9 10* *(11)*

This bird is not to be seen in January, February, and December, and only occasionally in March and November.

The chart for a typical winter visitor might be this:

1 2 3 4 (5) . . *(8) 9 10 11 12*

This bird does not breed in Britain, and does not sing during its winter residence.

Ad., adult; Juv., juvenile; Imm., immature; M., male; F., female are used throughout.

The names in the captions to the colour plates are arranged to correspond with the place of the birds on the plate: for example, the top left name in the caption refers to the top left bird on the plate, and so on. The numbers correspond to the numbers on the text page.

DIVERS

1 GREAT NORTHERN DIVER (*Gavia immer*). The largest of the divers has a body 17 to 20 ins. long. Its summer plumage and stout black bill are unmistakable; but in winter, small and juvenile birds are hard to distinguish from black-throated divers. If seen fairly close, their underparts are less uniform and have a barred appearance. By the early spring great northern divers are usually showing the spotted back and black head. The pointed bill, white on the face, and shorter neck separate the divers in winter from cormorants and shags (p. 11), and the thick neck also distinguishes them from the larger grebes (p. 3). Juvenile gannets sitting on the sea may be confused with them, but the gannets swim much higher and have dark necks and mottled plumage.

The great northern diver bred in north-west Scotland in 1970, and pairs and single birds remain off the Scottish coast all summer; in winter, though commoner in the north, they occur all round Britain and sometimes on lakes and reservoirs inland.

They swim and dive like black-throated divers and feed on fish and other sea creatures, taking perch and roach in fresh water. They need a long stretch of open water for their take-off and cannot rise from small ponds. The call in flight is like that of other divers. Most birds seen in British waters in winter must come from North America or Iceland, the nearest breeding places.

1   2   3   4   5   6   7   8   9   10   11   12

WHITE-BILLED DIVER (*Gavia adamsii*). This is the Old World counterpart of the great northern diver, though it nests in north-west America too. Except for the white up-turned bill, it is almost identical in appearance and habits, but is believed to feed almost entirely on fish. About 25 have occurred in British waters, most of them since 1946, and all on the east coast from Yorkshire up to Shetland, in winter, spring, or early summer.

2 BLACK-THROATED DIVER (*Gavia arctica*). This is a large black-and-white diving bird, 14 to 17 ins. long. In summer the plumage pattern and straight black bill distinguish it from other divers, though the small black throat-patch may be hard to see; but in winter it is difficult to tell from the great northern diver, partly because they both vary so much in size that this is no safe guide; juveniles, which are the most likely to be seen in Britain, often cannot be told apart unless they are handled.

The black-throated diver is the rarer of the two British breeding divers; it nests in south-west Scotland and from central Perthshire northwards, and on islands and headlands in the larger lochs up to 1,500 ft.; but it may fish in other waters and the sea. Outside the breeding season, numbers appear off the east coast, and odd birds elsewhere, occasionally inland.

Divers usually lie low in the water, showing only their heads, necks and the round of their backs. They normally submerge quietly, but sometimes they will spring up before diving. Black-throated divers remain under water about ¾ minute, and may use wings as well as feet to pursue the fish which is their chief food; they also take crustaceans, shellfish, and worms. In winter they patrol some yards offshore, usually alone, though in late summer they may be in parties up to twenty.

The call is a repeated *kwak kwak kwak*, uttered in flight between breeding and feeding waters. The pair take off into the wind and fly with quick beats of their short wings, legs stretched, and head held low. They lay two long, greasy-looking, dark-brown eggs with black spots in a lined scrape close to water; both sexes share the 4-week incubation and feed the chicks, which take to the water at once and can fly in about 9 weeks.

*1   2   3   4   **5**   **6**   7   8   9   10   11   12*

3 RED-THROATED DIVER (*Gavia stellata*). This is the smallest diver, with a body 14 to 15 ins. long, a slightly up-turned bill, and, at all seasons, rather light-coloured upperparts. In breeding plumage the uniform grey-brown of neck and back is distinctive, and the red throat-patch may look quite black in poor light. In winter the outline of the bill is the best way to tell this species from a small black-throated diver, though it almost always looks much paler.

Red-throated divers now breed over most of the north-west Highlands of Scotland, the main island groups, and in one small area of north-west Ireland. They prefer small lochs, usually close to larger waters or to the sea where they can fish. In winter they can be seen all round the coast, showing no particular choice of shore, and they appear on lakes and reservoirs more often than other divers.

Their behaviour in general is like that of their relatives. They swim fast under water and may dive for up to 1½ minutes. They eat mainly fish, though they take other sea creatures, bringing them to the surface to swallow. They walk awkwardly and usually heave their bodies along, sometimes with flapping wings. But they take off from water easily and fly more than other divers, uttering a repeated quacking call when high overhead. They have other calls and cries, most of which are heard only during the breeding season displays, which may include several birds or only a single pair. They build more substantial nests than do black-throated divers, and lay two greasy brown, cigar-shaped eggs with small black spots. The parents share incubation for 3½ to 4 weeks and feed the young at first by bringing food up from the gullet; later they bring whole fish. The young can fly in about 8 weeks, when the family leaves for the sea, where they are joined by birds which have bred elsewhere.

*1   2   3   4   **5**   **6**   7   8   9   10   11   12*

1a GREAT NORTHERN DIVER, summer
3a RED-THROATED DIVER, summer
2b BLACK-THROATED DIVER, winter

2a BLACK-THROATED DIVER, summer
1b GREAT NORTHERN DIVER, winter
3b RED-THROATED DIVER, winter

1 GREAT CRESTED GREBE (*Podiceps cristatus*). The largest British grebe, with a body 12 ins. long, has a unique breeding plumage from February onwards, with dark ear-tufts and red ruffle or tippet. In flight, with crest flattened, and neck and legs stretched, it looks very slender and shows a prominent white wing-bar. In autumn the adult adornments are lost, but the juvenile has a striped head. The great crested grebe is a little larger than the red-necked grebe, and its bill is not so thick-looking and is reddish, not black and yellow; the dark crown is narrower and there is a white stripe over the eye. Seen at sea with divers, cormorants, or shags, grebes look much slimmer, but when moulting they may be easily confused with the red-headed ducks and juveniles of goosanders and red-breasted mergansers (p. 29).

Great crested grebes now breed on suitable waters nearly all over Britain, up to central Scotland, and they are common in Ireland, preferring shallow lakes or ponds at least 3 acres in area with plenty of vegetation, especially reeds and horsetails. They sometimes nest in the reeds of slow-flowing rivers or on quite bare reservoirs. Numbers have increased in England with the increase in worked-out, water-filled gravel pits. On some Irish loughs and on the Continent they are found in colonies. In winter some remain on inland waters, but many go to the sea and to estuaries, chiefly on the east and south coasts.

Great crested grebes are famous for their spring displays, in which male and female play equal parts, and which include shaking heads when facing each other, chasing over water, and presenting nest material; they will also attack other pairs fiercely.

They make various noises during the display period: a bark, a double note from cover, a groan, and others; but the most often heard note is the hunger call of the young, a repeated *pee-ah, pee-ah, pee-ah*.

Grebes usually sink quietly when diving, but sometimes they spring up first; the great crested grebe stays under about ½ minute and does not go much deeper than 10 ft. Their food is varied: small fish, water insects at all stages, crustaceans, plants, even a few tadpoles and newts. Grebes usually dive when approached. They need a good take-off for flight and land on their breasts, not feet first, like ducks. They walk clumsily but better than divers. Breeding does not usually begin until the plant cover is high enough to hide the floating mass of stems which makes the nest. The female lays three to six elongated white eggs, which both sexes incubate for about 4 weeks; they become very dark from staining. The striped young

are fed at first by both parents, who may split the brood, and regularly carry them on their backs. The young begin to dive after 6 weeks and can look after themselves about a month later. There may be two broods in a season. In autumn great crested grebes either go to sea or collect on favourite wintering places inland; there seems to be no migration to and from Britain.

1 2 **3 4 5 6 7 8 9** *10 11 12*

2 RED-NECKED GREBE (*Podiceps griseigena*). About 10 ins. long and slightly smaller than the great crested grebe, the red-necked grebe is usually seen in British waters in winter plumage when it is best distinguished by its curiously top-heavy appearance, due to the thick black-and-yellow bill, the large head, and the relatively short body. At all times its neck is usually rather dark and there is no white stripe over the eye. It is much bigger than the Slavonian grebe (p. 5), and is quite distinctive in summer on the water, though when flying it is not easy to tell from a great crested grebe.

Red-necked grebes are winter visitors chiefly to the east coast of Britain from the Firth of Forth southward; but odd birds may be seen in all months. They are rare in the west and in Ireland. They keep close to the shore or in estuaries, coming occasionally to inland waters. In Britain they are usually solitary, though several may be found in the same area, swimming and diving like other grebes; at sea they feed on fish and crustaceans. They seldom take wing, but walk better than great crested grebes. Their ordinary call-note is *kek kek*, but winter visitors tend to be silent; they arrive from northern and eastern Europe from September onwards and leave again in March, by which time the summer plumage is sometimes to be seen.

1 2 3 4 (*5 6 7 8*) **9** *10 11 12*

PIED-BILLED GREBE (*Podilymbus podiceps*). There have been seven records, probably referring only to three individual birds, of this North American species since 1963, from Somerset, Yorkshire and Norfolk. It is a stockily built bird, 9 ins. long, characterised by a notably deep bill, pale in winter and with a dark band in summer. The plumage is predominantly dull brown at all seasons, but the throat is white in winter and almost black in summer.

1a GREAT CRESTED GREBE, winter
1b GREAT CRESTED GREBE, summer
2b RED-NECKED GREBE; summer

2a RED-NECKED GREBE, winter
1c GREAT CRESTED GREBE, Juv.
   moulting to first winter

1 BLACK-NECKED GREBE (*Podiceps nigricollis*). This grebe is 7 ins. long, being slightly smaller than the Slavonian grebe from which it can be distinguished in summer by its black neck and upper breast, in winter by its darker head and back of the neck, and at all times by the up-tilted bill. Juveniles are browner, but always more black-and-white than little grebes. Both black-necked and Slavonian grebes show a white wing-bar in flight.

As well as being a winter visitor and passage migrant, the black-necked grebe has bred in a number of British and Irish counties, but seldom for more than a few years. Outside the breeding season it is generally seen in very small numbers on lakes, reservoirs, and the sea coast. Black-necked grebes prefer breeding waters with more cover than those chosen by Slavonian grebes, and they may make large colonies.

Though in winter black-necked grebes may behave like other grebes, they are shyer when breeding, but they come into the open when they are displaying. Their display resembles that of the great crested grebe in certain performances—for example, in head-shaking with bodies raised. Their food in fresh water consists of insects, small shellfish, and crustaceans, with small fish for the young, and they dive for these, staying under water for half a minute. The usual call note is a quiet *peep*, but there is a harsher *wit wit* of alarm and a rippling note in spring at the breeding water. They lay three to five white eggs in a typical grebe nest, and these are incubated by both parents for 3 weeks. The striped young are independent after about a month; they have a distinctive hunger call. There may be two broods in a season, after which the birds disperse; winter visitors begin to arrive in September, and passage birds go through in spring and autumn.

*1   2   3   4   **5   6   7   8**   9   10   11   12***

2 LITTLE GREBE (*Podiceps ruficollis*). The smallest, roundest grebe is often called a dabchick. It is only 6 ins. long and is much browner than its relatives at all seasons. It has a shorter neck and no head ornaments, though the yellow-green skin where the mandibles join shows up brightly in the breeding plumage. It is possible to confuse the striped-headed young with those of other grebes or with young coots and moorhens, but these are always much darker. Only a faint wing-bar shows in flight.

Dabchicks are breeding residents over most of the British Isles, except some of the highland areas and Shetland, where they are winter visitors; they are also found round sheltered coasts in winter. They nest in thick cover on a lake, pond, or slow-flowing river, though occasionally they will build with open water round them.

In summer the presence of little grebes is often revealed only by a loud whickering call from thick cover; but in winter they are easier to see. They may form parties of up to forty birds on larger lakes, but are also often solitary. They swim fairly high in the water and dive by sinking or by springing up and going in head first. Their food is insects, small shellfish, crustaceans, and fish. When approached, dabchicks may beat away over the water with wings flapping and legs paddling, taking flight for a short distance; but they cannot take off on land, though they can stand and walk quite well. Their displays are not as elaborate as those of other grebes, but there are violent chases between rivals and trilling duets between pairs. The alarm call *wit wit* resembles that of the black-necked grebe. Dabchicks lay four to six, sometimes more, white eggs in a floating nest, and both parents incubate. Each egg hatches in under 3 weeks, but as the eggs are laid at intervals, the incubation lasts about $3\frac{1}{2}$ weeks. The parents look after the young for about 6 weeks, though the female may start a new nest within the period, as there are regularly two and sometimes even three broods a year. The young continue to pester the male for food with a loud *pee-ah* call even when they are as big as he is. In autumn, some birds leave the smaller waters for rivers, estuaries, and the sea, returning in March, and overseas visitors arrive from October, staying until the spring.

1   2   3   4   5   6   7   8   9   10   11   12

3 SLAVONIAN GREBE (*Podiceps auritus*). Though noticeably smaller than the red-necked grebe (p. 3), the Slavonian grebe, 8 ins. long, is rather larger than the black-necked grebe, from which it can be told in summer by its chestnut neck and breast, and at all times by its rather short, straight bill. In winter it has less black on the head and neck and, until the spring moult begins, it has distinctly white cheeks. But at a distance the birds are difficult to distinguish, and both show the white wing-bar in flight.

The Slavonian grebe is a resident, a passage migrant, and a winter visitor. It breeds in northern Scotland on a few lochs which have shallow bays with sedges or horsetails growing in the water. But it may be seen all round the coasts in winter and quite often inland.

Like the other less common grebes, the Slavonian grebe is usually seen offshore, alone or in pairs, swimming buoyantly and diving for food. What food it takes at sea is not yet known; on fresh water it eats insects and small crustaceans about equally. It allows a closer approach than its relatives and flies more readily, though it needs a good take-off distance. On the breeding lochs the birds display like great crested grebes (p. 3), but they have been less studied. They use a variety of cries and notes, but the typical spring call is a rippling trill. Both parents build the floating nest and share incubation of the three to five white eggs for 3 to $3\frac{1}{2}$ weeks. The young become independent after a month, during which they pester for food with an insistent call. The families then disperse to the coast, where they are joined from September by winter visitors; passage birds go through in late spring and again in autumn.

*1   2   3   4   **5   6   7**   8   9   10   11   12*

1a BLACK-NECKED GREBE, winter
2a LITTLE GREBE, winter
3b SLAVONIAN GREBES, summer

3a SLAVONIAN GREBE, winter
2b LITTLE GREBE, summer 2c Juv.
1b BLACK-NECKED GREBE, summer

PETRELS

1 FULMAR (*Fulmarus glacialis*). The fulmar looks like a medium to large gull, but has a rounder head, a big dark eye, and a darkish bill with tube nostrils. It is about 18 ins. long, and the dark grey wings, which have no black tips, are usually held straight in gliding flight. There are dark varieties not often seen in British waters.

The original colony of fulmars was on St. Kilda, but during the last 100 years they have spread all round the British Isles, though there are still more of them in the north. They may nest anywhere, from steep cliffs to old buildings and flat ground on islands, and they have colonised inland crags and quarries in several areas. At sea they scatter widely to north and west. Storm-driven birds have turned up in many inland counties, and one laid an egg on a lawn in Northants!

They follow fishing, whaling, and other boats and probably owe their increase in numbers to offal from this source, though their natural diet is a mixture of plankton and small fish from near the surface. Fulmars glide for long distances, using air currents, and often following in and out of a line of cliffs a few feet away, or tilting over the surface of the sea from wing tip to wing tip; at intervals, especially in calm weather, they have to flap to gain height or speed. They become noisy at their nest-sites, gurgling and cackling as they display to each other, jerking and bobbing their heads with bills open. The nest is a scrape with little lining, and both sexes sit on the single white egg in long spells of about 4 days for 6 to 8 weeks; they feed the fluffy grey-white chick for another 6 to 8 weeks, and then leave it to fledge by itself. After the breeding season they disperse out to sea, but begin to return in late autumn.

1   2   3   4   5   6   7   8   9   10   11   12

BLACK-BROWED ALBATROSS (*Diomedea melanophrys*). Albatrosses are birds of the southern hemisphere which occasionally wander north of the equator. This is the commonest species, with over a dozen records, including one bird which appeared among gannets on the Bass Rock for several years from 1967. About 18 more, not assigned to species, have been sighted. The adult plumage resembles that of a great black-backed gull (p. 87), with a yellow bill and a dark line through the eye; this species is about 2½ ft. long, with a wing span up to 8 ft.

2 LEACH'S FORK-TAILED PETREL (*Oceanodroma leucorrhoa*). This small petrel, about 8 ins. long, is a little larger than a storm petrel. It is browner in colour, with a forked tail and a dark line dividing the white rump. The best means of identifying it at sea is by its buoyant, springy flight, with rapid changes of direction, and bouts of gliding and beating.

Leach's petrels can be seen over British seas all through the year and come to their breeding colonies on four remote Scottish island groups in May. Otherwise they occur inland as storm-driven casualties, sometimes in hundreds. They do not follow ships as storm petrels do, and are known to British bird-watchers chiefly at their breeding colonies which they visit by night, calling in flight and from the nest-

holes, which are burrows excavated in peaty soil, under rocks, or in old walls. The male makes the burrow and the female lays one roundish white egg on a pad of nest material. Both birds sit in spells of 4 days for about 7 weeks, and they feed the fluffy chick for another 7 weeks or more before leaving it to fledge. The parents croon on the nest, and the chick calls plaintively. They feed almost entirely on surface plankton. After breeding, the birds scatter out to sea, keeping in loose gatherings, and swimming as well as flying. Anyone rescuing a petrel should not try to feed it but should hand it over at once to the R.S.P.C.A., who will release it at the coast.

1   2   3   4   5   6   7   8   9   10   11   12

3 STORM PETREL (*Hydrobates pelagicus*). The best known of all small petrels is only 6 ins. long. It is sooty-grey, except for its white rump, and has a narrow wing bar in fresh plumage and some white under the wings not seen in flight; the tail is square ended, and the black legs relatively short.

Like Leach's petrel it is to be seen in British waters all the year, but is much more widely distributed in the breeding season, with colonies up the west coast from Scilly to Shetland and off Ireland. Nearly all are on rocky islands, very occasionally on mainland cliffs. Birds have been seen in many British and some coastal counties of Ireland after storms in autumn, spring, and occasionally winter.

Storm petrels zigzag behind ships with a fluttering flight and short glides, occasionally descending to the water and pattering over it or settling and swimming buoyantly. Noisy displays take place over the breeding colonies at night, while birds in the nest-holes may give up to 1,000 purrs, each one ending with a sharp *chikka*. Most nests are under loose stones or boulders, or in walls, but some pairs excavate burrows. Both parents in spells of about 1½ days incubate the single egg, which is round and white, usually with a zone of faint brown spots. The young one hatches after 5 weeks and fledges after 8 or 9 weeks, the parents feeding it by regurgitating food. They eat mainly plankton picked off the surface of the sea, with little offal; when storm-driven over land, they take insects. After the breeding season, the petrels spread out into the Atlantic. Birds rescued inland should be handed over to the R.S.P.C.A.

1   2   3   4   5   6   7   8   9   10   11   12

WILSON'S PETREL (*Oceanites oceanicus*). A small petrel resembling the storm petrel but with long yellow-webbed feet extending beyond the tail in flight. It breeds in the Antarctic and migrates up the west side of the Atlantic, whence some spread over into British waters; but fewer than ten have been definitely recorded. Travellers across the North Atlantic in summer have a good chance of seeing one because they follow ships.

MADEIRAN PETREL (*Oceanodroma castro*) **FRIGATE PETREL** (*Pelagodroma marina*). These two small petrels breed on islands off North West Africa. The former has been recorded twice in the British Isles, the latter once.

2   LEACH'S FORK-TAILED PETREL

1   FULMAR

3   STORM PETREL

SHEARWATERS

1 MANX SHEARWATER (*Puffinus puffinus*). A black and white sea bird, 14 ins. long, and the only common member of the group. Shearwaters can be recognised from their flight, a burst of fast wing-beats followed by long spells of gliding low over the sea, tipping from side to side so that the wings seem to 'shear water'. Manx shearwaters are distinguished by the alternating light undersides and dark upperparts. The rare Balearic race is much lighter above and darker underneath; the other species likely to be seen in Britain are larger.

Manx shearwaters are seen all round British coasts in summer, though they are known to breed only up the west side of Britain from Scilly to Shetland, and in Ireland. They have recently returned to the Isle of Man after an absence of over 150 years. Most colonies are on islands, but some are on headlands and in Rum (Inner Hebrides) on the hilltops 2,000 ft. up. After breeding, shearwaters migrate southward, and they are often seen inland in England during autumn gales; they winter off France and Spain.

During the breeding season great masses of shearwaters sit on the sea near their colonies, and dive or fly a short distance when boats approach; but they do not follow ships. They visit the land at night to avoid their enemies, especially big gulls which kill many of them, and on Rum, golden eagles. The noise at the colony is a bedlam of wild *rookooing* calls as birds in the nest holes answer those on the wing. The nest is at the end of a tunnel which may be several feet long, either excavated in the soil or under stones. One elongated white egg is laid, and both sexes take long turns at incubating for a total of 7½ weeks. The bird not incubating flies enormous distances to find small fish and squids, which it takes from the surface or by shallow dives. The fluffy chick is left after 8½ weeks to make its perilous way to sea alone. Thousands of British Manx shearwaters have been ringed; several have turned up on South American coasts, and one reached south of Australia. Birds have sometimes been released in places they do not normally visit and have shown remarkable homing powers.

(1 2) 3 4 5 6 7 8 9 10 (11 12)

2 SOOTY SHEARWATER (*Puffinus griseus*). Though slightly smaller (about 16 ins. long) this species looks heavier than the great shearwater. Its general sooty plumage is distinctive, but a white line along the underside of the wing separates it in flight from the darker petrels.

Sooty shearwaters are autumn visitors to British seas outside their breeding season in the Southern Hemisphere. They may be seen in the Channel, off the south-west of Britain and the Hebrides, and in the North Sea. They often accompany great shearwaters, which they closely resemble, and they feed on squids, small fish, and fish offal, using their wings underwater, as do most shearwaters.

3 GREAT SHEARWATER (*Puffinus gravis*). It is easily distinguished at long range from the Manx shearwater by its size (about 18 ins. long) and from Cory's shearwater by its brown cap against white cheeks and throat and by a white band on the tail. Birds in moult show a wavy white wing-bar. It has a powerful dark hooked bill.

This non-breeding visitor is seen mainly in summer and autumn on the western approaches of Britain and sometimes on the North Sea, but seldom close to land. It breeds in the islands of Tristan de Cunha in the south Atlantic.

Great shearwaters fly like Manx shearwaters, often gliding for half a mile and sometimes twice as far; but they have difficulty in rising off the water, especially in calm weather when they have to flap and paddle vigorously. They feed on squids, small fish, and fish offal from the surface, or by diving rather clumsily.

. . . . . 6 7 8 9 10 . .

4 CORY'S SHEARWATER (*Puffinus diomedea*). This non-breeding visitor is about the same size as the great shearwater, but its brown upperparts merge with the white underside, the cheeks are dark, there is no white on the tail, and the bill is yellowish. There are two similar races, one breeding in the Atlantic islands off North Africa, and the other in the Mediterranean region, from which parties appear in autumn, generally off the south-west coasts of Britain and Ireland.

Cory's shearwater is similar to the great shearwater in flight, though its wing-beats in calm weather are slower. It follows schools of whales and dolphins, which stir up the squids that are its principal food.

LITTLE SHEARWATER (*Puffinus baroli*). This rare visitor is 11 ins. long, smaller than the Manx shearwater, shorter in the wing, and showing more white on the face. It has been recorded over 30 times in the British Isles mostly since 1964. Its nearest breeding places are on the Atlantic islands off North America.

BULWER'S PETREL (*Bulweria bulwerii*) from islands off North-west Africa has been recorded three times, most recently in August 1965 off Cape Clear, Co. Cork.

CAPPED PETREL (*Bulweria hasitata*). This species from the West Indies was recorded once in 1850, when a bird was caught in Norfolk.

3 GREAT SHEARWATER   4 CORY'S SHEARWATER

1 MANX SHEARWATERS   2 SOOTY SHEARWATER

GANNETS AND CORMORANTS

1 GANNET (*Sula bassana*). Adult gannets are the largest, whitest British sea-birds; they are 3 ft. long and have a wing-span of 6 ft. In flight, the pointed tail and pointed bill held forward give their bodies a characteristic cigar-shape. Their black wingtips are conspicuous, and light reflects strongly from their white bodies. The sexes are alike. The juveniles are brown, white-speckled, and the immature birds gradually become whiter. At these stages they can be confused with divers (p. 1) or with the larger shear-waters (p. 9). The four toes point forward and are webbed together to give a large splay foot; the straight bill is bluish-white with a special structure to withstand the impact of diving, the nostrils being closed in adults.

About two-thirds of the world's breeding gannets nest in the British Isles in fourteen colonies, mainly off the west coasts and in the Northern Isles; the most famous colony is the Bass Rock in the Firth of Forth, and the only mainland one is at Bempton, Yorkshire. There is also a colony off Alderney. Gannets are in British waters throughout the year and may be seen all round the coast; they have been recorded from most inland counties after storms. They are usually seen on the wing, gliding, flapping, and then diving like plummets, sending up a thin column of spray and reappearing in a few seconds. They also make shallow dives when inshore or following ships after refuse, on which they feed as readily as on their natural diet of fish. They rest on the water but, except for breeding, only land when ill or oiled.

They begin to occupy their breeding sites in December. As with many birds where male and female are alike, the pair face each other in display, wing-waving, head-wagging, and finally clashing bills. Their growling call is used for display, for anger, and for recognition. The nest of seaweed and flotsam is built just out of pecking range of those around it. Both parents sit in turn on the single white egg, which becomes stained during the 6½ week incubation. The chick, at first naked, blind, and helpless, feeds by putting its head inside the parents' throat, as they regurgitate. It soon gets a coat of down, which it sheds during the 2 months in the nest. When fledged, it is deserted by its parents and makes its own way to sea. Some immature birds migrate slowly down the west coast of Europe and Africa as far as Senegal, but each year fewer immature birds migrate, and nearly all adults are resident.

1 2 3 4 5 6 7 8 9 10 11 12

2 SHAG (*Phalacrocorax aristotelis*). Smaller than the cormorant, the shag is 2½ ft. long with a wing span of 3½ ft. The differences between them are described under cormorant. The sexes are alike. They are found round most of the Scottish, Irish, Welsh, and south-west English coasts; there are colonies also in Northumberland and Cumberland. They seldom go far inland unless driven by storms, and then a few may remain for a time. Their colonies are either on steep cliffs, especially with big caves, or under loose boulders at the top or bottom of cliffs.

The shag has similar diving methods and feeding habits to the cormorant but it comes to land less often, and then usually to rocks near water. Its display, calls, and breeding behaviour are also similar, although the three to five eggs do not take so long to hatch. If the adult is approached on the nest, it opens and closes its yellow mouth and hisses. Shags disperse after breeding, and some British birds cross to France.

1 2 3 4 5 6 7 8 9 10 11 12

3 CORMORANT (*Phalacrocorax carbo*). This is the largest black-looking British sea-bird, 3 ft. long with a wing-span of 4½ ft. In flight, it looks like a big duck, but has broader wings. In spring the white thigh patches of the adult and, at closer range, the whitening of the head and lack of crest distinguish cormorants from shàgs, and they are heavier, thicker-necked birds with a bronze-blue rather than a dark green sheen. The sexes are alike. Juvenile cormorants are easy to confuse with shags, though their underparts are always paler and may become quite white. It is sometimes possible to count the fourteen tail feathers of a sitting cormorant (the shag has twelve). Both species have black legs and long, hook-tipped bills which are grey above and yellowish below.

Non-breeding cormorants may be seen all round British coasts, and on lakes and reservoirs and up some rivers, especially the Severn. Inland, they roost in trees. They breed on cliffs or rocky islets along western and northern coasts and on the Farne Islands, and in the Firth of Forth. In Ireland and also on the Continent they often nest in trees. Several Irish colonies and one in South-west Scotland are on fresh water, and a Welsh crag some miles from the sea has been used for centuries.

Cormorants fly rather heavily and low, mainly by flapping, and with necks held slightly upward; but they may travel high in V formation, like geese. They swim at several levels, sinking when alarmed until only their necks show; they tilt their bills upward, whereas grebes and divers hold them straight. They use their feet underwater to chase fish, which they usually swallow on the surface. On land they sit upright like so many black bottles, though they often spread their wings, either to dry them or to assist digestion. The female leads the display, which begins at the colonies early in spring; she either flaps her wings with head drawn in, or shakes her head at birds flying over. The male responds by raising his head feathers and extending his throat sac. They utter deep growling calls at the colony, and build their nests of seaweed and dead plants close together. The clutch is of three to five long, chalky eggs, which both parents incubate in turns for about 4 weeks. The chicks are helpless at first and are fed by regurgitated food; they fledge in about a month. Most British cormorants do not migrate, but some wander as far as Portugal.

1 2 3 4 5 6 7 8 9 10 11 12

MAGNIFICENT FRIGATE BIRD (*Fregata magnificens*). An immature female of the American race was found in Tiree in the Inner Hebrides in July 1953. It has a wing-span of up to 8 ft., white underparts, and a forked tail. The adult male is purplish-black

3a CORMORANT, Juv. 3b Ad.   1b GANNETS, Imm. in flight
1   GANNET, Ad., summer   2a SHAG, Ads., with and without crests 2b Imm.

1 HERON (*Ardea cinerea*). Measuring 3 ft. long, this is the largest common bird in Britain next to the mute swan. It is unmistakable in outline, at rest or in flight, when the dark undersides of its wing are conspicuous. The sexes are alike, but immature birds have less crest and less black, and juveniles (1a) are brownish grey. The legs are brown, eyes yellow, and the bill, normally yellowish, may turn red for a time in spring.

Herons nest in almost every British and Irish county, but are commonest in the south and east of England. They like slow-moving rivers and streams, shallow lakes, marshes, and sheltered tidal waters. Most heronries (breeding colonies) in the south are in tall trees near water, but elsewhere they may be in bushes, reed-beds, on cliffs, or even on the ground.

Herons often stand motionless beside shallow water, heads sunk in their plumage or necks raised in an S-bend. If disturbed, they take wing with heavy flapping and legs trailing, uttering a *kaark* of alarm. Their eyes can focus together along the bill, enabling them to stab at their prey with great accuracy and speed. Each bird has its own beat along a river or ditch; they are most active at dawn and dusk, stalking slowly after fish, frogs, voles, and young birds, which they swallow head first. They also take molluscs, crustaceans, and insects, and are accused of eating trout eggs. Very early in spring, pairs begin to display at the heronry, greeting each other with neck movements, bill snapping, and various calls. They use the same nest year after year, the female building it up into a huge saucer of sticks, lined with twigs, grass, or bracken. The parents sit in turn on three to five chalky blue eggs, which hatch in about 3½ weeks. The young, which are fed by food regurgitated, keep up a loud clacking chorus between feeds. They fledge in about 8 weeks and then are often seen in parties standing in fields or perched in trees, before dispersing in autumn. Some herons from abroad pass through or winter in Britain, and there is known to be some interchange between heronries.

1 2 3 4 5 6 7 8 9 10 11 12

2 BITTERN (*Botaurus stellaris*). Smaller than a heron, the bittern is 2½ ft. long. In flight its rich brown plumage streaked with black and its rounded wings suggest a huge owl. It can extend its long neck feathers into a fan. The sexes are alike, and the juveniles differ little from adults.

Having almost ceased to breed in Britain, the bittern now nests in East Anglia and very locally in Lancashire, Kent and Anglesey; occasionally elsewhere. Odd birds turn up in winter in reed-beds anywhere.

The bittern seldom comes into the open and only flies short distances, so it is not easy to observe; it is liveliest at dawn and dusk. When alarmed it 'freezes' with bill pointed upwards and blends well with the reed stems. Though it walks slowly, it can travel quite fast through reeds by grasping the stems. It hunts its varied food in thick cover, and cleans itself after eating fish with 'powder' from patches on its breast. The male's early spring booming sounds like a distant foghorn and carries up to 3 miles on calm days. Both sexes also utter hoarse calls. The female builds the nest platform from vegetation around her and lays four to six olive-brown eggs, sitting on them for 3½ weeks; she tends the young, dropping food from her crop when they pull at her bill. They soon wander from the nest among the reeds but cannot fly for about 8 weeks, after which they usually disperse from the breeding area.

1 2 3 4 5 6 7 8 9 10 11 12

AMERICAN BITTERN (*Botaurus lentiginosus*). A rare visitor, rather smaller than the European bittern, with a brown instead of a black crown and finer black markings on the body. It has been recorded about fifty times, mostly from Ireland and the west side of Britain.

3 LITTLE BITTERN (*Ixobrychus minutus*). A very small 'heron', about 14 ins. long, which looks like a miniature night heron, but is buff where the other is grey and white. The female is browner, and the juvenile looks like a tiny common bittern.

It probably bred in East Anglia about 80 years ago, but is now a rare visitor, mainly to the south-east and in spring or autumn, haunting reed-beds and scrub near water. It flies buoyantly, with a short call note *kwer*; it also utters harsh calls from cover. It breeds all over Europe.

4 NIGHT HERON (*Nycticorax nycticorax*). The adult is smaller and more compact than a heron, about 2 ft. long, with glossy greenish-black upperparts and greyish-white below. Juveniles have a brown plumage like the bittern. In flight adults look black above with grey wings and tail.

In recent years wandering birds from Edinburgh Zoo have occurred in Scotland; but genuine wild night herons are visitors from Holland and France and are usually seen in the south, especially in spring and late autumn. They prefer woodland or scrub near marshes or lakes.

Night herons are active at dawn and dusk, roosting in trees or bushes by day, when they sometimes give their hoarse call, rather like the croak of a raven. They can climb among branches and twigs agilely but slowly; and feed on the same variety of small animals as other herons.

5 SPOONBILL (*Platalea leucorodia*). This unmistakable bird in flight or at rest is nearly 3 ft. long, with a body of 15 ins. The juveniles have black ends to the primary flight feathers and, at first, a flesh-coloured bill.

Up to 300 years ago spoonbills bred in East Anglia; now they are regular visitors there and, less commonly, to the south of England and to Wales, and are usually seen along estuaries or on coastal marshes. There are two colonies in Holland. They stand in the open, often on one leg and with their heads sunk in their breasts. They feed by sweeping their bills from side to side and gripping anything edible, both small water animals and the fruits of plants. They have a graceful flapping flight and also glide and soar.

4a NIGHT HERON. Juv. 4b Ad.   3 LITTLE BITTERN. M.
5 SPOONBILL. summer   2 BITTERN
1a HERON. 1st winter   1b HERON. Ad.

LONG-LEGGED WADING BIRDS. 2

1 LITTLE EGRET (*Egretta garzetta*). This pure white heron is rather under 2 ft. long from bill to tail. Its legs and bill are black, and it has yellow feet which show when it takes to flight. The juvenile does not have the long head plumes of the adult.

The beautiful little egret from southern Europe has been seen in Britain more often in recent years, mainly on the east and south coasts, but it is still a very rare visitor. It usually occurs on coastal marshes, not associating with other birds. In habits it is a typical heron and feeds on a variety of small creatures from ditches and ponds.

GREAT WHITE HERON (*Egretta alba*). Another pure white heron, which is a very rare visitor from eastern Europe, is nearly 3 ft. long, and can only be confused with the little egret at a distance. It is slim, with black feet, a yellow bill, and no long crest feathers. About a dozen have been recorded in Britain, recently always on the south coast of England.

2 PURPLE HERON (*Ardea purpurea*). Darker and somewhat smaller than the common heron (p. 13) which it very much resembles, this heron is rather over 2½ ft. long. At close range, it is seen to be much browner than any juvenile common heron, though the young birds are rather paler. It has longer toes than the common heron has, a difference which shows in flight.

Purple herons, which breed in France and Holland, are rare visitors to Britain, mainly to the east coast, nearly 200 having been recorded altogether. They frequent reed-beds or bush cover near lakes and marshes. They are fonder of thick cover than common herons and spend more time on the ground, their long toes enabling them to walk over soft ground and floating weeds. They hunt and feed on much the same variety of small animals as common herons do.

CATTLE EGRET (*Ardeola ibis*). Another very rare heron, about the same size as the little egret but with a shorter neck, and in summer a buff back and breast. Its crown is buff all the year, and its bill and legs are yellow, but become red in the breeding season. Juveniles are white, with dark legs. Although only two had been recorded in England up to 1962, that year a party appeared in Sussex in spring, and more may be expected as cattle egrets have begun to nest in France. Their headquarters are in Africa, and they have now colonised Brazil and North America. They perch on the backs of cattle, picking parasites and insects off them as they graze.

SQUACCO HERON (*Ardeola ralloides*). A small, light-brown heron from the Mediterranean area with greenish legs and bill; in flight it shows white wings and tail. It is about 1½ ft. long, and when settled is a squat-looking bird. It becomes paler in winter, and the juvenile is streaked with brown. About 100 have been recorded in Britain mainly in East Anglia and the south-west, in spring and summer. The birds become active in the evening, and feed on fish and insects.

3 GLOSSY IBIS (*Plegadis falcinellus*). This rare visitor from eastern Europe looks like a black curlew (p. 69) with rounded wings. It is about 22 ins. long and has a glossy summer plumage which becomes duller in winter, with white streaks; the young birds are browner. It was once a fairly regular autumn visitor on the south and east coasts, and occasionally elsewhere, but now it is very seldom recorded. It used to be found on shores and coastal marshes, feeding on small insects and molluscs by probing in the mud.

4 WHITE STORK (*Ciconia ciconia*). This bird is quite unmistakable and very handsome with its white plumage, black wings, and long red bill and legs. It is nearly 3½ ft. long. The young birds have dark-brown wings, and their legs and bills are duller than the adult's. Storks, which usually appear on spring or autumn migration in East Anglia and southern England, have become rarer in recent years, as they have in France, Holland, and Germany where they breed. A pair nested on St. Giles Cathedral, Edinburgh, in 1416, and after a spring influx in 1967 two remained for several months in Norfolk.

Storks hunt frogs in marshes and ditches, snapping them up in their stride, and take many other small animals. They fly with legs and neck stretched, and may soar for long periods in wide circles.

5 BLACK STORK (*Ciconia nigra*). A little smaller than the white stork, but like it in shape. It has glossy-black upperparts and white underparts. Its bill is a darker and the legs a brighter red than the white stork's. It flies and walks like a white stork, but is much shyer, and it feeds on a variety of small animals. About thirty have been recorded in Britain, mainly in the east and south and in spring. They breed from central Europe eastward.

6 CRANE (*Grus grus*). Another enormous and unmistakable bird, over 3½ ft. long from beak to tail. It is related to the rails (p. 58). It is a very rare visitor, and some of those seen may be escapes. It bred in East Anglia up to about 1600, and seems to be occurring more often in recent years, usually in the south-east of England. Such visitors are probably genuine passage migrants on their way to or from Scandinavia, where they breed.

1 LITTLE EGRET   2 PURPLE HERON
3 GLOSSY IBIS   4 WHITE STORK
6 CRANE   5 BLACK STORK

DABBLING DUCKS. 1

1 MALLARD (*Anas platyrhynchos*). Nearly 2 ft. long, this is the typical 'wild duck' and ancestor of most farmyard varieties. Both sexes have a dark purplish-blue wing speculum with white edges, which shows up in flight. The duck's almost black bill usually has some orange at the side. Drakes when young or in eclipse look like dark females; the fluffy ducklings are dark brown above and yellow below.

Mallards are found throughout the British Isles, both as residents and winter visitors, by all types of fresh water, on marshes and estuaries, and along sheltered coasts. They may nest a long way from water. Many are also bred for sport.

Mallards may be wild and wary or completely tame. They feed by day or night, dabbling in mud or shallows, up-ending in deeper water, and grazing on fields, eating parts of many plants. They rest and preen on or near water, often perching on low branches, and they are at home on land, though they waddle rather awkwardly. They dive usually only if injured or excited and, if alarmed, take off almost vertically and fly with rapid, noisy beats and necks stretched. On migration they move in loose formations, not in V's. The duck has a loud *quack quack*, and the drake's call is higher pitched. When courting, several drakes will display round a duck on the water, and also chase her in the air. They form pairs in autumn and begin nesting very early in spring, the duck choosing the site under cover on the ground, in a pollarded tree or old nest, and even on buildings in cities. She lays six to twelve or more greenish-white eggs in a nest lined with down from her breast, and sits closely for about 4 weeks, covering the eggs with down when she leaves the nest. The ducklings feed themselves at once with her guidance and take nearly 2 months to fledge. During the heavy moult which follows breeding the birds cannot fly and stay hidden; but in late summer they fly again, and in autumn are joined by many overseas visitors.

1 2 3 4 5 6 7 8 9 10 11 12

BLACK DUCK (*Anas rubripes*). This close relative of the mallard from North America has been recorded five times between 1954 and 1969. Drake and duck are similar and look like dark female mallards, but they have no white on the tail, and no white edge to the wing speculum. The pale underside of the wings shows up against the very dark body in flight.

2 GADWALL (*Anas strepera*). Although smaller than a mallard (20 ins. long), it looks a big duck. The drake's dark plumage is attractive in detail; the duck is greyer and more mottled than a mallard, with a bright orange line along the bill. The red, black, and white speculum is distinctive, and in flight the belly shows white. The drake in eclipse is like a dark female.

Gadwalls have been successfully introduced to East Anglia and the London area, Gloucestershire, and Somerset; some also breed on Tresco in the Scillies and in east Scotland. But they are mainly winter visitors in small numbers to lakes and quiet rivers.

They resemble mallards in habits, but beat their more pointed wings faster, and the duck's quack is quieter. The drakes croak and whistle when displaying. The eight to twelve creamy eggs, laid in a well-concealed nest near water, hatch in about 4 weeks, and the young, looked after by the female, take 7 weeks to fledge. Residents do not move about much; winter visitors arrive from September onwards and leave in March and April.

1 2 3 4 5 6 7 8 9 10 11 12

3 PINTAIL (*Anas acuta*). Length about 22 ins. without the tail feathers. The drake has an unmistakable plumage, and the duck can be distinguished from a mallard by her slimmer form, lighter colour, grey bill, pointed tail, and dark brown speculum. In flight her narrow wings with their light trailing edges show up. Both sexes have green legs.

Pintails are residents, passage, and winter visitors, most numerous in Ireland and western Britain, both on coasts and fresh water. They breed somewhat irregularly in parts of Scotland, in eastern England, and occasionally in Ireland.

They feed on a variety of plants, including eel-grass (*Zostera*) at low tide. They are shy and take wing quickly, with faster beats than a mallard. The duck has a quiet *quack*, and the drake whistles during the displays, which resemble those of the mallard. The duck nests on the ground, sometimes in the open, and the seven to ten creamy-yellow eggs hatch in about 23 days. The drake stays nearby during incubation and usually helps with the brood, which takes about 6 weeks to fledge. Breeding birds do not as a rule migrate; winter visitors come from eastern Europe and Asia.

1 2 3 4 5 6 7 8 9 10 11 12

4 SHOVELER (*Anas clypeata*). About the same size as a gadwall, its distinguishing features are the very broad bill, light-blue forewing, and green speculum, and the white breast and chestnut flanks of the drake. Drakes in eclipse have lighter wings and darker backs than ducks, and young drakes attain full plumage slowly, causing confusing mixtures.

The shoveler breeds, mainly as a summer visitor, in most English, Irish, east Scottish, and a few Welsh counties, on marshes and by lakes. On passage and as a winter visitor it haunts shallow waters in lowland regions.

Shovelers work their broad bills along the water surface and dabble in mud to take small animals and plants, and they also snap insects in the air. They fly readily but walk badly. They are usually silent, though the duck quacks, and the drake has a double call: *tuk tuk*. The eight to twelve greenish or buffish white eggs are laid in a nest some way from water and sometimes quite exposed. The duck hatches them in 3½ weeks, and the drake sometimes helps with the young, which fledge in 6 weeks. Birds bred in Britain migrate as the passage and winter birds arrive, and return early in spring before the others leave.

1 2 3 4 5 6 7 8 9 10 11 12

1a MALLARD. F.
2a GADWALL, M.
3a PINTAIL, F. 3b M.

2b GADWALL, F.
1b MALLARD, M.
4b SHOVELER, M. 4a F.

1 WIGEON (*Anas penelope*). The wigeon is a stoutly built bird, 1½ ft. long, smaller than a mallard (p. 17) and larger than a teal. It has a rather rounded head and small bill. The drake has a buff and chestnut head, a broad white patch extending to the front of the wing, and a dark green speculum with black borders. The duck is a much richer brown than most ducks and has a pointed tail and a dull, white-edged speculum. Young and eclipse males are like females, and the ducklings are blackish-brown above and mixed lighter browns below.

In winter wigeon are to be seen all round British coasts and on many inland lakes and reservoirs, preferring those with grassy shores. Some breed in Britain, mostly in highland country, near sheets of water, especially those with islands.

Wigeon eat almost entirely vegetable matter, grazing both on grassland and on eel-grass beds between the tides, often feeding at night. They fly fast in close parties, the drakes uttering their famous whistling call: '*whee-oo*'; the females growl, sometimes in unison. In display, the drakes surround a duck and whistle, but do not make any very striking movements. In spring, the flocks break up, and small groups may nest near each other, building in heather, bracken, and other thick cover, usually near water. The duck incubates the six to ten creamy eggs for up to 4 weeks, the drake generally staying near. Both look after the young, which fly in about 6 weeks. The parties then move to the coast and are joined by winter visitors and passage migrants.

*1　2　3　**4　5　6***　7　8　9　*10　11　12*

AMERICAN WIGEON (*Anas americana*). The 'baldpate' of North America is so named because the drake's head is buff with a broad green band from eye to nape. The rest of the plumage is brown instead of grey but otherwise resembles the European wigeon. The ducks are more alike, the American being paler above and white instead of grey under the wing. About 60 have now been recorded, including a party of thirteen in Co. Kerry in 1968; some southern occurrences are probably escapes from collections.

2 TEAL (*Anas crecca*). This is the smallest of the common British ducks, being about 14 ins. long. The drake's head pattern is unmistakable, as is the buff and black patch towards the tail. The white stripe along the drake's side is absent in the American race, which occasionally appears in Britain. Both sexes show a green and black speculum. Young drakes and old ones in eclipse look like dark females, and the ducklings are like small mallards.

Teal are common throughout the British Isles in winter, but more local in the breeding season. They like the shores of shallow lakes, bogs, and marshes, gathering particularly on flooded land, and less commonly on estuaries and muddy coasts. They nest near small ponds and pools, or sometimes a long way from water.

Though they may rest on the water, teal spend most of their time on land, feeding on plants and small animals, in muddy ground. Their quick actions, rapid flight with twists and turns, and small size make them resemble waders (pp. 60 - 65). A party of teal used to be called a 'spring' because of the speed with which they rise. On the wing, the musical, double call of the drakes, *shrit shrit*, can be heard a long way off; the duck is rather silent, usually quacking only when alarmed. Their display is much like mallard's and pairs form in autumn but remain in the flock until the spring, when they go to the breeding area. The nest is usually well hidden on the ground, and the eight to ten pale buff eggs are incubated by the duck for about 3 weeks; the drake generally remains near and helps look after the young, which fly after 3½ weeks. After the moult, British teal wander, but seldom further than France, while thousands arrive from eastern Europe in autumn; many pass through in autumn and again in March and April.

*1　2　3　**4　5　6***　7　8　9　*10　11　12*

3 GARGANEY (*Anas querquedula*). Though a little larger than the teal (15 ins. long), this summer visitor can easily be mistaken for it. In spring the broad white stripe over the eye and a sharp division between the brown breast and pale grey flanks distinguish the drake, and he always has a very pale forewing and a white border to the green speculum. The duck's very dull speculum distinguishes her from the teal. Except for the forewing, young and eclipse drakes resemble ducks, and the ducklings are like teal ducklings. Garganeys breed in small numbers in several southern counties and East Anglia, and occasionally further north, in the rich vegetation found round shallow lakes and in river valleys and fenland. They occur on passage elsewhere. They are like small shoveler (p. 17) in habits, and eat both plants and a good many animals, including small fish, frogs, insects, and worms. In spring the drake has a remarkable croaking call, often heard in flight, while the duck utters a quiet quack. They often arrive in England in pairs and nest in long grass in a marsh or close to water; the clutch is seven to twelve creamy eggs, which the duck sits on for about 3 weeks. She alone looks after the young, which fly in about 4 weeks, leaving the country in small parties during the autumn.

*.　.　3　**4　5　6***　7　8　9　10　.　.*

BLUE-WINGED TEAL (*Anas discors*). The drake of this American garganey has a white stripe in front of the eye, a white border above the green speculum, and a brightish blue forewing; the duck's wing pattern is similar but duller. About 35 have been recorded, mostly from Ireland but the rest widely scattered, and usually in autumn or winter.

1a WIGEON, F.
1b WIGEON, M.

2c TEAL, F.
2a TEAL, M. summer   2b in eclipse

3a GARGANEY, M.
3b GARGANEY, F.

ORNAMENTAL WILDFOWL

1 EGYPTIAN GOOSE (*Alopochen aegyptiacus*). This big relative of the shelducks (p. 29) is a popular ornamental species which has become naturalised in Norfolk and perhaps elsewhere, and is now considered to be a British bird. It is likely to be seen only near park lakes in small parties or in nesting pairs. It has a double quacking call, often uttered on the wing.

2 MUSCOVY DUCK (*Cairina moschata*). The domestic form is the most likely to be seen at large in Britain, as it is kept by many people, whereas the black wild form is not. Owing to domestication, there is a good deal of variation in colour: black, black-and-white, white, or grey. The crest, the bare red wattle, and the knob on the bill, as well as its clumsy form, make this bird quite distinctive. Muscovies seem able to establish themselves for a time, for example on the Thames. They fly with difficulty and usually nest on the ground, but they sometimes build at a height, for example, on a thatched roof.

3 RUDDY SHELDUCK (*Tadorna ferruginea*). Although a number of records of this shelduck from southern Europe and Asia are accepted as genuine wild birds, many more must be due to escapes, for its brilliant plumage makes it a favourite ornamental wildfowl. They have turned up in a number of Scottish and English counties, and there was evidently quite a large genuine invasion in 1892. With a total length just over 2 ft., they cannot easily be mistaken for any other bird likely to be seen in Britain, except possibly the Egyptian goose. The sexes are more or less alike. They feed mainly on vegetable matter with some small animals, and are most likely to be seen near shallow fresh water. They make their nest in a hole or burrow, as the common shelduck do (p. 29)

4 RUDDY DUCK (*Oxyura jamaicensis*). This North American species is a member of the group of small ducks called stiff-tails. They have rather round bodies and they hold their stiff fan-shaped tails upright when they are displaying on the water. The drake have white faces surrounded by a black crown and nape; and their bills are blue and their bodies chestnut red, with white under the tail. The drake cannot be confused with any native species. The duck are light brown and black, with a black crown and the characteristic tail. Ruddy ducks can now be seen in several reservoirs and gravel-pit lakes from Somerset to Staffordshire, and are breeding successfully, so the species is recognised as British by naturalisation

5 MANDARIN (*Aix galericulata*). This spectacular looking duck is the Asiatic counterpart of the American Carolina or Wood Duck. Both are commonly kept in collections in Britain, but only the mandarin has naturalised itself successfully. The drake in full plumage is quite unique; and the duck, though much less conspicuous, can be distinguished from any native ducks by the row of white spots along her underside, the blue speculum, and the white on her face. Mandarins have established themselves round Virginia Water and Windsor Park, round Woburn in Bedfordshire, and also in Scotland near Perth; and they do not move far away. They are dabbling ducks feeding both on the surface and up-ending, but chiefly grazing on land. In flight, the duck looks very pale. Mandarins perch freely and nest in holes in trees

1   EGYPTIAN GOOSE   2 MUSCOVY DUCK

3a RUDDY SHELDUCK, M. 3b F.

4a RUDDY DUCK, F. 4b M.   5a MANDARIN, M. 5b F.

DIVING DUCKS. 1

1 RED-CRESTED POCHARD (*Netta rufina*). One of the bigger diving ducks found on fresh water, with a total length of 22 ins., the drake is easily identified by his bright chestnut head, rather thin red bill, black breast, grey back, and white on the flanks. In flight, a broad white bar shows on the wings. The duck has an obvious but duller wing patch and very pale cheeks, and she has pinkish legs, while the drake's are reddish. With her generally brown plumage, she resembles the duck common scoter (p. 27). Drakes in eclipse, which comes on in May, retain the red bill but otherwise look rather like the ducks.

These pochards are fairly regular winter visitors in small numbers to the southern half of England, though some that are recorded are almost certainly escapes, as they are popular ornamental wildfowl. Pairs bred in Lincolnshire in 1937 and in Essex in 1958 but it is doubtful if they were wild birds. Red-crested pochards may be seen either on deep or shallow lakes, usually with reed-beds or other surrounding cover; they spend more time on land than most diving ducks and walk quite well, but they normally feed by diving after underwater plants. They rise from the water with some difficulty but are fast fliers, making a whistling sound with their rapid wing-beats. They are silent birds in Britain, but occasionally they show part of their display; the drake lifts his body from the water while resting his bill on his neck and spreading his crest. Drakes and ducks also swim round each other.

2 POCHARD (*Aythya ferina*). Considerably smaller than the red-crested pochard, the common pochard is only 1½ ft. long. It has a round body, smooth head, and, in side view, tapering bill, which give it a distinctive outline. The drake's plumage pattern of dark red head, bluish bill, red eye, black breast, and grey body is unmistakable; and the dull brown plumage and shape of her head make the duck also easy to identify. They show no wing-bar in flight. Eclipse drakes and juveniles resemble the duck. The duckling is blackish-brown above and greenish-yellow below.

As a breeding species pochards are concentrated on the east side of Britain, but they are widespread in winter. They are found on a variety of waters of medium depth, but seldom on rivers, unless very slow-running, or at sea. They nest by quiet lakes and ponds, especially those with islands or large tussocks in the water.

Like other diving ducks, pochards tend to swim away from an intruder rather than fly, and they find it difficult to take off. They fly in bunches, sometimes swooping down suddenly to land. They swim low in the water, hardly showing their short tails, and dive with a jump or by submerging. They feed on many water plants and some small animals. They come on land at times and walk quite well. Drakes surround a duck in display and stretch their necks, filling them with air, and then expel the air with a noise like a groan. The duck has a hoarse, growling call in the breeding season. She builds close to or right over water, laying six to twelve large greenish-white eggs, on which she sits closely for about 3½ weeks. The young take about 8 weeks to fledge and are looked after entirely by the duck. After breeding, parties collect and move towards the south, while winter visitors from eastern Europe arrive in autumn and stay until March or April.

*1 2 3 **4 5 6** 7 8 9 10 11 12*

3 FERRUGINOUS DUCK (*Aythya nyroca*). This rare visitor is smaller than a pochard, being about 16 ins. long, and looks rather like a female tufted duck (p. 25). The sexes resemble each other, but the drake has a richer chestnut colour and a white instead of a brown eye. Both birds have a curving white wing-bar which shows in flight, and white under the tail which shows on the water. Some female tufted ducks also show a patch under the tail.

There have been about 200 records, mainly from southern and eastern England, of this east European duck. It is most likely to be seen on quiet waters with plenty of vegetation surrounding them. Escapes from collections may also be seen.

The ferruginous duck is a shy bird, which behaves in general like the pochard; it is a good diver in rather shallow water, feeding both on water plants and small animals. The calls are like those of the pochard, and the display is also similar.

1a RED-CRESTED POCHARD, F.   1b M.
2a POCHARD, M.   2b F., winter
3a FERRUGINOUS DUCK, M.   3b F.

DIVING DUCKS. 2

1 SCAUP (*Aythya marila*). A fairly large duck, 19 ins. long. The drake has a black head, breast, and tail, a blue bill, a pale grey back, and white flanks; it can be distinguished from the tufted drake by its back and smooth shaped head. The duck also has a smooth head, and she has a larger white blaze round her bill than any tufted duck; but she may be hard to distinguish except at close range. Both sexes have yellow eyes. Immature plumages are also confusing, but the drake in eclipse is less like the female than most of his relatives. The duckling is like that of the pochard, with lighter upperparts.

The scaup is a winter visitor all round British coasts, though commonest in the east. It occasionally appears inland, usually after storms. Up to 1913 it bred occasionally in Scotland, and is now nesting again sporadically.

Large flocks of scaup form in winter and may be seen off-shore sitting or flying close together. They dive deep and stay down about half a minute, feeding on small water animals, sea-weeds, and fresh-water plants. They sometimes feed on shallow water and occasionally come on land, walking quite well. After the winter visitors have gone, odd birds or pairs may stay into spring on fresh water. They are seldom heard to call outside the breeding season.

1   2   3   4   5   (6   7   8)   9   10   11   12

2 TUFTED DUCK (*Aythya fuligula*). This well-known British diving duck is about 17 ins. long, with a round body like the pochard (p. 23); but the purplish black plumage of the drake, the white flank patch, and yellow eye make it distinctive. The duck is a rich dark brown with a less bright eye, and both sexes have the tufted head, from which they get their name. Some ducks have white round the bill, like a duck scaup, others have white under the tail like a ferruginous duck (p. 23), and there are puzzling plumages when drakes are moulting. They have a broad white wing-bar and a narrow white line near the trailing edge of the wing. Eclipse and young drakes resemble but are darker than females. The duckling is very dark above, and pale yellow below.

Tufted ducks now breed over a wide area, except in highlands, and they are even commoner as winter visitors to lakes, reservoirs, slow-flowing rivers, and ponds in parks, but seldom to salt water. The tufted ducks of St. James's Park in London are mostly wild birds from eastern Europe.

While in general they resemble the pochard in habits, tufted ducks become much tamer and will take food from man in parks. They obtain their natural diet of water plants and some small animals by diving, sometimes for ¾ minute. Their display also resembles that of the pochard and of ferruginous ducks, but is less violent. The duck has the harsh call typical of the group, and the drake a rather pleasant quiet whistle. The nest is often built on an island or on shore in wet places near water; sometimes several are near together. The clutch of six to fourteen rather large greenish eggs are incubated by the duck for about 3½ weeks. She looks after the young, which soon learn to dive for their food and fledge in about 6 weeks. Parties collect after nesting and may build up into flocks, while the winter visitors arrive in numbers in autumn and return from February onwards.

*1   2   3   4   **5   6**   7   8   9   10   11   12*

RING-NECKED DUCK (*Aythya collaris*). This American counterpart of the tufted duck has been recorded about fifteen times since 1955, but some may have been escapes. The drake has a high domed head, no tuft, and the pale slaty-blue bill has a dark tip and a thin white band at the base. The duck has the same shaped head and bill pattern and a white ring round the eye.

3 GOLDENEYE (*Bucephala clangula*). Between a scaup and a tufted duck in size, the goldeneye is about 1½ ft. long. In any plumage it has a distinctive peaked head shape. The drake in full plumage is unmistakable at close range, but at a distance can be confused with a drake goosander (p. 29), which also shows a great deal of white. The duck with her reddish head, white collar, and pale patch on the small bill, is not difficult to identify, though young drakes (3c) resemble her. A big white wing-bar shows in flight. The duckling is dark brown above, and almost white below.

The goldeneye is a widely-distributed winter visitor both to the coasts and inland, usually in small parties or odd birds. Although pairs often remain into spring, there were no certain breeding records until 1970, when a duck with four young was seen in Inverness-shire.

Goldeneyes swim higher than other diving ducks and rise more easily from the water into a rapid flight, their wings making quite a loud singing noise. They dive to moderate depths for ½ minute or more, and feed almost entirely on small animals of many kinds. Their displays, which consist of males swimming round females with head-jerkings and of various developments from this beginning, are often seen in Britain before the birds leave. This is a species in which the proportion of drakes to ducks varies in different parts of the country. Goldeneyes nest in holes of trees, and they have used nest-boxes in Scandinavia for hundreds of years. Nest-boxes have been put up on suitable lochs in Scotland, but so far without success.

1   2   3   4   5   (6   7   8)   9   10   11   12

BUFFELHEAD (*Bucephala albeola*). This small North American relative of the goldeneye has been recorded about six times round British coasts, and once recently in Buckinghamshire. The drake has a broad white band across its big head down to the eyes, which is reduced to a pale patch in the duck.

3a GOLDENEYE, F. 3b M. 3c M., 1st winter
2a TUFTED DUCK, M., moulting 2b M. 2c F., two types
la SCAUP, M. 1b F.

DIVING DUCKS. 3

1 EIDER (*Somateria mollissima*). These biggest sea-ducks, nearly 2 ft. long, are unmistakable even at quite long range on water, especially the drake. The duck has a dull speculum with light borders. The shape of the head, with the almost straight line from crown to bill-tip, is also distinct. Young drakes have varied plumages (1b), and drakes in eclipse have a pale band running from the bill to the crown of the head. The ducklings are dark smoky grey.

Eiders are resident and breeding almost all round the Scottish coasts, in Northumberland, Lancashire, and in Northern Ireland. Non-breeding birds spread much further south in summer. They congregate off low rocky and sandy coasts and in sea-lochs and estuaries, but are seldom seen inland.

Parties in spring are a mixture of white and dark birds. The drakes swim round the ducks and utter the crooning *oo-oo* calls which sound like distant human conversation; they jerk their heads and sometimes raise their bodies. Eiders feed in company, diving and surfacing one after the other, regularly using their wings underwater, and bringing up shell-fish and small crabs. They eat very little vegetable matter. They fly, powerfully but heavily, in long lines low over the waves.

Several or many eider ducks nest close together, in cover or right in the open, as on the Farne Islands, where they will allow a visitor to stroke them on the nest. The duck incubates the four to six large, rather shiny green or cream eggs, which are bedded in the famous eiderdown; she sits almost continuously for about 4 weeks. The very independent young join up in large groups ('creches') with several females in charge. They take about 2 months to fledge.

*1 2 3 **4 5 6 7** 8 9 10 11 12*

KING EIDER (*Somateria spectabilis*), **STELLER'S EIDER** (*Polysticta stelleri*). The king eider occasionally visits northern Scotland from the edge of the Arctic; it resembles the common eider in general habits, but is rather smaller (about 22 ins. long), and has a rounder head. The drake has bright head colours, a big orange bill and a black-edged shield on the forehead. The duck is brighter than the common eider duck. Steller's eider from northern Asia is only about 18 ins. long. The drake has a black and white pattern above, with long black-and-white shoulder feathers, and is rich buff underneath. The very dark duck has a purplish speculum. Seven recorded, last in 1970.

2 COMMON SCOTER (*Melanitta nigra*). This round-bodied sea-duck, about 19 ins. long, has a pointed tail and a simple plumage pattern. The drake looks black at sea except for the orange-pink area on the knobbed bill; the duck is very dark brown with pale cheeks. There is no wing-bar, and the drake does not have a full eclipse. Young males are dark brown at first, as is the duckling.

The scoter is best known as a winter and non-breeding visitor, occurring all round British coasts, though it breeds in small numbers on fresh-water lochs in the north of Scotland, the Inner Hebrides, and in the north and west of Ireland. At sea, scoters are usually seen off low sandy and muddy coasts, and occasionally they turn up inland, usually singly. They may form dense black 'rafts' out to sea, before taking wing in long ragged lines, usually low over the water but sometimes at a height. Like eiders, they dive in company for shellfish, their main food, but they swim higher out of the water, often showing their pointed tails. The duck has a hoarse call, the drake a musical 'song' in spring, when displaying. The duck nests in long heather or other thick cover, often on an island, and she hatches the five to seven creamy eggs in about 4 weeks. The young, which she alone looks after, fly in about 1½ months. They then return to sea and are joined in autumn by passage migrants and winter visitors.

*1 2 3 4 **5 6** 7 8 9 10 11 12*

3 VELVET SCOTER (*Melanitta fusca*). Both drake and duck, about the same size as an eider, have distinct white wing-bars, and the drake has white under his eye and orange legs. The young drake is dark brown, like a duck, but has white on his face.

These scoters are winter and passage visitors from Scandinavia, mainly in small parties, to the north and east coasts of Scotland and the seas round the Isle of Man. They are less wild than common scoters and occur off rocky coasts. They feed by diving on shellfish and seldom come to land unless oiled.

4 SURF SCOTER (*Melanitta perspicillata*). This rare visitor from North America, a little smaller than the velvet scoter, is most often recorded from the north of Scotland. It can be recognised by its long-snouted appearance, though in other ways the duck is very like a common scoter.

HARLEQUIN DUCK (*Histrionicus histrionicus*). A very rare visitor from North America or Iceland. The drake, about 18 ins. long, is a gay mixture of black and white, with chestnut-red flanks, and red above the eyes. The duck is mottled brown and white, with white patches on face and wings. Both sexes have blue legs. It has been recorded eight times.

5 LONG-TAILED DUCK (*Clangula hyemalis*). Not including the drake's long tail, this sea-duck is about 17 ins. long. There are distinct summer and winter plumages. In winter, both sexes are dark brown and white. In summer the drake's upperparts become mainly light brown (5a), and the duck becomes browner. The drake loses his long tail-feathers in eclipse.

Long-tailed ducks are winter visitors, mainly to northern coasts, though they may be seen all round Britain and occasionally inland, and a few stay on in the north all summer. The birds feed in flocks out at sea on shellfish, diving sometimes for as long as 1½ minutes. They are noisy, even outside the breeding season, the drakes having a musical yodelling call. In flight they beat their wings mainly below their bodies and sometimes pitch breast-first on the water, then swim buoyantly with tails up.

5a LONG-TAILED DUCKS. M., summer 5b F., moulting 5c M., winter
4 SURF SCOTER M.   3a VELVET SCOTER, M. 3b F.
2a COMMON SCOTER, M.   2b F.   1a EIDER, M. 1b Imm. M. 1c F.

SHELDUCKS AND SAWBILLS

1 SHELDUCK (*Tadorna tadorna*). One of the biggest and most unmistakable of British ducks, about 2 ft. long. Unlike other commoner British ducks, the sexes look much alike, except for the pronounced knob at the base of the drake's bill. In flight, they show black wing-tips, white forewings, and a metallic green speculum. Both drake and duck have a duller eclipse plumage resembling that of immature birds, while juveniles have white faces, throats, and breasts. The ducklings are dark brown above and yellowish white below.

Shelduck are resident all round British coasts; they prefer sand dunes for nesting, but at other times concentrate in muddy estuaries. Most adults leave in July to carry out their moult in the Heligoland Bight; but some remain in Bridgwater Bay, Somerset.

Pairs or parties of shelduck scatter over muddy beaches when the tide is out, standing up like geese. They feed mainly on shellfish, crustaceans, and insects, with some vegetable matter. They fly with rather slow beats and a whistling sound, often uttering their quacking call. They have complicated displays with various head movements, both in pairs and in groups. Even in the breeding season they spend much time resting in parties above the shore in favourite spots, which become littered with feathers; they can swim buoyantly and dive if necessary. The nest, lined with a mass of light down, is built down an open rabbit-hole, under stones and bushes, or in a hollow tree, and eight to sixteen large creamy eggs are laid. The duck, called off twice a day by the drake, sits for about 4 weeks. The young later unite in parties, as eiders do (p. 27), and fledge in about 2 months. Some birds pass through Britain going northwards and winter visitors from the north arrive in autumn.

*1 2 3 **4 5 6** 7 8 9 10 11 12*

2 SMEW (*Mergus albellus*). The drake of these small sawbills is about 16 ins. long; the duck is smaller and may be confused with the smaller grebes (p. 5). In full plumage the drake is unmistakable, but immature birds may be puzzling, for some have quite dark heads. The duck has a chestnut and white pattern on her head, and in flight both sexes show a double white wing-bar separated by black.

Smew are winter visitors from Scandinavia east to Asia, and are most common in south-east England, usually single birds or small parties being seen, with few adult males. They frequent reservoirs and lakes, and occasionally big rivers and estuaries, but seldom the open sea. Like other sawbills, they are underwater fish-hunters, diving for only ¼ minute. They swim well, are active on land, and fly with a rapid noise-less beat. They are silent in winter, except for the drake's croak or grunt in its complex display, which includes head movements and dashes over the water.

3 GOOSANDER (*Mergus merganser*). This is the biggest of the 'sawbill' group, the drake being about 26 ins. long and the duck rather smaller. The drake's thin red bill and beautiful salmon-pink underparts distinguish it from similar birds such as mallards, and the duck's red head with its shaggy crest, grey upper-parts and pinkish underparts are distinctive. In flight, the duck shows a white speculum, while the drake's white wings have black tips. In his long eclipse he resembles the duck except for a white fore-wing. Young drakes are also like the female, and the ducklings are dark above, whitish below, with small chestnut patch on the neck.

In winter goosanders are distributed widely on fresh water and are common in London; they now nest all over Scotland and the extreme north of England, preferring lochs, rivers, and quite small streams, usually in wooded country. Fish form most of their diet, which they search for with heads under water and then dive after with a jump or by submerging. They usually swim low in the water and fly low with a rather fluttering action. Small parties remain together until they break up into pairs, after complicated displays, during which the usually silent drake gives a croaking call. The duck has a harsh call. She nests in a hollow tree, under big boulders, or in a bank, and lays a clutch of seven to twelve eggs which she hatches in about 5 weeks. The young flutter out of the nest hole and fledge in another 5 weeks. They then go down to larger lochs or the coast, where they are joined by winter visitors.

*1 2 3 **4 5 6** 7 8 9 10 11 12*

4 RED-BREASTED MERGANSER (*Mergus serrator*). About 3 ins. shorter than the goosander, the merganser drake is easily recognised by its rather wispy crest and streaked chestnut breast. Unlike the goosander, the duck has no definite break in colour between the brown head and the body. Both sexes show a broad white wing-bar in flight, crossed by black bands. During its long eclipse the drake looks like a duck except for the white fore-wing; juveniles also look like ducks, and the ducklings are like goosander ducklings.

In winter mergansers are to be seen in sheltered places round most British coasts, but rarely inland. They are residents in Scotland and Ireland, and now also nest in parts of north-west England and Wales, both on fresh and salt water, especially where there are islands.

In general behaviour and diet mergansers are like goosanders; they can dive for as long as 2 minutes. Their display, more spectacular than the goosander's, includes violent head movements and is the one occasion when the drake utters a call. The duck has the usual harsh note and a quack of alarm. The nest, though well-hidden, is rarely deep in a hole like the goosander's. The duck incubates the seven to thirteen pale-buff eggs in about 4 weeks, the drake taking no part. The young fly in about 5 weeks and tend to form packs, and the families move down to tidal water where they are joined in autumn by winter visitors.

*1 2 3 4 **5 6** 7 8 9 10 11 12*

HOODED MERGANSER (*Mergus cucullatus*). This smaller colourful merganser from North America has been recorded six times, though only once in recent years. The drake has a white, black-edged fan crest, and the duck a pronounced brownish crest.

1a SHELDUCK, Juv.   1c SHELDUCK, F.

         1b SHELDUCK, M.

2a SMEW, M.   2b SMEW, F.

    3   GOOSANDER, F. and M.   29

    4   RED-BREASTED MERGANSER, F. and M.

1 GREYLAG GOOSE (*Anser anser*). The greylag is the typical goose, ancestor of farmyard geese and the biggest of the 'grey' group, 2½ to 3 ft. long. Wild grey geese are hard to identify, for they all have the same general plumage pattern of grey-brown with pale edges to the feathers and a large white area round the tail. Adult greylags can be told in flight by their pale fore-wings and, if not too far away, by their heavy heads and bills. The pink-footed geese also have light fore-wings but darker heads than bodies. Greylag have orange bills with white nails (tips), and pink legs, as well as a more-or-less even tone of colour over head, neck, and body. First winter birds resemble the adults.

Greylags are winter visitors to parts of central and eastern Scotland and, less commonly, to some eastern English and Irish counties; elsewhere they are rare. Truly wild pairs breed in the northern Highlands of Scotland and the Hebrides, but are decreasing; on the other hand, 'colonies' of released birds have become established in Norfolk (where greylags bred up to 1800), in south-west Scotland, the English lakes, and elsewhere. Their winter haunts are marshes, pasture and arable fields, bogs, and lakesides; and they breed round moorland lochs and on small islands.

All grey geese follow a fairly regular routine in winter in Britain. They fly out early in the morning from their roosting areas, which may be close to the sea or by a loch, to feed in the fields. They travel short distances in wavering lines, honking and cackling, with deceptively slow-beating wings; then they circle round, plane downward, check their flight with rapid flaps, lower their feet, and settle. Small parties follow each other until several hundred birds may be grazing one field, walking slowly forward, often in silence. When alarmed, they jerk their heads nervously, then rise almost straight upward, calling loudly, wheel round in companies, and fly away. Grey geese can swim well. Their displays are not spectacular, but the gander, as domestic ganders do, chases off an intruder with head lowered and loud hisses, then 'reports back' to his mate.

The greylags breeding in Scotland lay four to six eggs, usually in long heather; the goose lines the nest with down and sits for about 4 weeks, the gander staying on guard near her. The fluffy goslings take about 2 months to fledge and, after the parents have moulted, the family remains together for the winter and even longer. The winter visitors leave in April and fly north in the famous V formation.

1 2 3 4 5 6 7 8 9 10 11 12

2 WHITE-FRONTED GOOSE (*Anser albifrons*). Smaller than the greylag, about 2 to 2½ ft. long, this is the easiest grey goose to recognise when adult because of the white 'front' between its bill and eyes and the black bars on its underparts. Two distinct races visit Britain; that from northern Europe has a pink bill and is lighter in plumage than the Greenland race, which has a yellow or orange bill. Both have white nails. Juveniles of both races have no white fronts nor barring underneath.

White-fronted geese are the commonest grey geese in winter down the west side of Britain; the Green-

land race is found in the west of Scotland and Irelan[d] the north European race in England and Wale[s] Their haunts are low moors, 'mosses', saltings such [as] the famous Dumbles by the Severn, and fields.

They seem more active than the greylag or pin[k]-foot, particularly on the wing, and their laughin[g] cackle, consisting of a double *wick wick* continuous[ly] repeated, is distinctive. The flocks often split up in[to] family parties.

1 2 3 4 5 . . . . 10 11 12

3 LESSER WHITE-FRONTED GOOSE (*Ans[er] erythropus*). Though smaller than the white-fronte[d] (about 2 ft. long) the lesser white-fronted is not ea[sy] to pick out in a big flock. It is darker all over, has [a] bigger white front when adult, and a prominent yello[w] ring round the eyes, which shows up well; it h[as] relatively longer wings.

Until 25 years ago, the lesser white-fronted w[as] considered to be extremely rare; now it occurs fai[rly] regularly, though in very small numbers, in sout[h] west Scotland and by the Severn in company with t[he] eastern race of white-fronted geese. A few have al[so] been recorded in eastern England. They behave li[ke] other grey geese, but can sometimes be picked out [by] their quicker grazing movements, and more hig[h] pitched voice.

4 PINK-FOOTED GOOSE (*Anser brachyrhynchu[s]* About the same size as the white-fronted goose. [In] flight, the fore-wings are pale, but the dark head a[nd] neck and small bill distinguish it from the greylag [at] reasonable distances. The bill is black and pin[k], sometimes almost black, and the legs are pin[k], but young birds have greyish, light pink, or yellow[ish] legs and look more mottled.

The pink-footed goose is a winter visitor in some te[ns] of thousands to the east of Britain and a few places [in] the west, but there are now very few by the Seve[rn] (mainly in late autumn). Its habits are similar to t[he] greylag in winter; it roosts on the coast or [in] estuaries, sometimes forming very large flocks. [Its] call is usually a double *ink ink*, between the calls [of] greylag and white-front in pitch. Most British pin[k]-feet nest in Iceland.

1 2 3 4 (5 6) . . 9 10 11 12

5 BEAN GOOSE (*Anser fabalis*). A rare goose vary[ing] in size between the greylag and the pink-footed goo[se]. It is the brownest and darkest of the group, and [the] pale edges of the feathers on the upperparts show [up] at close range. Its legs are bright orange, and its b[ill] varies in colour, but in Britain is usually orange w[ith] a black nail. Some regard it as a race of the pinkfo[ot].

The bean goose is a winter visitor, and is ve[ry] rare except in one area in south-west Scotland and o[ne] or two in eastern England. Its habits are like those [of] the greylag; it is the least talkative of the grey gee[se] with a call resembling the pink-foot, but gruff[er]. It tends to roost inland rather than go down to [the] shore, but associates with other geese in day time.

1 2 3 4 (5 6) . . (9) 10 11 12

GREYLAG GEESE   2a WHITE-FRONTED GEESE. Greenland race, Juv.   2b Ad.
a PINK-FOOTED GEESE, Imm.   3b Ad.   2c WHITE-FRONTED GOOSE. N. European race, Ad.   2d Imm.
BEAN GEESE, Ads.   4a LESSER WHITE-FRONTED GEESE, Ad.   4b Imm.

GEESE. 2

1 SNOW GOOSE (*Anser caerulescens*). Length 2 to 2½ ft. Though grouped with the grey geese (p. 31), the snow goose (1a) looks quite distinct with white plumage, black wing-tips, red and black bill, and pink legs. There are greater and lesser races, and a 'blue' colour phase (1c) of the latter with a white head and tail and a dark grey body has also occurred. Immature snow geese are dull brown and white, but the immature blue geese (1b) are dark except for the tail area.

Snow geese in all forms are very rare visitors from North America to Scotland, chiefly the south-west, and England and Ireland, especially Wexford, and sometimes the birds recorded have in fact, escaped from collections. In Britain they are usually seen with grey geese and behave like them. The call note is a single *aw*.

2 RED-BREASTED GOOSE (*Branta ruficollis*). This very rare 'black' goose, 21 ins. long, has an unmistakable plumage, though it can be confused with a brent from behind unless the head is seen. About twenty have wandered from Asia, mostly in winter, to various parts of Britain, and several have appeared with the other geese by the river Severn; but one or two of these may possibly have escaped from captivity.

3 CANADA GOOSE (*Branta canadensis*). Length over 3 ft. (body 2 ft.). This big goose has a grey-brown body with darker wing-tips, a white area round the tail, a black head and neck with a white chin patch, and black bill and legs.

The large eastern race of Canada goose was introduced as an 'ornamental wildfowl' from North America about 250 years ago; several thousand now live wild in flocks in the English Midlands, East Anglia, and elsewhere. Some hundreds, in small flocks or single pairs, have been moved in recent years from waters where they had become too numerous to other suitable places. Their adopted habitat is usually a lake or large gravel pit, especially if it has islands, and the surrounding marshland. A few birds of a smaller race have reached the west of the British Isles from North America.

Canada geese swim far more than grey geese and feed on water weeds by submerging their heads or up-ending; they also graze in fields, doing some damage to crops. They are tamer than other geese, and do not migrate as Canada geese do in their native country; but they may move to different waters in winter. They utter a loud, distinctive *a-honk* in flight or when

alarmed. In Britain Canada geese nest on the groun on islands or the shores of lakes; the goose lays fou to six creamy-white eggs in a nest of down and sits fe about 4 weeks with the gander on guard near he The young fly after 6 weeks.

*1 2 3 **4** **5** **6** 7 8 9 10 11 12*

4 BARNACLE GOOSE (*Branta leucopsis*). Up to 2¼ long with a body of 1½ ft., the barnacle comes betwee the brent and the Canada goose in size, and is di tinguished by its cream-coloured face and beautiful barred upperparts. Juveniles have darker faces tha the adults. They are winter visitors from Greenlan Spitsbergen, and Novaya Zemlya, chiefly to th Hebrides, Solway Firth, and some parts of Irelan but birds on passage are seen elsewhere. Their typic habitat is the green sward (*machair*) of the Hebride but they are also found on saltings, fresh marshe and fields near the sea.

Next to the Canada goose, barnacle geese are th least wary of British geese and spend much more tin on land than the brent do. Their call note, heard fro a flock on the wing, sounds like a pack of small dog They feed mainly on grass, often by night, and seldo mix with other geese.

1 2 3 4 5 (6 . . 9) 10 11 12

5 BRENT GOOSE (*Branta bernicla*). Two races of th small goose, about 2 ft. long, are seen as wint visitors in Britain, one race having darker (5a) an the other paler (5b) underparts. Their size, dark upperparts, and absence of a chin patch distinguis them from the Canada goose, and their black fac and uniform upperparts from the barnacle. Th juvenile has no white streak on its neck.

The dark-breasted race is, in general, found to th east, and the pale-breasted to the west of Britain an in Ireland, but they often mix. They winter on coast mudflats and depend very much on the eel-gra *Zostera*; when it disappeared for a time, bre geese became very scarce. They breed in the far nor all round the world.

Brent geese live in tight flocks, and a flock m look like a solid black island when at rest on the s They fly in rather ragged wavy lines, not in a Their call is a growling croak. They feed by paddli among the *Zostera* beds or by dipping their heads a up-ending in deeper water. They roost at sea a seldom come far inland.

1 2 3 4 (5 . . 8) 9 10 11 12

2 RED-BREASTED GOOSE
1a SNOW GOOSE
3 CANADA GOOSE

1b SNOW GOOSE Imm. blue 1c Ad. blue
4 BARNACLE GOOSE
5a BRENT GOOSE, dark 5b Imm. pale

33

SWANS

1 MUTE SWAN (*Cygnus olor*). Adult male (cob) swans are the largest British birds, weighing 20 lbs. or more and measuring 5 ft. from beak to tail, with a body 2½ ft. long. Their distinguishing features are the orange beak with black nail and knob at the base, the large head, and the graceful S-curve of the neck. The young birds (cygnets) have grey-brown plumage, and they become progressively whiter over several years. There is a 'Polish' variety which is white at all ages. Swans with rusty-coloured heads are not a different variety, but have been feeding in water containing iron oxides.

There are about 20,000 swans in Britain; those in Ireland have not been counted but must number several thousands. They nest in every English, Welsh, and almost every Scottish county. But less than half of them breed in any one particular year. There is a swannery at Abbotsbury in Dorset where 200 to 500 birds live under protection. Elsewhere they concentrate for breeding in river valleys, and often along canals and on ponds, however dirty, near large towns. A few nest on estuaries and by the sea. Most of the swans that are not breeding live in 'herds', sometimes of several hundred birds, at the mouths of rivers and on lakes and reservoirs. Many people do not think of them as wild birds, though they are descended from wild stock and have colonised many places, for example the Scottish Hebrides, without being introduced; and visitors come from Europe from time to time. Swans used to be called 'birds royal' because only those with a licence from the King could keep them. Swans on the lower Thames still belong to the Crown and to two London livery companies.

Mute swans spend much time resting and preening between bouts of feeding. They feed by dipping their heads or up-ending to pluck underwater weeds or by waddling slowly to graze waterside meadows. They also eat some insects and small molluscs, but not fish eggs, though they may disturb spawning beds. They do not take flight easily from land and often splash and paddle a long way over water before getting airborne. Their flight is powerful with characteristic 'wing-music', and a group will sometimes fly fast and with necks outstretched in V-formation. 'Mute' is a misleading name, for they snort, hiss, and call, and cygnets pipe shrilly; but the 'swan-song' before death is pure legend. Their frightening display, 'busking', with wings raised, head back, and body pushed forward, is well-known; but there is also friendly bill-dipping between cob and pen (female). The cob brings material from which the pen builds the huge open nest, in which feathers collect, though it is not lined with down like the nests of geese and ducks. Both incubate the three to ten large pale-green eggs, the cob mainly at night. When the eggs hatch, in about 5 weeks, the parents take the cygnets to water where they tear up weed for them, and often carry them on their backs. The cygnets are fully fledged in about 4 months, but stay as a family through the winter until chased away by the old cob. They then often join a non-breeding herd.

1   2   3   4   5   6   7   8   9   10   11   12

2 BEWICK'S SWAN (*Cygnus columbianus*). This is the smallest of the three swans, with a total length of 4 ft. and a body of 2 ft. It is more goose-like in shape and its stout neck is noticeable from a distance. The yellow on its bill is rounded instead of extending towards the tip.

Bewick's swans, which are now quite frequent winter visitors, especially in severe weather, are found on wide rivers and estuaries, lakes, and reservoirs, in general further south than whoopers, stretching from the Wash, across England and Wales to Southern Ireland. They breed mainly north of the Arctic Circle all round the world. They resemble whoopers in habits, but their musical 'conversation' on the water and rather goose-like, low-pitched call on the wing help to distinguish them. They tend to gather in bigger herds than whoopers do, and their food is almost entirely vegetable.

1   2   3   4   10   11   12

3 WHOOPER SWAN (*Cygnus cygnus*). The whooper is as large as but slighter in build than the mute swan, and has a straighter carriage of the neck. It is hard to distinguish from Bewick's swan except by its larger size and the greater amount of yellow on the bill. Juveniles and immature birds are even harder to tell apart, but are usually seen with adults.

Whoopers are quite common winter visitors to shallow lakes and lochs, large rivers, estuaries, and sheltered coasts in parts of Scotland, the Lake District, and Northern Ireland. Family parties or small herds arrive in October, and odd pairs stay on until May, some remaining all summer without breeding. They breed in Iceland, Scandinavia, and within the Arctic Circle; an occasional pair used to nest in the Scottish Highlands and northern islands and there was a recent attempt in 1968.

In general habits whoopers are like mute swans but are more agile on land, do not arch their backs in anger, and make only a whistling sound in flight when they utter the characteristic 'whooper' call. The American race is called the trumpeter swan. Whoopers use several other calls on the water and in their spring display, when the male makes head and neck movements and may later rise breast to breast with the female.

1   2   3   4   5   (6   7   8   9)   10   11   12

3a WHOOPER SWAN. Ads. 3b Imm.
2 BEWICK SWAN. Ad.
1a MUTE SWANS. Ad. 1b Imm. 1c cygnets 1d 'Polish' cygnet

EAGLES

1 GOLDEN EAGLE (*Aquila chrysaetos*). This most splendid of British resident birds of prey is from 2½ to 3 ft. long, with a wing span of 6 to 7 ft. The females are usually larger than the males but are alike in plumage. In spite of their greater size, it is quite possible to confuse eagles with buzzards (p. 39), especially at a distance. Both spread their flight feathers when soaring, but the eagle's wing-beats are more measured and sweeping. Also, its wings and tail are longer in comparison with its body than are those of a buzzard; and at close range its powerful beak is distinctive. Young golden eagles have a white patch on the tail (1b), but it is smaller in extent than the white tail of the adult sea eagle, and the border of the tail is dark.

Golden eagles are believed once to have inhabited mountainous areas all over the British Isles, but now they nest only in the Scottish highlands and larger islands and in south-west Scotland; they have bred recently in one place in Northern Ireland. They are occasionally seen elsewhere, usually when immature, and, after failure in 1969, eaglets were reared in the Lake District in 1970 and 1971. After increasing over the past 30 years, golden eagles are threatened, like other birds of prey, by the effects of poisonous chemicals. They are still shot and trapped by sheep farmers, and their eggs are taken by collectors.

Eagles are usually first seen soaring over the hillside or perhaps perching in silhouette on the skyline. When they change from soaring to flapping flight the beats look slow and heavy, but, in fact, they can travel very fast. When hunting, they search the ground carefully, then swoop to grip the prey in their talons. They take hares, rabbits, grouse and other birds, and sometimes small lambs; and they have been known to attack young deer; they also eat carrion. Fights with wild cats have been recorded, but they are not usually courageous birds, even in defence of their nests. They are clumsy walkers, rolling from side to side.

Both sexes display by soaring to a great height, uttering a call like a buzzard's mew, and then diving, perhaps several thousand feet, with half-closed wings. The pair begin building the nest (eyrie) months before it will be used; it is a huge mass of sticks and heather, often lined with woodrush, and is usually on a wide cliff ledge with a commanding view, but at no great altitude. Sometimes the nests are in trees, generally pines, but not often on sea cliffs. A pair may have two, sometimes more, eyries, to which they return year after year, using them alternately. The one to three, usually two, eggs are dull white and rather round, and often one has brown markings. The female does most of the incubation, and each egg takes about 6 weeks to hatch. The eaglets take nearly 3 months to fledge, and the parents continue to feed them for some time after

this. The young birds, which are not adult until they are 3 or 4, tend to wander. Eagles in captivity have lived to about 20 years old, but very rarely for longer.

1   2   3   4   5   6   7   8   9   10   11   12

SPOTTED EAGLE (*Aquila clanga*). This eastern European eagle is a very rare wanderer to Britain, the last certain record being in 1915. It is smaller than the golden eagle, about 2 to 2½ ft. long, and the adult has dark brown plumage. The immature birds have spotted wings.

2 SEA EAGLE (*Haliaeëtus alibicilla*), also called the white-tailed eagle or erne. These very large birds are up to 3 ft. long, the female being bigger than the male but alike in plumage. The sea eagle has quite a different outline from the golden eagle, the wings being relatively longer, the wedge-shaped tail much shorter, and the beak even bigger and broader. The adult's head is lighter and greyer, and its white tail is conspicuous. The immature birds have dark tails (2b).

Over 100 years ago sea eagles were more common than golden eagles, but now they are only occasional visitors over fresh or salt water, and these are usually immature birds. The last recorded nest was in the island of Skye in 1916. On the Continent they nest in tall trees near water; the British eyries were mainly on sea-cliffs. The birds look enormous in flight and have a very slow wing-beat. They hunt mainly on the wing, snatching their prey from the water or making shallow noisy plunges. They will sit motionless for hours, perhaps watching for fish, their main food. On the Continent they also eat birds and some mammals. The shrill chattering call is rarely heard except in the breeding season.

GRIFFON VULTURE (*Gyps fulvus*). This large bird of prey, about 3½ ft. long, is an extremely rare visitor from Southern Europe, the most recent to be reported being two seen together in Derbyshire in 1927. It has a light-brown body, dark wing-tips and tail, and whitish head. In flight, the short neck and tail and the immense broad wings, with almost parallel edges which taper sharply at the ends, are distinctive.

EGYPTIAN VULTURE (*Neophron percnopterus*). Another small vulture which has been recorded twice in Britain, in 1825 and 1868 — on both occasions immature birds. This species is predominantly white with black wing-tips, though the immature birds are brown. They have rather pointed wings and long wedge-shaped tails.

1b GOLDEN EAGLE, Imm.
1a GOLDEN EAGLE

2a SEA EAGLE
2b SEA EAGLE, Imm.

BUZZARDS

1 BUZZARD (*Buteo buteo*). The commonest large British bird of prey, the buzzard, is between 1½ and 2 ft. long, the females usually being larger than the males. Buzzards are stout bodied and broad winged, and mainly dark brown, their lighter underparts streaked with brown. But the plumage is very variable, and some birds are dark, some almost white, underneath. Often there is a dark patch at the 'wrist' of the wing. The sexes look alike, and juveniles soon resemble the adults. The brown eyes and bare yellow legs are noticeable at close range.

The buzzard was an increasing resident throughout Britain until the coming of myxomatosis in 1953 began to destroy an important source of food — rabbits. Since then its distribution has changed a good deal, but it is still quite common in south-west England, Wales and its borders, north-west England, south-west Scotland, the Scottish Highlands, and Inner Hebrides. There are odd pairs elsewhere, and a few in Northern Ireland on the north coast. Single birds wander about in other parts of the country, but they make no true migration.

Like the golden eagle (p. 36), the buzzard is usually seen on the wing, when its shape and soaring flight sometimes lead to its being mistaken for an eagle in areas where they are both found. But apart from its smaller size, its wings and tail are relatively shorter and its beak relatively smaller. It may soar with extended flight feathers or with pointed tips, and then suddenly 'ball up' and dive headlong with wings bent and close to the body, at the end of the dive checking and sweeping up again. Sometimes it rolls and turns in the air, these movements forming part of the display flights of the pair over or near the chosen breeding area. Sometimes a bird will hang apparently motionless, in an up-current of air. At rest the buzzard looks dumpy, almost owl-like, especially when perched on a roadside telegraph pole. It takes off heavily with great flaps, lifting the yellow legs into its body feathers. It hunts on the wing or by pouncing from a perch. In general, voles are its chief food, but in Britain it relied on young rabbits to feed its young and has therefore been affected by their scarcity in recent years. It also takes small birds, lizards, snakes, and large insects, and is particularly fond of earthworms, pulling them out of the ground, on which it moves clumsily. The call, often given in flight, is always described as a plaintive mew, and is uttered at all seasons. Young birds have an even more piercing version, which from a distance, sounds rather like the call of the golden plover.

Like other birds of prey, buzzards are frequently mobbed by members of the crow family and, on the coast, by gulls. Often they seem to regard the chase as a kind of play and make little effort to avoid their pursuers, flapping lazily out of the way of their dive but not leaving the area. If the attack is pressed home, however, as it is, for example, by ravens nesting in the same line of crags, the buzzard turns over on its back in the air, presenting its claws to the enemy.

Buzzards nest either in firs or ivy-covered trees, or on sea cliffs or rock ledges, sometimes quite low ones; a tree growing out of a wooded crag is a favourite site. The nest is a large shallow cup of sticks, which may be used for several years, and is lined with fresh greenery, often renewed in the course of incubation. The two to four eggs are round and white with brown markings; they are laid at intervals, as with all birds of prey, and each takes about 4 weeks to hatch. The female does most of the incubation and feeds the young on prey brought by the male. Later, both feed the brood until after they fledge at about 6 weeks. Family parties eventually break up, but gatherings of up to a dozen buzzards may be seen after the nesting season.

1 2 3 **4 5 6** *7 8 9 10 11 12*

2 ROUGH-LEGGED BUZZARD (*Buteo lagopus*). This rare autumn and winter visitor is about the same size as the common buzzard, but can be recognized by its generally lighter underparts and especially by the broad white band on the black-edged and relatively longer tail. At rest, the feathered legs are a good distinction. There is often a dark band across the chest which the common buzzard does not have, and the head is lighter-coloured.

A few rough-legged buzzards from northern Europe are seen during the winter of most years in the north and east of Britain, but they are rare on the west side and in Ireland. Occasionally, as in 1966, there are small 'invasions', when many more than usual are seen. Their habits in winter resemble those of the common buzzard, though they are more inclined to hover. They also have a mewing call, but it is unlikely to be heard in Britain. They feed mainly on mammals, but will also take birds up to the size of a moorhen, swooping on them from the air.

1 2 3 4 . . . . . 10 11 12

1 BUZZARD
Two in flight

2 ROUGH-LEGGED BUZZARD
One in flight

HAWKS

1 SPARROWHAWK (*Accipiter nisus*). A typical yellow-eyed hawk, in which the male (less than 1 ft.) is smaller than the female (15 ins. or more). There is also considerable difference in plumage. The male (1a) is bluish grey above, with brown markings on the rounded wings and dark bars on the long tail, and with rufous bars across his light underparts; the female (1b) is fairly dark brown above, with dark bars across her underparts; also the pale strip over the eye and patch at the nape are more pronounced. Young males tend to be browner than the adults.

Sparrowhawks have become much scarcer in the south and east of Britain in recent years, at least partly due to their eating birds which have been poisoned by farm chemicals. In some counties they are extinct as breeding birds, but they are still widespread, though not common, along the west side of Britain and in Ireland. Because of the decrease, they were given legal protection in 1962. While preferring fir woods, they are found in wooded country of all types right to the coast or the edge of the moors, over which they often hunt. British sparrowhawks are resident, though they may wander in the winter; but there are others which pass through Britain on passage.

Sparrowhawks are not easy to watch; they are usually seen briefly as they flash along a hedge or across a road in pursuit of small birds, flying low with short bursts of three or four wing-beats followed by a glide. They also hunt amongst trees, jinking from side to side. They often take their prey by surprise, and also watch and pounce. They show a complete absence of fear which has sometimes led them inside houses. Usually they snatch their victim and are away at once. They take a variety of small birds (about ninety species have been recorded in Britain), including young game birds and ducks, and also a number of insects and a few small mammals such as field mice. The display, as with other birds of prey, consists partly of soaring flights over the nesting area, when the broad-winged, long-tailed outline and the difference in size between the sexes show up well; the male also makes mock attacks on the female and has a special, slow-flapping flight. The nest of sticks in a tree may be built months before laying begins; it is often on the foundation of an old nest or squirrel's drey and has a very shallow cup. The usual clutch is four to six, round, greenish-white eggs, with rich brown streaks. The female does most or all the incubation, rubbing off small white feathers on the nest until they form a lining; and she feeds the young when they hatch in 5 weeks from food brought in by the male. The young fly in 3 to 4 weeks. When disturbed, the female gives the loud alarm cry *kek kek kek kek*, which is the best-known call, though several others are used during the breeding season. The explanation usually offered for the difference in size between the sexes is that the smaller, neater male can hunt more efficiently, while the larger female is able to give a more efficient covering to the eggs.

1   2   3   4   5   6   7   8   9   10   11   12

2 GOSHAWK (*Accipiter gentilis*). This big version of the sparrowhawk is from about 1½ ft. (males) to 2 ft. (females) in length. The sexes are alike and resemble female sparrowhawks; in fact, a male goshawk (2a) is not easy to distinguish from a female sparrowhawk. The immature plumage (2b) is brighter brown and the underparts are streaked with darker markings, not barred as in the adult.

Goshawks are rare visitors from the Continent, mostly when immature and usually in spring or autumn. They are chiefly recorded down the east side of Britain, but occasionally elsewhere. About six examples of the American race have also occurred, four of them in Ireland. Goshawks probably used to breed in Britain, especially Scotland, and some bred in Sussex from about 1926 to 1951 — though these may have been escaped or released birds, as the goshawk is much used in falconry. It is possible that a few pairs may now be breeding elsewhere in Britain.

Their size and habit of soaring makes it easy to confuse goshawks with buzzards, but their longer tails and rounder wings should be distinctive. Their habits resemble those of the sparrowhawk, but they are able to take birds as large as pigeons regularly, though they will eat smaller ones, small mammals and even insects. The goshawk is a silent bird, though it has a loud alarm call near the nest. The nest is built of sticks, usually in thick woodland on a tree-site, and is used for many years in succession. The female incubates for over 5 weeks the clutch of three or four eggs, which are like large sparrowhawk's eggs. The young fledge in about 6 weeks.

1a SPARROWHAWK. M.   1b SPARROWHAWK. F.
2a GOSHAWK. M.   2b GOSHAWK. Imm.

KITES, HONEY BUZZARD AND OSPREY

1 RED KITE (*Milvus milvus*). The sexes of this rare bird of prey are alike in plumage and are the same size as a buzzard (p. 39) — about 2 ft. long. Kites have longer, narrower wings, usually showing a bend at the 'wrist', and a rather long, forked tail. (A buzzard with some central tail feathers missing may also appear to have a forked tail.) In a good light, the reddish-brown underparts and white patch under the dark-tipped wings are distinctive (1b). Young birds have darker heads than adults — indeed, some old birds have quite white heads.

Though widespread in Britain until the 18th century, breeding kites are now confined to mid-Wales, where about twenty-four pairs survive in hanging oakwoods on the sides of river valleys in hilly country. There have been odd nests elsewhere, and wandering birds are seen in various parts of the country.

Kites, like buzzards, soar, glide, and occasionally hover, but they look more buoyant in the air. They catch most of their food on the ground by pouncing, and eat small and young birds, frogs, small mammals, insects, and many earthworms. They are quite active on the ground, hopping rather than walking, but prefer to perch in trees, where they devour their prey. They have a mewing call and a circling display rather like that of other large birds of prey. The female, assisted by the male, builds the large nest of sticks, often in a tall oak but sometimes in a conifer. She lines it (rather as a crow does, though much less tidily) with wool, hair, and rags. The two or three eggs resemble those of the buzzard; the female hatches them in about 4 weeks. The young take 7 or 8 weeks to fledge and may wander in autumn, though the old birds stay in the area and roost in a group.

*1 2 3 **4 5** 6 7 8 9 10 11 12*

BLACK KITE (*Milvus migrans*). Though common in central France and Switzerland and possibly once the kite of the London streets, only 12 black kites have been reliably reported in Britain. They are a little smaller than red kites and dark brown all over, though with reddish underparts, and young birds have a pale patch under the wing. The slight fork to the tail disappears when it is opened. They are often found over water on the Continent, acting as scavengers, as gulls do in Britain.

2 HONEY BUZZARD (*Pernis apivorus*). The sexes are alike both in plumage and size, between 20 ins. and 2 ft. long. They resemble common buzzards but have longer wings and several broad dark bands on the tail seen from below, instead of only one (2b). The pattern of the underparts is both different and lighter, and the head looks thinner in flight and is usually rather light-coloured. At close range the yellow eye is distinctive. Young birds are very variable in plumage.

Once a regular summer visitor to southern England the honey buzzard is breeding again in very small numbers; and a few are recorded on passage in most years.

In flying habits it resembles the common buzzard but it spends much more time on the ground, where it walks agilely, searching for the wasps' nests which it attacks. It also takes other insects, small birds and their eggs, and small mammals. Its call is rather squeakier than the common buzzard's but the display in the air is similar. Honey buzzards like to build on the foundation of an old nest, but if they build a fresh one, it may be quite small. The clutch is usually two beautifully marked eggs, dark brown on white, and the young hatch in about 4½ weeks, fledging in about 6 weeks.

3 OSPREY (*Pandion haliaetus*). These magnificent birds are about the same size as a buzzard, the females usually larger than the males. The dark brown above and white below makes them distinctive, as well as the dark patch at the 'wrist', the rather broken dark bar on the underwing, and a dark band across the breast. Young birds differ only slightly in plumage from the adults.

The osprey is now a rare summer visitor (about six pairs) to the Scottish Highlands, where it once bred quite commonly until, in the early 20th century, it was exterminated by being shot and the eggs taken. It returned in the 1950's. It is also a regular passage visitor in spring and autumn, especially along the east side of Britain, appearing on quiet inland lakes and ponds as well as near the coast.

Ospreys spend much time at rest on a favourite tree perch, and then take wing and fly with strong flapping beats. On sighting a fish, the bird pauses in the air, then dives, entering the water with feet first and wings half-closed, making a tremendous splash, and rises almost at once, the fish held head foremost in its claws and its legs stretched (3b). Its usual cry is a thin whistle, hard to associate with so magnificent a bird. In display ospreys soar and chase each other, the male performing a series of dramatic stoops in the air without landing. Recent Scottish eyries have all been in pine trees (usually near water), but the birds used to nest on rocky islands and old buildings as well. Both sexes build the massive nest of sticks. The female normally lays a clutch of three finely-marked eggs, dark brown on white; she does most of the 5-week incubation, and feeds the young with food supplied by the male, which he often passes to her in the air, as a harrier does (p. 44). The young fly in about 7½ weeks and then start their southward migration.

*. . . **4 5** 6 7 **8** 9 10 (11) .*

3a, 3b OSPREY
1a, 1b RED KITE
2a, 2b HONEY BUZZARD

HARRIERS

1 MARSH HARRIER (*Circus aeruginosus*). The largest British harrier is about 20 ins. long, the male and female being the same size. It is somewhat like a buzzard (p. 39) in appearance, but has longer and more angled wings, and longer tail and legs. The very distinctive full male plumage is seldom seen in Britain (1b). Females and young males are rather alike, with light-coloured heads and 'shoulders' but darker wings and tail (1a). There is a good deal of variation among the males, some of which breed while still in immature plumage.

Once quite widespread, the Marsh Harrier, now breeds regularly only in East Anglia and one other southern county, though odd pairs nest elsewhere from time to time. It is mainly a summer visitor, but a few birds are residents or even winter visitors. Their favourite habitats are reed-beds and shallow lakes, but outside the breeding season they often hunt over open marshland.

Harriers are usually seen in flight, low over the reeds, gliding with wings raised above the line of the body, and then gaining speed with a few deliberate wing-beats. In spring they may soar to considerable heights and be mistaken for buzzards. They search the ground or water methodically, then drop on their prey, which includes a variety of marsh birds, their eggs and young, small mammals, frogs, and reptiles. Their long legs enable them to walk quite well on the ground, and they often spend a long time motionless on low perches. The display consists of flying tricks over the breeding area. Later, the male brings food to the female and for the brood, passing it to the female in the air, a manoeuvre for which harriers are famous. The male and female have different, rather feeble calls. The nest is built among reeds or other thick vegetation, and the clutch, usually of four or five white eggs which quickly become stained, is incubated mainly by the female, each egg taking about 5 weeks to hatch. The young are fed by the female and stay about 5 weeks at or near the nest. They finally fly about 8 weeks after hatching, when the whole family may be seen over the area before dispersing.

1 2 3 **4 5 6** *7 8 9 10 11 12*

2 MONTAGU'S HARRIER (*Circus pygargus*). This is the smallest of the harriers, up to 1½ ft. in length, the male and female being about the same size. It is also the most graceful. The black marks visible across both sides of the grey upper wing and the brown streaks on the flanks distinguish the male (2a) fairly easily from the male hen harrier; but the females (2b) are very difficult to tell apart. The unstreaked brown underparts distinguish the young birds of both sexes. Montagu's harrier is a rare summer visitor, a few pairs breeding in widely separate parts of England and Wales, and occasionally in Scotland. They are most often found in newly planted forestry areas where there is thick mixed ground vegetation, but also breed on open moors or marshes with reed-beds.

Their general behaviour, food, and display resemble those of the hen harrier, but the alarm call is even higher-pitched. The female builds most of the simple nest in thick cover, and lays three to six white eggs; she also does most of the incubation, which takes about 4 weeks for each egg. The young fledge in about ⁊ weeks, but they scatter from the nest before then and are fed separately.

. . . 4 **5 6** *7 8 9 10 . .*

3 HEN HARRIER (*Circus cyaneus*). The male is smaller than the female, their lengths ranging from 17 to 20 ins. The male (3b) and female (3a) are remarkably unlike each other, and respectively far more like the male and female Montagu's harrier. But the male hen harrier has no black marks across the upper wing and no brown streaks on the flanks and the white patch on the rump is larger than on the male Montagu's. But it has the same black primary flight feathers and a dark trailing edge to the secondary feathers. The female hen harrier, apart from her larger size and larger white rump patch, can hardly be distinguished from the female Montagu's. Young birds look like the females and can be told from young Montagu's by the brown streaks on their underparts.

Both as a resident and a winter visitor, the hen harrier is more common than it was 20 years ago, and now breeds on heather and rushy moorland, often in newly afforested areas, in several parts of the Scottish Highlands and Borders, as well as in its old strongholds in Orkney and the Hebrides, in six Irish, in two English, and in two Welsh counties. In winter it is more widely distributed, though in very small numbers, and may be seen on marshes and open country of all kinds.

Hen and Montagu's harriers are much more graceful on the wing than marsh harriers. They fly and hunt in the same way, though the hen harrier sometimes chases as well as pouncing on its prey, mainly small and young birds and mammals. The display consists of flights by both sexes and spectacular dives by the male. The most usual call is the alarm given near the nest: a repeated high-pitched *kek, kek, kek*. The female builds most of the nest, a pad of grass and rushes fairly well hidden in heather, and lays from three to six blue-tinted eggs, which she alone incubates and which soon fade to white. Each egg hatches in about 30 days, and the young fledge in about 6 weeks, though the parents stay with them longer.

1 2 3 **4 5 6** *7 8 9 10 11 12*

PALLID HARRIER (*Circus macrourus*). About 1½ ft. long, this very rare visitor from eastern Europe and Asia is paler than most male hen harriers, has less black on the wing-tips, none along the trailing edge of the wing, and a greyish-white rump patch. The female is very like a female hen harrier, and the young birds cannot be told in the field from young Montagu's harriers. Its habits resemble those of the two commoner 'grey' harriers. The four British records were between 1931 and 1952, two of them on Fair Isle

3a HEN HARRIER, F.   3b HEN HARRIER, M.

    2a MONTAGU'S HARRIER, M.   2b F.   2c Juv.

1a MARSH HARRIER, F.   1b MARSH HARRIER, M.

1 HOBBY (*Falco subbuteo*). One of the smallest of the falcons, 12 to 14 ins. in length, the female being usually bigger than the male. The sexes are alike in plumage, which resembles that of the peregrine, except for the reddish thighs and under tail-coverts. Hobbies have relatively long wings and short tails, so that in flight they look rather like giant swifts (p. 119) without a forked tail. The young birds are very dark brown above, and the conspicuous light edges to the feathers of the juvenile plumage gives the head, in particular, a scaly appearance; the underparts are creamy-brown, heavily streaked, but with no red (1b).

Hobbies are rare summer visitors to the southern counties of England, though pairs have nested in the Midlands and on the Welsh Border and odd birds turn up much more widely. Their haunts are farmland or heathland with small woods, clumps of trees, and hedgerows with standard trees.

Like most birds of prey, a hobby is usually first seen in flight, when the female can be distinguished from the male by her less fluttering wing-beat. Hobbies are very fast fliers; they often hunt by direct chase and can take swallows and swifts in this way; sometimes they dive or 'stoop' in true falcon manner on their prey or even seize it from below. Swallows and martins, well aware of their danger, often mob passing hobbies. As well as birds, hobbies eat many large insects, especially dragonflies. The display consists of flying evolutions, which may also be seen outside the breeding season, and the male presents food to his mate when they are perched on a tree, uttering the call note *wer wer wee wee wee*, which resembles the call of a kestrel. Hobbies are seldom seen on the ground. They nest late, often taking the old nest of one of the crow family and flattening it out. The female does most of the incubation of the two or three round, red eggs, which take about 4 weeks to hatch; the male brings her food and later helps feed the brood, which take about 4½ weeks to fledge. Family parties are seen about until they migrate in the autumn.

2 GYR FALCON (*Falco rusticolus*). A rare visitor even bigger than a peregrine, 20 to 22 ins. long. Three races have occurred in Britain. The commonest comes from Greenland (2b) and in full plumage is an unmistakable big white bird with black spots; but most birds seen here are likely to be young, with more dark markings. These are almost regular winter and spring visitors to Scotland and Ireland. North European birds are like large pale peregrines, the females being bigger than the males. Only two of these have been definitely identified in Britain. Birds of the Iceland race (2a) have occurred mainly in the north, with a few elsewhere.

Gyr falcons have broader, less pointed wings and are more deliberate in flight than peregrines, which they resemble in general habits. When at rest, the wing tips do not reach to the end of the tail. In Britain they prey on several species of waders, gulls, and rock doves, and also rabbits and water voles.

3 PEREGRINE (*Falco peregrinus*). The finest of the British resident falcons is from 15 to 19 ins. in length, the female being considerably bigger than the male and rather darker in plumage. The contrast of the blue-grey upper and light underparts is noticeable at a distance, especially when the bird is perched, and the black 'moustache' can be picked out in flight at reasonable range. The young birds are dark brown above and streaked underneath.

In recent years the peregrine has suffered a catastrophic decline in numbers and is almost extinct in south-west England. There are a few pairs in Wales and the north of England, but most are now to be found in the Scottish Highlands and parts of Ireland. They are thought to have decreased in numbers partly because of eating birds which have themselves been poisoned by chemicals. Outside the breeding season peregrines wander extensively, and two of the North American race have turned up in England. The breeding habitats are craggy moorlands or rocky coastlines.

It is possible to mistake a pigeon flying towards you for a peregrine because they both have stout bodies (3b). But the falcon tapers away neatly, has a much shorter tail, and usually alternates spells of fast flapping with long glides. The wings are long and pointed and, when soaring against the clouds, the bird has a crossbow silhouette. Its best-known hunting method is to circle high over its victim and then to make a lightning dive, usually striking it in the air; it then forces or follows its victim down to the ground and plucks it on a convenient stone. It often chases a bird in the air with dramatic twists and turns. It may take any of nearly a hundred kinds of birds, and also some mammals, frogs, and insects. A peregrine will sometimes sit motionless for a long time on a conspicuous perch. Its call, a loud, ringing *kee-kee-kee*, is a magnified version of the kestrel's and may be given continuously near the nest. Peregrines pair for life and make their nest on a ledge often at a great height, but sometimes quite close to the ground. The clutch of three or four magnificent red eggs is incubated mainly by the female, who is fed by the male. Each egg takes about 4 weeks to hatch, and the young fledge in 5 or 6 weeks and stay with the parents for some time afterwards, but scatter in the autumn. Some birds from further north pass through Britain at this time.

*1   2   3   **4   5   6**   7   8   9   10   11   12*

1a HOBBY. M.   1b Juv.   1c in flight
2a, b GYR FALCONS in flight
3 PEREGRINE. M. and in flight

1 **KESTREL** (*Falco tinnunculus*). Easily the commonest British falcon. Both sexes at all stages have a general light-brown appearance, though the grey head and tail of the adult male (1c) distinguishes it from the female (1b) and young (1a), and from any other bird except the very rare lesser kestrel.

Young males have brownish heads for the first 2 years. The sexes are about the same size, 13 or 14 ins. long.

Kestrels are residents, generally distributed throughout the British Isles in all types of habitat, even in central London. There are also passage migrants, and birds from northern Scotland come south in winter with others from overseas.

The hovering kestrel is a characteristic sight of the countryside; no other British bird hovers so often or so expertly (1d), dropping like a stone to the ground and rising to go on hovering in a new position, if unsuccessful. It also constantly changes its place in the air without stooping, and holds itself against the wind by winnowing wings and small movements of its spread and depressed tail. In flight it alternates quick beats with glides, as do other birds of prey, but its long, pointed wings and tail distinguish it. When it is soaring in circles, however, wings and tail are rounded and, from underneath in a poor light, it is possible to confuse it with a sparrowhawk, though it usually looks much lighter. Kestrels often perch on telegraph poles and wires and on the tops of bushes and fence posts, from which they drop on their prey. They feed mainly on mice and voles, with large insects, some small birds, and worms; in London they feed almost entirely on house sparrows. Their flying display over the nest site and their loud *kee kee kee* call resemble that of other falcons. The nest scrape may be in a hollow tree, in a hole of a building, on a cliff ledge, occasionally in a big nestbox, or in the old nest of crow or magpie. Four to six round reddish eggs are laid at intervals of 2 or more days, incubated mainly by the female, and hatched in about 4 weeks. The young fledge in 4 to 4½ weeks and remain nearby before dispersing. The discarded nest is full of the remains of pellets thrown up by the young, from which it is possible to discover what food they eat.

1   2   3   4   5   6   7   8   9   10   11   12

LESSER KESTREL (*Falco naumanni*). A rare visitor from southern Europe which looks like the common kestrel but is smaller, about 1 ft. long, and the male has an unspotted back and mantle. The females are almost identical except for their size. The whitish claws can seldom be seen. Only about a dozen have been recorded in Britain, mainly in England in spring or autumn. Their habits are like those of the common kestrel, but they hover less and chase insects more. They nest in colonies in old buildings or cliffs.

2 **RED-FOOTED FALCON** (*Falco vespertinus*). Both male and female of this rare visitor are about the same size, 1 ft. long, but their plumage is different. The adult female (2a) is not unlike a kestrel, but is much greyer above and has less streaked underparts. The young birds are rather like young hobbies (p. 46) but are paler above and less heavily marked below.

This falcon from eastern Europe has been much more often observed in the past 15 years and in very small numbers is almost a regular visitor to the south of England on spring passage, when it may be met almost anywhere with trees or open woodland. It is much rarer in autumn, and in the west and north. It feeds on insects and is most active at dusk. In flight it looks like a lightly-built kestrel, and it also hovers, though not so frequently. It perches on wires, bushes, fences, and even on the ground, and sometimes drops on its prey. Its call is like a kestrel's but is seldom heard in Britain.

.   .   .   4   5   6   7   8   9   10   .   .

3 **MERLIN** (*Falco columbarius*). The smallest of the British falcons, the male being about 10 ins. long, the female over 1 ft. The male (3b) is rather like a very small male sparrowhawk (p. 41), but with pointed wings and streaked, not barred, underparts. The female looks a darkish brown bird, with her heavily streaked breast and barred tail (3a); and the young birds resemble females (3c).

Merlins are scarce residents or summer visitors in the west and north of Britain, as far as Orkney, and in Ireland, breeding principally on heather and bracken moorland, and occasionally on sand dunes; at other times they may appear almost anywhere, but especially on coastal dunes and rough ground. Birds from Iceland are regular visitors on passage, and some winter here.

They have a quite distinctive tripping flight, as though they were continually changing step; they generally fly low, rather like sparrowhawks, chasing the small birds which are their particular prey, and which they strike from above. They occasionally take small mammals, birds, and insects off the ground. Like peregrines (p. 46), they pluck their victims in the open, and often stay still on a stone or fence for long periods. The chattering call is more rapid and shrill than that of other falcons. The male displays by flying over the nest site and by feeding the female, as a hobby does. The nest is a scrape in long heather or other vegetation, or sometimes in a crow's discarded nest in a tree or crag. The clutch is usually four eggs, of the round red falcon type, and both parents incubate. The young hatch in about 4 weeks and fledge about 4 weeks later. The family parties then desert the moors for lower ground.

1   2   3   4   5   6   7   8   9   10   11   12

1d KESTREL, M., hovering
1a KESTREL, Juv. 1b F.
1c M.

2a RED-FOOTED FALCON, F. 2b M.
3d MERLIN, M. in flight
3a MERLIN, F. 3b M. 3c Juv.

1 RED GROUSE (*Lagopus lagopus*). A game bird of which the sexes are more or less alike, though in summer the hen (1b) is much paler than the cock (1a), Cocks become darker in winter, though the differences are hardly noticeable in the field, and there is a good deal of variation. Juveniles look like summer females, but by the autumn are very much like the adults. Grouse in Ireland and the Hebrides are paler in winter than those on the mainland. Males are from 14 to 16 ins. long, and females 13 to 14 ins.

Red grouse were introduced to Dartmoor and Exmoor and are resident in parts of Wales, the north Midlands, north of England, Scotland and many of its islands, and parts of Ireland. Until recently, British red grouse were considered to be a distinct species, the only species of bird unique to Britain, and called *Lagopus scoticus*; but they are now considered to be a race of the willow grouse of Europe, which has a white winter plumage like the ptarmigan and white wings even in summer. Red grouse are confined to moorland and bogs with heather, crowberry, rushes, and rough grass; but they sometimes visit fields. They prefer drier areas and are much more numerous on the east than on the west side of Britain.

The first sight of red grouse is usually as they take off from the heather, the cock probably calling *go-back, go-back*, and skimming away at speed, showing the curved wings and dark, slightly fanned tail. But often their necks are seen as they peer above the vegetation, and cocks may stand prominently on rocks, mounds, or walls. They visit roads to pick up grit for their crops, like poultry. Their flight is alternate rapid wing-beats and glides, with a final flap as they land. Their principal food is heather at all stages: shoots, flowers, and seeds; but they eat other moorland plants, grass-seeds, a variety of insects, spiders, and earthworms. Even in late autumn cocks may be heard calling against rivals. In display the cock flies up from his stance, then glides down, beating his wings before landing, and as he does this he sings an elaboration of the *go-back* call.

Grouse have been decreasing in Scotland for many years, and a scientific investigation into the causes of this began in 1957. It is probably due to the gradually increasing number of wet summers and to a loss of fertility in the moorland soils, both of which factors affect the heather on which grouse depend for food and cover. It used to be thought that birds of prey and members of the crow family reduced their numbers, and, indeed, crows, which take eggs and young chicks, are partly responsible. But birds of prey are more likely to be useful in preventing numbers from becoming too large, for when there are more young grouse than there is food to support them, they suffer from an epidemic disease.

Pairs are often formed in winter and remain on their territories, except in very hard weather. The hen selects the nest site in long heather, rushes, or grasses, but adds very little lining to it. The clutch varies in number, but six to ten is usual; the eggs are shaped like small hens' eggs with dark red-brown blotches over a creamy-white background. They hatch in about $3\frac{1}{2}$ weeks, incubated by the female with the male often near. The young leave the nest almost at once, following the parents, and they can fly before they are 2 weeks old. The female attempts to distract possible enemies from her young by pretending to be injured. Family parties (coveys) move about the moor and may join up into packs, which desert the higher ground in severe weather.

1 2 3 4 5 6 7 8 9 10 11 12

2 PTARMIGAN (*Lagopus mutus*). About the size of a female red grouse, the ptarmigan can always be told by its white wings and underparts. There are three different plumages: in winter both sexes are white all over, except for black tails and the black eye patches of the cock (2c); in spring and summer the cock has brownish-yellow and grey mottled upper-parts (2a), and the hen is yellower with black markings (2b); in autumn both become much greyer, though the hen remains lighter-coloured. Juveniles resemble the adult's summer plumage, but with very dark primary flight feathers.

Ptarmigan are now confined to the Scottish Highlands and a few of the larger islands with high hills; their habitat is the bare mountain top with loose stones and close vegetation, above 2000 ft. They are the only British birds to show complete adaptation to snowy conditions; they can burrow in the snow to get at the plants on which they feed and to take cover. Their general behaviour resembles that of the red grouse, and their display is similar, though the cock's call is more like a vulgar cough. The usual note is a croak, which may be lengthened to a sort of rattle. The nest is a scrape in the bare ground; the five to nine eggs are smaller and paler than those of the red grouse; they and the sitting hen blend so well with their surroundings that they are quite difficult to see. Incubation lasts from $3\frac{1}{2}$ to 4 weeks, and at first both parents look after the brood, the hen feigning injury to distract attention from her young, as the hen grouse does. The young can fly after only 10 days, after which the old cocks join into packs, and so do the families later.

1 2 3 4 5 6 7 8 9 10 11 12

2a PTARMIGAN. M.
2b PTARMIGAN. F.
1a RED GROUSE M.

2c PTARMIGAN, autumn and winter plumage
1b RED GROUSE F.

1 BLACK GROUSE (*Lyrurus tetrix*). The male, generally known as the blackcock, is considerably bigger than a red grouse, about 21 ins. long; and the female or greyhen is about 16 ins. The blackcock can be distinguished from a cock capercaillie by its lyre-shaped tail and the greater amount of white in the plumage (1a). The greyhen (1b) resembles a red grouse and a hen capercaillie or, indeed, a pheasant, unless the forked tail or broad white wing-bar can be seen. For a time in late summer, the blackcock has a sort of mottled eclipse plumage, as ducks have; and first-winter cocks are browner than adults. The juveniles look like the females.

Black grouse in general have been decreasing in Britain in recent years, but increasing in a few areas; there are now very few in Devon and Somerset and they are only local in North Wales and northern England; but they have become commoner on the Scottish Border and in parts of the central Highlands where afforestation is taking place. Their habitat is on the edge between woodland and moorland, and they have become particularly associated with newly planted areas of conifers. They do not move about much.

Parties of black grouse may be seen perched on the tips of young fir trees or roosting in taller trees; when disturbed they fly more silently than most game-birds, with bursts of rapid beats and long glides on curved wings, often circling round as though trying to return, and they may be found in the same spot regularly unless driven out. They do much of their feeding on tree shoots and buds, and are consequently regarded as a pest by foresters. They also visit stubble fields in autumn, but move rather slowly on the ground. Their display at the 'lek', an open space in a wood or a grassy patch in moorland, is famous. The cocks gather before dawn and at dusk and threaten each other, fanning their tails, fluffing the white feathers underneath, dropping their wings with 'wrists' bent, and lowering their heads with the red wattles over the eyes raised. They seldom fight seriously, and all the time they keep up their *rookooing* calls, which can be heard a long way off as a sort of wavering chorus. The hens come to the leks and mate there but otherwise spend very little time with the cocks, who often form parties of their own sex and may return to the lek for milder displays in autumn. The hens, therefore, undertake all the nesting duties, selecting a well-hidden site, usually on the ground, and laying six to ten speckled brownish eggs. The eggs are laid at quite long intervals and not in-cubated until the clutch is complete. The young hatch in about 4 weeks and can fly 2 or 3 weeks later. Hybrids with other game birds have been recorded.

Packs seldom of more than thirty birds form in the autumn.

*1 2 3 4 **5** **6** 7 8 9 10 11 12*

2 CAPERCAILLIE (*Tetrao urogallus*). The male or cock is one of Britain's biggest land-birds, nearly 3 ft. long. His size, his thick, shaggy-looking head and neck, and turkey-like fan tail distinguish him. But the hen, which is only about 2 ft long, is very like a greyhen except for her larger size, rounded tail, and redder breast. The juvenile resembles the hen, and the first-winter cock is like a small, duller adult.

The British stock died out in Scotland and Ireland about 1750, but Swedish birds were reintroduced to Perthshire from 1837 onwards, and the 'caper' is now well-established in the central Highlands and has occurred and bred in parts of the Lowlands, though there has been some decrease in recent years. Caper-caillies are birds of the conifer forest and seldom found far away, though they sometimes visit deciduous woods with birches.

In general habits capercaillies resemble other grouse. Owing to their size the cocks rise noisily, but are silent on the wing and swerve expertly among trees. They feed in winter almost entirely on conifer shoots and buds, but eat many kinds of plants on the ground in summer, and also some insects. They walk or run quite fast. Several cocks may display together, but often one 'sings' alone a remarkable phrase, starting with a series of clicking sounds and ending with a noise like a cork being drawn from a bottle, with rattling of the wings added. While singing, the cock may sit on a perch or may parade about with wings lowered, tail fanned, and head up.

The song may be repeated many times and is used when attacking a rival. In recent years several solitary cocks, living on or near the southern edge of the capercaillie's range in the Highlands, became famous for their attacks on humans, whom they would peck or buffet with their wings fiercely. One knocked a man off a bicycle. But they would not go near a dog. This curious behaviour seems to be unknown on the Continent, where the bird is regarded as very shy and hard to approach. It may be due to a lack of other cocks as natural rivals.

A cock may have several mates but takes no part in nesting duties. The hen lays five to eight eggs, rather like those of the black grouse, in a scrape often close to a tree trunk, and sits on them for about 4 weeks. The young may fly when less than 2 weeks old. Where capercaillies are fairly common, parties of either cocks or hens may form in autumn.

*1 2 3 **4** **5** **6** 7 8 9 10 11 12*

1a BLACK GROUSE. M.
    and in display
2a CAPERCAILLIE. F.

1b F.

2b M.

PHEASANTS

1 PHEASANT (*Phasianus colchicus*). A cock pheasant is unmistakable, though the number of different strains introduced have produced a great variety of plumage. Probably most cock pheasants now have a white collar or some white feathers between the glossy blue head and the copper-coloured body. They may be nearly 3 ft. long, of which half or more is the long pointed tail. The much duller female (1c) may be a foot shorter, including a tail of up to 10 ins. Hen pheasants can be confused with females of the grouse family (p. 50) unless the tail is seen, especially one strain which is as dark and red-looking as a red grouse. Juveniles before their tails grow are easy to confuse with partridges. In autumn young males can be seen in all stages of plumage up to that of the adult.

The 'old English' pheasant without a white collar (1b) was introduced from near the Caspian Sea before the Norman Conquest, but did not reach Scotland and Ireland for another 500 years; the Chinese ring-necked race (1a) came in 1785, and other races since. Pheasants are now found living wild throughout England and Wales, much of Scotland, and parts of Ireland, but are continually reinforced by birds bred for sport. Their original habitat included reed-beds and forest, and they flourish in mixed countryside in England; they can survive in thick low scrub in the wilder parts of Scotland, Ireland and Wales.

The loud *kok kok* call of the cock pheasant is one of the familiar sounds of the English countryside, and in winter and autumn he is often conspicuous on bare fields and roadsides, sometimes with other males or parties of females. But in summer pheasants are harder to see, remaining in long grass or other cover until, almost under one's feet, they explode into the air. They can rise almost vertically at great speed, 'towering' or 'rocketing', which is largely the reason for their popularity as sporting birds; but they can keep this up only for short distances, and often instead of flying they run away, crouching low. There are many cases of pheasants flying out over lakes during shooting drives and coming down exhausted on the water after a mile or less, though they do sometimes make longer flights. They spend most of their time on the ground, where they eat seeds, grain, roots, and leaves, and also some insects, worms, and slugs. But they often roost in trees, even when they are bare, and sometimes perch in them in daytime.

The male displays by crowing — an extended form of the *kok* call — followed by half-a-dozen rapid flaps of his wings; he courts the female by erecting his ear-tufts, swelling the red skin round his eyes, and spreading his wings and tail. Males spar with heads and tails down and rumps raised. Probably because of the artificially high numbers, many males have several mates, but very rarely take any part in nesting duties. The female makes a simple nest in cover on the ground or occasionally at a height on a stack,

wall, or tree stump, and lays up to sixteen rather glossy, olive-brown eggs. Often two or more females lay in one nest, or sometimes a pheasant may lay in a partridge's or mallard's nest. Incubation lasts from 3 to 4 weeks, and the beautifully marked chicks are active at once and can fly in 2 weeks. Pheasants do not form packs as grouse do, but, again owing to artificial numbers, many may be seen together.

*1 2 3 **4** **5** **6** 7 8 9 10 11 12*

JAPANESE PHEASANT (*Phasianus versicolor*). A bird very like a dark common pheasant, but the male is dark green above rather than dark brown. The females are almost impossible to tell from hen common pheasants, and some authorities consider that they are not a separate species but only a race of the common pheasant.

2 LADY AMHERST'S PHEASANT (*Chrysolophus amherstiae*). This species was introduced for sporting and ornamental reasons. The males are very distinctive, but the females are like common pheasants except that they have longer tails, and can be distinguished from female golden pheasants by the grey-green wattle round the yellow eye. These pheasants are naturalised in parts of Bedfordshire and Buckinghamshire near Woburn Abbey, living in thick rhododendron coverts, with habits in general like those of the common pheasant. But they keep much lower when flushed and are therefore dangerous as sporting birds. The bird shown on the plate is a hybrid or cross with the golden pheasant. Such mixed matings are common among game birds.

3 GOLDEN PHEASANT (*Chrysolophus pictus*). Another ornamental bird with an unmistakable male plumage. The female resembles the female Amherst pheasant but has a red wattle round the eye. Golden pheasants are naturalised and numerous in central East Anglia and are found in south-west Scotland and elsewhere round big houses; but they are not popular as sporting birds, because, like Lady Amherst's pheasant, they fly low when put up, and efforts have been made to exterminate them.

SILVER PHEASANT (*Gennaeus nycthemerus*). This and other species of pheasant have been introduced from time to time, and may occasionally be seen, especially near Woburn Abbey. The male is black and white, and the female has a black crest and black and white tail; both have red legs.

REEVES'S PHEASANT (*Syrmaticus reevesii*). This is now most likely to be seen near Woburn Abbey. It is a big bird with a very long tail; the male has a black and white head, and the female's head is chestnut and buff.

2 LADY AMHERST'S PHEASANT.
    hybrid cock

3a GOLDEN PHEASANT. cock 3b hen

1c PHEASANT. hen

1a, b PHEASANT. cocks

PARTRIDGES, QUAILS, AND CORNCRAKE

1 **COMMON PARTRIDGE** (*Perdix perdix*). This round, compact game bird, about a foot long, is a resident throughout the British Isles, though more patchily distributed in northern Scotland and Ireland. It is a typical bird of agricultural, particularly arable, land and, though protected as a game bird, is not usually artificially bred. The cock is more strikingly marked than the hen on head and breast.

In fields partridges crouch to avoid notice, but as you approach, they run, then take wing with typical game bird flight, skimming over hedges and gliding to the ground several hundred yards away to run again and stop. They cannot fly long distances. They feed mainly on plants and grain, and eat insects in the summer, and they come to the roads for grit and for dust baths. Their call is a hoarse *chirrick, chirrick*, heard especially during their early spring display, when parties break up into pairs with many calls, chases, and sparrings. The pairs spread out into chosen territories where in late spring they nest. The well-hidden nest on the ground, with a faint track leading to it, holds a clutch of eight to twenty olive-brown pointed eggs, which are incubated by the hen only for about 3½ weeks. Both parents look after the young, which can fly in about 2 weeks. They stay as family coveys through the summer, and later often several coveys join together.

1   2   3   4   5   6   7   8   9   10   11   12

2 **RED-LEGGED PARTRIDGE** (*Alectoris rufa*). These birds, rather larger than the common partridge, were introduced to Britain in the 18th century from Europe, and are often called French partridges. They are easy to recognise from a distance by the white throat, and close to, by the red bill and legs. The sexes are alike. From behind, their backs are less rounded than the common partridge, and they look bigger and stand taller. The juveniles of both species look much alike, except for the difference in leg colour.

Red-legged partridges are found mainly in the south and east as far north as Yorkshire, and they prefer drier areas: sandy and stony fields, heath and downland, sand dunes, shingle beaches, and old quarries. They will often run rapidly rather than take flight, and may scatter when they do fly. They may perch high, and their loud *chuck chu-car, chuck chu-car* from the roof of a barn or a wall carries a long way. Their alarm call in a short *chuck chuck*. They feed like common partridges but are more often to be seen scratching in heaps of chaff. Female redlegs lay ten to sixteen eggs, sometimes at long intervals, in simple nests on the ground. Sometimes they lay two separate clutches, in which case the male incubates and looks after one of them. Isolated redlegs may associate and even mate with common partridges.

1   2   3   4   5   6   7   8   9   10   11   12

3 **QUAIL** (*Coturnix coturnix*). Quails are small plump birds, about 7 ins. long, the sexes being much alike except that the male's colours are brighter. Immature birds resemble the female. They are irregular summer visitors to farmlands, especially grass and clover, all over the British Isles, but more commonly in the south. Occasionally birds appear in the winter.

Quails are seldom seen as they remain hidden in crops and do not flush easily. But the call of the male, which sounds like 'wet my lips' and is generally uttered on the ground, but occasionally on the wing, at night, can be heard half a mile away, even above the noise of farm vehicles. Their feeding habits are like those of partridges. The nest, well hidden in crops, holds seven to twelve yellowish eggs with dark markings, and only the hen incubates and looks after the brood. The eggs take about 3 weeks to hatch, and the young about 10 days to fly. A pair may hatch two broods in a season, and the broods stay together in 'bevies' until they migrate.

*(1   2   3)   4   **5   6   7   8   9**   10   (11   12)*

4 **CORNCRAKE** (*Crex crex*). These birds, also known as landrails because they are the least aquatic of the British rails (*see* p. 58), are distinguished by their short, deep bills and bright chestnut wings which show up in flight. The juveniles are lighter in colour, and the nestlings have black down. Corncrakes are summer visitors, but are far less common than they were 50 years ago, being now mainly confined to the extreme west of Wales, northern England, north and west Scotland, and the islands. They are still common in parts of Ireland. Their decline is probably because mechanical cutters destroy the nests and young in the hayfields, which are their favourite habitat. They also nest in drier bogs. They are seen on passage, generally in the autumn when corn crops are cut.

The monotonous *crek crek* call of the male both day and night reveals the corncrakes' presence in spring, though when they are common, they do appear in the open. When flushed, they rise heavily and soon settle again in cover. The males can be attracted by an imitation of their call, and will then fluff themselves out in display and attack their own image in a mirror. The corncrake's food is mainly insects and other small animals. The well-hidden nest, which may have an awning of woven stems over it, holds eight to twelve brownish red-spotted eggs, which the female incubates for 2 weeks or more. Both parents feed the young who soon look after themselves, but do not fly for at least 4 weeks. There is sometimes a second brood.

*(1   2   3)   4   **5   6   7   8   9**   10   (11   12)*

BOB-WHITE (*Colinus virginianus*). A small North American game bird, much like a quail but with white markings on the face and a very dark tail. Several attempts have been made to introduce it to English farming country — Cotswolds and East Anglia — and to Tresco, Isles of Scilly. Its presence is most likely to be revealed by its call, from which it gets its name

3a QUAIL, M. 3b F.
2 RED-LEGGED PARTRIDGE
1a COMMON PARTRIDGE, F.

4 CORNCRAKE and chicks
1b COMMON PARTRIDGE, M.

RAILS

1 **MOORHEN** (*Gallinula chloropus*). A very common water bird, about 13 ins. long, much larger than a water rail, and smaller and more colourful than a coot. Its long unwebbed toes have flaps of skin which open when it swims. Juvenile and first-winter birds are much browner (1b), with greenish bills and frontal shields, and are distinguished from juvenile coots by the white round their tails.

Moorhens are found throughout the British Isles as residents, and there are some winter visitors and passage migrants from abroad. They live near fresh water, including ponds in city parks, but not on fast-flowing streams or high lochs and tarns. They sometimes breed up to a mile from water.

Though a familiar sight crossing a river or pond, with its jerky, bobbing swimming action, a moorhen tends to keep close to the bank and spends much time in cover. When alarmed, it dives and remains submerged with the bill just on the surface. It walks and runs well. Many moorhens may graze together in a field and often come to henruns for food, which is mainly vegetable. Their usual calls are a loud *kurruck* or a single *kik*, with variations. They have a variety of display actions, making use of the white tail patch, and they fight fiercely, sitting up in the water and striking at each other with their feet. They build several platforms before completing the true nest, which is made of any available plants and holds a clutch of five to twelve brown, red-speckled eggs. Both parents incubate for about 3 weeks, and the active nestlings, which swim almost at once, fly in about 6 weeks. There are at least two broods.

1   2   3   4   5   6   7   8   9   10   11   12

AMERICAN PURPLE GALLINULE (*Porphyrula martinica*). An immature bird was found in the Isles of Scilly in November 1958. The adult, about the size of a moorhen, has a purple glossy plumage.

2 **COOT** (*Fulica atra*). The biggest British member of the rail family is about 15 ins. long. It looks black on the water except for its white shield and bill, but shows a narrow white wing bar in flight. The juvenile has a pale throat and breast and no shield. Coots are not so widespread as moorhens, and do not breed in northern Scotland, though they may appear there in winter, when large flocks form, including birds from abroad. They are found on lowland lakes and ponds of fair size, and also on the larger, slower rivers.

Coots swim more smoothly than moorhens, but they jerk their heads more than ducks do, and their pointed bills and rounded, tailless outline distinguish them further. They feed largely by diving after water plants, but also graze on land. They appear to fly better than moorhens, lifting their legs behind their tails and beating their wings fast. Their usual call is a loud *kyowk*, sometimes repeated quickly. Coots display on the water and attack each other with heads low and wings half-raised. They build more substantial nests than moorhens do, often well out in the reeds; the clutch of six to nine brown, black-speckled eggs is incubated by both parents for 3 weeks or more. The young, which have brilliant red heads,

begin to dive for their own food after 4 weeks, though they stay with the parents for longer.

1   2   3   4   5   6   7   8   9   10   11   12

3 **SPOTTED CRAKE** (*Porzana porzana*). This bird is smaller than a water rail (about 9 ins. long), has a shorter bill, and white spots on the breast and upper parts; but from behind it is possible to confuse them. It is much darker as well as smaller than a corncrake (p. 57), and the female is duller than the male.

Spotted crakes are passage migrants and occasional winter visitors, though a few pairs may breed in bogs and marshes. They behave like water rails, but feed more on small animal life than plants. They have a loud call and a monotonous *tick tack*, both heard in the evening or at night.

4 **WATER RAIL** (*Rallus aquaticus*). About 11 ins. long, this is the only long-billed British rail. It rather resembles a snipe (p. 67), but can easily be distinguished by its slow walk, heavy flight, and the white on its tail. The three long front toes are not webbed. The female is similar to the male but duller in colour. The nestling is covered with black down.

Water rails are residents, winter visitors, or passage migrants. As breeding birds they are probably commonest in East Anglia and parts of Ireland, but they are local everywhere, being confined to reedy, sedgy, and other swampy areas, even to quite small patches in winter. They are usually seen stalking delicately in an open space or flying up with dangling legs, but they crouch and make for cover when alarmed. A grunting squeal, called 'sharming', announces their presence. Their food is both plant and animal. The nest is well-hidden and contains six to eleven brown eggs, like small moorhen's eggs. Both parents share the incubation for nearly 3 weeks and look after the young, which fledge in under 2 months. There are usually two broods.

1   2   3   4   5   6   7   8   9   10   11   12

5 **BAILLON'S CRAKE** (*Porzana pusilla*). The smallest British rail, about 7 ins. long, can be distinguished from the little crake by white marks on the upper parts and white bars on the flanks. The sexes are alike. It used to breed occasionally in East Anglia, but no nest has been recorded for many years. It lives, like its relatives, in dense cover near water, and has a purring call.

6 **LITTLE CRAKE** (*Porzana parva*). This is a very small bird though slightly larger than Baillon's crake. The female (6a) has distinctive buff underparts, and the male (6b) is like Baillon's crake, but without the white markings on back and flanks. The juveniles of both species are alike. The little crake is occasionally recorded from spring to autumn, and is most likely to be recognised by its call, two or three quiet notes followed by a trill, and uttered mainly by night. It breeds as near as Germany. In general habits it resembles its close relatives.

SORA RAIL (*Porzana carolina*). A North American bird, much like the spotted crake except for its yellow bill. It has only been recorded five times in the British Isles in the last 100 years.

1a MOORHEN.Juv. 1b Ad. and chicks 2 COOT. Ad. and Juv.
3 SPOTTED CRAKE 4 WATER RAIL
5 BAILLON'S CRAKE 6a LITTLE CRAKE. F. 6b M.

1 OYSTERCATCHER (*Haematopus ostralogus*). A big wader, 17 ins. long, and the only British member of its family. It is easy to recognise at any time of year, though the pattern of wings and tail in flight resembles that of the black-tailed godwit (p. 69). The white half-collar is a mark of an immature or non-breeding bird (1b) rather than a winter plumage, and may be seen at all seasons.

Oystercatchers breed round most of the British coast. In winter they concentrate in areas like Morecambe Bay, Lancs. and north Norfolk, and are occasionally seen inland. They nest both on rocky coasts and beaches of sand and shingle; inland round lakes and lochs, on river shingle-beds, and fields and moorland up to 2,000 ft. in Scotland.

They are noisy birds at all times, forming huge flocks in winter and mobbing intruders on their breeding ground when they have young. On the coast they feed at low tide on the exposed mussel-scaups or probe in the mud for cockles, when they are accused of damaging the cockle fisheries. They take limpets and other shellfish and can deal with oysters; they also eat worms, small crabs and insects, even the eggs and young of other birds nesting near them. At high tide they rest in packed groups. Their best-known display is the piping of several birds together with necks stretched and bills pointed downward. Parties fly excitedly over the breeding area early in spring, and the male has a 'butterfly' song-flight. Their *bleep bleep* is one of the best known calls of the shore, alternating with a short *pic pic*. The piping notes become speeded up into a continuous trill.

Pairs usually spread out when nesting, but sometimes form small groups with ringed plovers and terns. They may make several scrapes and choose one, though in rocky areas the same site may be used for years, lined with shells, pebbles, rabbit droppings, or flowerheads. The eggs, usually three, are rounder than most waders' eggs, and have a light brown ground colour covered with dark spots, streaks and pothooks. Incubation, mainly by the female, lasts 3½ to 4 weeks.

Families begin to collect on the coast in July, and about September they start moving southward. In the meantime birds from further north arrive, some passing on and others remaining. The first oyster-catchers return to their breeding areas in February, but non-breeding flocks stay by the shore all the year.

*1 2 3 **4 5 6 7** 8 9 10 11 12*

2 LAPWING (*Vanellus vanellus*), also known as peewit and green plover. The most familiar British wader, though not typical because of its crest, rounded wings, black-and-white appearance, and short bill which is characteristic of the plovers (*Charadriidae*). Lapwings are unmistakable in spring, but in autumn the duller plumage of the juveniles (2a) may be puzzling. Flocks in flight can be easily recog-nised by their flapping beat and the twinkling of the white undersides.

Lapwings breed in every British county but are now scarce in the south except in winter, when they concentrate in pasture fields and round lakes, reservoirs, and estuaries. They prefer to nest on ploughed fields, often with young crops or stubbles, or in marshes, moorland, and bogs up to 3,000 ft. In late summer they appear on the aftermath of hayfields, and in hard weather in parks and on playing fields.

Lapwings scatter over a field to feed, running a few steps, stopping to peck, then standing up straight; they are often seen with starlings, rooks, or gulls (which may try to rob them of their food). They feed by night at full moons, resting by day, sometimes in very large flocks. They are friends to the farmer because they feed mainly on insects in the soil. In spring they spread out over the breeding ground, and the males attract attention by their tumbling flights and 'song', which is built up from the usual *peewit* call and fits the dashing flight. The alarm and mobbing call is also an extreme *peewit*. Flocks at rest, apparently asleep, often call quietly.

After early displays, several pairs may settle down to nest in one field or moorland area. The males each make several scrapes, the females choose one and line it with local material; it is generally quite exposed, often on a slight mound. Four eggs are the usual clutch, with dark-brown ground colour and heavy markings, which makes them hard to see, especially when smeared with mud in wet weather. Incubation, mainly by the female, lasts 3½ to 4 weeks or more. The young leave the nest as soon as they are dry and are equally hard to find; when bigger they sometimes run away, the parents mobbing overhead. In mid-June they begin to form small parties. The breeding birds slowly move off the higher ground towards the coast or big river valleys, and the flocks build up into hundreds, even thousands. Many migrate to Ireland and lapwings from the Continent winter in Britain. They may move on again ahead of severe weather but are sometimes caught by it. They begin to return to their breeding areas in February.

*1 2 **3 4 5 6** 7 8 9 10 11 12*

SOCIABLE PLOVER (*Chettusia gregaria*). A very rare wader from Asia only recorded eleven times in Britain, though once in 1963 and twice in 1968. It is 11½ ins. long, a little smaller than a lapwing, with no crest and more pointed wings. In winter it looks like a long-legged golden plover (p. 62), with olive-brown upper parts and a pale stripe over the eye; the breast is mottled and the underparts white. The primary wing feathers are black, the secondaries white, and the tail white with a black band across it, and this shows distinctly in flight. In spring the crown of the head becomes black and there are patches of black and chestnut on the belly. The harsh triple call sounds like *reck reck reck*.

2a LAPWING, Juv.
2b LAPWING, M.   2d chicks
1a OYSTERCATCHER, Ad.

2c LAPWING, F.

1b Imm.   1c chick

PLOVERS. 2

1 GOLDEN PLOVER (*Pluvialis apricaria*). A medium-sized rather plump wader, 11 ins. long. In spring and summer (1a, b) the amount of black on the face and neck varies, the darker birds being of the northern race which passes through Britain to Iceland and Scandinavia; in autumn (1c), when the black is lost, the two races look alike. In flight the tail and rump are dark, and there is no bar on the pointed wings. Juveniles can be distinguished from grey plovers because they have no black patch under the wing.

Golden plovers breed on peat and grass moors up to 3,000 ft. from Devon to the Scottish Highlands and Islands, and are probably commonest on the Pennines and south Scottish hills. They are much more widely distributed in winter when they haunt grassland and drier moors, stubbles and ploughed.land, going to the coast mainly in hard weather.

Winter flocks are of all sizes up to several thousand birds, and often mix with lapwings and starlings. They feed, like lapwings, on insects, worms, small molluscs, and spiders; they also eat some grass stems and seeds. They often sleep in daytime, bills tucked behind wings, but when disturbed they flash away from the slower lapwings, wheeling to show their light under-sides and dark upperparts alternately. In spring the male flies above the future breeding ground with slow wing-beats and song, then bursts of rapid flight, ending in a dive to earth; or sometimes several display together on the ground. The note used throughout the year is a musical whistling *tloo-ee* in two syllables; the display song has a mournful sound. The male selects the breeding ground before pairing, but the female chooses the final scrape, often on a low hummock, and lines it with grasses. The clutch is usually four eggs, larger than lapwing's eggs, with fewer bolder markings on a paler ground colour. Both sexes incubate in turns for about 4 weeks. Some birds slip off when an intruder is far away and return to call plaintively; others sit close and when flushed pretend to be injured. The chicks, perhaps the most beautiful of all young waders, are very hard to find. As soon as they can fly, the families leave the high moors and move to lower grassland, reaching southern England in September. Some cross the Channel, especially in hard weather. Immigrants from further north follow the British birds southward. The return movement begins in February.

*1 2 3 **4 5 6** 7 8 9 10 11 12*

LESSER GOLDEN PLOVER (*Pluvialis dominica*). A very rare visitor from Asia and North America. It is rather smaller (9½ ins. long) than the European golden plover; and in spring is like the northern race, except for a grey, instead of white, underwing. In winter it looks duller and resembles a juvenile grey plover, but with a darker rump and tail and no black patch under the wing. It has appeared in Britain 18 times, four of these birds, identified when shot, being of the Asiatic race.

2 GREY PLOVER (*Pluvialis squatarola*). A winter visitor and passage migrant to most British and Irish coastal counties, but rare inland, as it prefers rather muddy shores and estuaries. It is a little larger than a golden plover (11 ins. long), but very like it in build. Its summer plumage (2b), which sometimes lasts into the autumn, is strikingly beautiful and unmistakable; but grey plovers are usually seen in Britain in winter plumage (2a) when the adults have greyer backs than golden plovers, though juveniles are easy to confuse on the ground. In flight the black patches under the wings, pale rump and tail, and wing-bar are distinctive.

Grey plovers form small parties rather than big flocks. They search for their food — insects and other small creatures in the mud — like other plovers and mix with groups of smaller waders along the tide-line, their stouter figures standing out amongst dun-lins and ringed plovers. Parties can be identified in flight by the call note in three syllables: *tlee-oo-ee* They arrive from July onwards, gradually working south, mainly down the east coast. Many remain all winter, starting north again in March, but a few non-breeding birds can be seen all the year round. They breed in countries of the far north.

1 2 3 4 5 6 7 8 9 10 11 12

3 DOTTEREL (*Eudromias morinellus*). Smaller (9 ins long) than the golden and grey, but larger than the ringed plovers (p. 65). In spring and summer the pattern of the under-parts and white stripe over the eye are distinctive; in winter dotterels can be distinguished from ringed plovers by the absence of a black collar, and from the golden and grey by the lack of mottling on the back. In flight the rump is dark and the tail very dark with white spots; there is a faint wing-bar. The female in summer is generally brighter than the male.

The dotterel is a summer visitor and passage migrant in small numbers, breeding in the central Scottish Highlands and occasionally elsewhere on bare areas 3,000 to 4,000 ft. high, among loose stones and low vegetation. During spring and autumn migration dotterels visit lower downland and bare fields and are fairly regular in East Anglia.

Dotterels on passage are usually seen in small parties or 'trips'; they feed mainly on small insect from the soil. On the breeding ground they are remarkably tame. The female is the dominant bird taking the male part in display flights and chasing her prospective mate. After making trial scrapes, the female selects one and lays usually three eggs, leaving the male to sit. The eggs are rather rounder than those of other plovers. They take 3 to 3½ weeks to hatch, and the young leave the nest a day later. Both sexes, but especially the male, pretend to be injured i disturbed from the nest or young. The trips leave the hills in July and travel southwards until the autumn mainly near the coast; they start northwards again in late April.

*. . (3) 4 **5 6** 7 8 9 10 (11)*

62

3a DOTTEREL, Ad. 3b Juv. 3c chick   1a, b GOLDEN PLOVER, summer 1d chick

2a GREY PLOVER, winter   1c   GOLDEN PLOVER, autumn

2b GREY PLOVER, summer

1 KENTISH PLOVER (*Charadrius alexandrinus*). This bird, which is just over 6 ins. in length, can be distinguished from the ringed plovers by the white throat of the adult and the dark legs at all ages. The female is less strongly marked on the head than the male. A narrow white wing-bar shows in flight.

A few Kentish plovers used to nest on the south-east coast, but there have been no recent records, though they still nest in the Channel Isles. They are now occasional visitors to the coast on passage. Their breeding habitats are extensive beaches of sand, shingle, or dry mud. In habits they resemble the ringed plovers, though they do not form large flocks as the common ringed plovers sometimes do. They have a slow-beating song flight rather like that of the little ringed plover, and the nest is similar; but the clutch is usually of three eggs.

2 RINGED PLOVER (*Charadrius hiaticula*). This is one of the most familiar small shore birds, about 7½ ins. long. It is a typical plover, with its short bill and round head. It can be told from the little ringed plover and the rare Kentish plover by the white wing-bar in flight, by its brighter orange legs, and by its call. It is larger and stouter, but that is not of much value for identification unless two species are together. The juveniles of all three species are easy to confuse, but the ringed plover (2b) always has a better developed collar. The sexes are alike.

The ringed plover is to be seen on most British coasts; it breeds inland in East Anglia, the north of England, and parts of Scotland and Ireland, and occasionally elsewhere, and birds on passage occur inland in England at lakes, reservoirs, and gravel pits. The breeding habitats are sandy and shingly beaches, flinty 'brecks', and shingle beds by rivers. In winter birds, including visitors from abroad, move to muddy shores and estuaries.

Ringed plovers are often seen running along looking for food close to the sea's edge with other small waders, especially dunlins, their heads sunk into their bodies. But they also feed higher up the beach, searching for small insects, molluscs, and worms,' moving a few steps, pecking, then looking up or stretching their wings. They often fly in mixed parties, uttering their musical call: *too-i*. The male displays to the female, showing his plumage to advantage by puffing his breast, stretching his wings and fanning his tail, and making scrapes in the sand. Several birds will also join in chases, calling excitedly. Finally the female chooses a scrape and lays usually four grey-brown eggs with black spots. Both parents share the incubation for 3½ weeks, and may feign injury to distract attention from the nest or the chicks. The chicks are active at once and fly in about 3½ weeks. There are two or even three broods a year. Ringed plovers sometimes nest in small groups near groups of little terns.

*1   2   3   **4   5   6   7**   8   9   10   11   12***

3 LITTLE RINGED PLOVER (*Charadrius dubius*). A slim little bird, about 6 ins. long, with paler legs than the common ringed plover, no bar on its wing, and a prominent orange rim to the eye which can be seen at close range. The juveniles (3a) can be best distinguished from ringed plover juveniles by their wing pattern.

The little ringed plover is a summer visitor, now spreading west and north, breeding in Scotland in 1968 and regularly in north-east England. It has colonised Britain since 1938, its favourite habitat being shingle stretches in gravel pits; it also nests on river shingle, and occasionally by shallow pools. The arrival of the little ringed plovers at a gravel pit is often announced by the male's song flights over it, with repeated *tirra tirra* calls as well as the ordinary *teew*, higher pitched than the call of the common ringed plover and quite distinctive. They run about rapidly, searching for small invertebrate animals or the edge of the pools. The nest is a tiny scrape, and the four eggs are smaller than but the same colour as those of the ringed plover, and take about the same time to hatch. The chicks fledge in about 3½ weeks. There may be two broods in a season. The birds stay about the nesting area for a time after the young can fly, but are not often seen elsewhere.

*. .   3   **4   5   6   7**   8   9   (10)   . .*

KILLDEER (*Charadrius vociferus*). This North American plover, about 9½ ins. long, is rather like a dotterel (p. 63). It has two black bars across the chest, a noticeably long tail with a reddish rump, and pale legs of variable colour. About a dozen have been recorded in the British Isles, mostly on the west side. In America the killdeer breeds on farmland much as the lapwing (p. 61) does in Britain.

CASPIAN PLOVER (*Charadrius asiaticus*). An Asian plover, 7½ ins. long, which is smaller than a dotterel but larger than a ringed plover. It has no black on the face and the chestnut band across the breast is higher up than on the dotterel, from which it can be told in winter by its white forehead. It has only occurred once in Britain – in 1890: when a pair were seen near Great Yarmouth in Norfolk, and the male was shot.

1a KENTISH PLOVER, Juv.
2a RINGED PLOVER, Ad.   2c chick
3a LITTLE RINGED PLOVER, Juv.

1b KENTISH PLOVER, M.
2b RINGED PLOVER, Juv.
3b LITTLE RINGED PLOVER, Ad.   3c chicks

1 WOODCOCK (*Scolopax rusticola*). The woodcock is over 13 ins. long, 3 ins. of which is bill. It looks like a large, round-winged snipe with a high domed head, in which the big black eye is set far back. As it flies away, its beautifully blending plumage suggests a small owl, until the long bill is seen.

The woodcock is a resident, summer and winter visitor, and passage migrant. It usually breeds in woodland of oak, beech, birch, or conifers, with light undergrowth of bracken and brambles; but it may nest in long heather on the moorland edge. In winter it is found even on treeless islands, but not as a rule far from wet ground.

At dusk in spring and summer, and sometimes also before dawn, male woodcock make 'roding' flights (1b) round their chosen territories. As they seem to falter in their rather slow, flapping flight, they utter a low croak followed by a high-pitched *chissick*, and repeat this at intervals, sometimes the *chissick* being given without the croak. Woodcock also fly out at night from the woods to feed in marshes and bogs, probing after worms in the mud. They take insects and other small animals, and some seeds and leaves. By day, except in hard weather when they have to go on feeding, they lie up in cover, rising rather noisily when disturbed and flying off low among the trees. They nest on the ground, usually in dead leaves under light cover, and the four light-brown eggs with reddish streaks are rounder than those of most waders, and blend with their surroundings. The female alone incubates them for about 3 weeks, though the male may be nearby, and she looks after the young, who can fly after about 3 weeks. Before that, she will carry them out of danger. There may sometimes be a second brood. Woodcock do not form flocks, and it is rare to see more than two together once the young are fledged.

1 2 **3 4 5 6 7** 8 9 10 11 12

2 SNIPE (*Gallinago gallinago*). Its remarkably long bill, $2\frac{1}{2}$ ins. out of a total length of about $10\frac{1}{2}$ ins., and dark plumage with light stripes distinguish the snipe from all other waders, except its close relatives. The pale stripe in the centre of its crown, longer bill, and more pointed wings separate it from the jack snipe. It has less white on its tail than have adults of the rare great snipe.

Snipe are residents, summer and winter visitors, and passage migrants all over the British Isles; birds from the Faeroes regularly come to Britain and the American race, Wilson's snipe, has occurred once. They · like wet habitats of all kinds from valley marshes to high moorland, although their actual nesting ground may be quite dry.

A snipe usually gives a fleeting view as it rises almost at the feet and twists away, calling a sharp *whist*.

Sometimes it turns high in the air and circles roun flying more regularly with rapid beats. Several m get up together and form a small flock, and hundre collect in winter in good 'snipe bogs'. In early spri 'drumming' flights (2b) start and may be heard day or night. The snipe rises steeply, then div twisting and turning and making a bleating noise the air passes through its extended outer tail-feathe Snipe give their *chipper chipper* call in spring both flight and also from a perch. They feed by probing the mud for worms with their sensitive bills, but th also eat some insects, molluscs, and plant seeds. T simple nest is well concealed on the ground, and t four olive-brown eggs, richly marked with da streaks and spots, are incubated by the female f nearly 3 weeks. Both parents tend the beautifu marked, downy chicks, which begin to fly when or 2 weeks old. There may be two broods in the seaso Families leave the drier areas after nesting.

1 2 **3 4 5 6** 7 8 9 10 11 12

3 JACK SNIPE (*Lymnocryptes minimus*). Mu smaller than a common snipe, being $7\frac{1}{2}$ ins. lor of which $1\frac{1}{2}$ ins. is bill. In flight (3b) the shorter bill a more rounded wings are obvious. The plumage darker and glossier, there is no central stripe ov the head, and the tail is more wedge-shaped. The tw light stripes down the back are prominent when it on the ground.

The jack snipe is a winter visitor and passa migrant which sometimes stays through the summe It has favourite spots, often quite shallow drains a ditches in open marshes, but when it crouches it difficult to find. Flushed, it usually flies only a sho way, but almost always rises again close to the observ before he can see it. Several may be found in the sa area, though they do not generally form parties. Th are silent birds in winter but have a weak form of t common snipe's call. Their food is much the sam but they may take more seeds.

1 2 3 4 (5 6 7 8 9) 10 11 12

4 GREAT SNIPE (*Gallinago media*). This snipe loo heavier and darker than the common snipe, and t adult shows a good deal of white on the sides of t tail. It is also slightly longer and has more barr plumage. Juveniles are very difficult to identify. T great snipe used to be a scarce but regular passa visitor to south and east England, but is now rare a was recorded about two dozen times between 19 and 1970. It haunts drier habitats than the commo snipe does. Its habits are similar, but it is more sile occasionally uttering a croak on rising, and its flig when flushed is slower and straighter.

(In flight) 2b SNIPE, drumming   1b WOODCOCK, roding
2c SNIPE   3b JACK SNIPE   4 GREAT SNIPE
3a JACK SNIPE   1a WOODCOCK, on nest   2a SNIPE and chicks

1 CURLEW (*Numenius arquata*). The largest British wader is about 1½ ft. long and its curved bill may be another 5 ins. Its size, long legs, and grey-brown plumage make it easy to recognise, though in flight the wings look dark, and the rump and tail white, and it is possible to confuse it with immature gulls.

Curlews now nest in most British counties, being rarest in the south-east. In winter they are found mainly round the coast. Their breeding habitat in the north and west, to which they are largely summer visitors, is moorland and rough pasture; in the south they nest in river valleys, crop fields, and among sand dunes. There are many winter visitors and passage migrants.

Its *coor-lee* call is often the first sign of a curlew in flight; then a party may be seen high up travelling in line formation, their wing-beats slow compared to smaller waders. They plane down to ground and walk rather deliberately with necks stretched when alarmed. They scatter over the shore among other birds, probing into the mud for worms or picking small animals out of shallow water. The bubbling song in flight is one of the characteristic spring sounds on moorland, and the sharp alarm call has led to the Scottish name *whaup*. Both birds may join in the fluttering courtship flight, and share incubation of the three or four pear-shaped, rather shiny, olive-green, brown-marked eggs, laid in a big saucer of dry grass on quite open ground. Then they boldly defend the young, which hatch after 4 weeks and fly after 5 weeks or more. The families gradually move away to the coast, where large flocks may build up. Some later migrate overseas.

1 2 3 4 5 6 7 8 9 10 11 12

2 WHIMBREL (*Numenius phaeopus*). About 2 ins. shorter than a curlew, with a bill of 3½ ins., the whimbrel looks generally darker. It has a distinguishing head pattern: two almost black bands divided by a pale stripe. As with the curlew, the plumage does not vary much at any stage.

Whimbrels breed as summer visitors in Shetland, in Lewis, and perhaps elsewhere too; and they are passage migrants, more numerous in autumn than spring and seen mainly along the coast, where they haunt muddy and sandy shores and salt marshes. Their breeding habitat is boggy moorland.

The whimbrel's usual call is a rapid titter, which is sometimes heard inland at night during migration. On the shore whimbrels allow a closer approach than curlews but resemble them in their feeding and general habits, though their wing-beats are noticeably faster. The nest and three to four eggs are also similar to but smaller than the curlew's; both sexes share the incubation for about 3½ weeks, and the young fly when about 4 weeks old, after which the family leaves the breeding ground for the coast.

. . . 4 5 6 7 8 9 10 . .

ESKIMO CURLEW (*Numenius borealis*). Very few of this North American curlew have been seen in recent years, and it is on the verge of extinction. It is like the American race of whimbrel in having no white rump, and the central stripe on the head is not well marked. There were seven British records between 1852 and 1887.

3 BLACK-TAILED GODWIT (*Limosa limosa*). Godwits can be distinguished from curlews by their long straight or slightly up-turned bills and slimmer figures. This is the larger British species, about 16 ins. long with a further 4 ins. of almost straight bill. As soon as it flies, its white wing-bar, black and white tail, and long legs trailing beyond the tail separate it from the bar-tailed godwit, but on the ground in winter plumage (3b) they look much alike, though this species is darker. In summer (3a) the chestnut on its breast is more extensive. The juvenile looks like a winter adult with a reddish tinge to the breast.

After being a 'lost' breeding bird, this godwit has now returned to a small area in East Anglia and also occasionally nests in north Scotland; but it is best known as a passage migrant and winter visitor to shallow bays and estuaries. The breeding habitat in the south is lush pasture, and in Scotland, boggy moors.

The black-tailed godwit 'stands tall' among other waders, often in groups or large flocks, and it wades quite deep to feed on small animals, as well as probing the mud for worms. It calls *quick quick quick* as it takes wing, but on the breeding ground utters a lapwing-like *kee-vit* and a tittering note when beginning its display flights, in which the female joins the male. The nest-scrape is often well-hidden in grass; the four well-marked olive-brown eggs are sat on for 3½ weeks by both parents who defend the young vigorously until they fly at about 4 weeks old.

1 2 3 4 5 6 7 8 9 10 11 12

4 BAR-TAILED GODWIT (*Limosa lapponica*). An inch or so less in length than the black-tailed godwit, this species has an up-turned bill and shorter legs. In flight it shows a white rump, barred grey tail, no wing bar, and a stouter shape; at rest in winter it looks rather like a small pale curlew but in summer (4b) the male has rich chestnut underparts, the female being duller; young birds resemble her. It is a winter visitor and passage migrant all round British coast, but is rare inland. It likes sandy and muddy shores where it is often seen with knots, dunlins, and other waders. Flocks call *quirrick quirrick* in flight and perform complicated movements over the sea's edge where they land to feed like their relatives. Non-breeding birds may be seen in summer.

1 2 3 4 5 (6) 7 8 9 10 11 12

1 CURLEW 2 WHIMBREL
3a BLACK-TAILED GODWIT, summer 3b winter 4a BAR-TAILED GODWIT, summer 4b winter

1 REDSHANK (*Tringa totanus*). This typical medium-sized wader, 11 ins. long, is distinguished in all plumages by the barred tail with a white rump and white patches along the trailing edges of the wings (*see* bird in flight). The upperparts look greyish-brown in winter and darker in summer. The sexes are alike but the juvenile (1b) has yellow legs.

Redshanks breed throughout Britain and Ireland except in the extreme south-west and on some islands, but are often local. They are common round all coasts in winter, but scarce inland. The breeding habitats range from moorland, rough pastures, and marshes to gravel pits and sand dunes.

The redshank's *tew tew tew, tewi-tewi-tewi* gives the alarm over the marsh, as the bird leaps into the air from a ditch and flashes away, showing dark and white; even on the ground it bobs up and down in apparent excitement. When feeding it runs rapidly over the shore, bending to probe the mud or wading and even swimming; it takes a mixture of small shell-fish, crustaceans, worms, and insects, with a little plant material. There is a song-flight in spring and wing-flapping display on the ground near the nest-site, which is chosen from several scrapes. Both parents incubate the four creamy-buff, red-speckled eggs for over 3 weeks, and the young fly in a month. The parents defend them vigorously. Redshanks often nest near lapwings and slip off quietly as the plovers rise — the only time they are silent. Large flocks form in autumn, but few emigrate from Britain. Birds from Europe and Iceland are winter and passage visitors.

*1   2   3   **4   5   6**   7   8   9   10   11   12*

LESSER YELLOWLEGS OR YELLOWSHANK (*Tringa flavipes*). This American wader is now a fairly regular autumn wanderer to the south-west of Britain and Ireland. It is about an inch shorter than a common redshank, more slender, but with longer, yellow legs, and it has no white wing-bar. The upperparts are dark in summer, with lighter spots, and become greyer and more uniform in winter. It is most usually found on muddy shores or pools near the coast.

GREATER YELLOWLEGS OR YELLOWSHANK (*Tringa melanoleuca*). A somewhat larger North American visitor which has been recorded nearly twenty times, mostly on the west side of the British Isles. It is best distinguished by its stouter bill; it is more spotted than a greenshank and shows less white on the lower back.

2 GREENSHANK (*Tringa nebularia*). Slightly larger than a redshank (about 1 ft. long) and usually greyer looking, except for its dark wings, the greenshank shows a white rump and tail and no wing-bar in flight (*see* bird in flight). At closer range, its long green legs and slightly up-turned bill distinguish it. In winter the head, neck, and breast look almost white while in summer (2a) the back can look almost black and the breast is spotted. Juveniles are darker than adults.

As a summer visitor the greenshank breeds in the central and northern Highlands of Scotland; elsewhere it is a passage migrant, and occasional winter visitor to some coastal areas. It nests on boggy, rocky, or tree-clad moorland, usually not far from water; on passage it occurs inland by lakes, reservoirs, and pools, and on the coast along muddy shores and estuaries, where it may also spend the winter.

The loud *tew tew tew* call is lower-toned than that of the redshank and is given as the bird, usually solitary, takes wing and flies away, low and fast. Its habits on passage resemble those of the commoner bird, but, when feeding, it often uses the side to side action of the spotted redshank. There are a variety of displays, with 'songs', at the breeding area, where the birds perch on stones and trees. The nest is almost always made close to a stone or dead branch in open moorland; the four eggs, larger and more richly marked than redshanks' eggs, are incubated mainly by the female for 3½ weeks, but both parents look after the young, which fly when about a month old. Small parties then move down to the coast to begin their migration.

*1   2   3   **4   5   6**   7   8   9   10   11   12*

3 SPOTTED REDSHANK (*Tringa erythropus*). A little larger than a common redshank and with noticeably longer bill and legs which show well beyond the tail in flight. This species has no wing-bar though it has a white rump. In its summer plumage 'black' (3b) it is unmistakable, but in the winter grey plumage (3a) it resembles the common redshank though usually paler. Juveniles are darker than adults in winter.

The spotted redshank is a passage migrant which sometimes winters in Britain and is more numerous in autumn than spring, either as single birds or in parties or flocks. It is commonest in south-eastern England, but may occur almost anywhere on estuaries and sheltered coasts or inland at reservoirs, sewage farms, and gravel pits. It breeds in northern Europe and Siberia.

Spotted redshanks are taller, more elegant, and less excitable birds than common redshanks. They wade in shallow water, turning their heads from side to side and pecking at the surface for small insects and water animals. As they rise, they call a double note *choo-et* which is distinctive, and they often land just out of sight.

(1   2   3)   4   5   (6)   7   8   9   10   11   (12)

(In flight) SPOTTED REDSHANK; REDSHANK, winter; GREENSHANK

1a REDSHANK, summer
1b REDSHANK, Juv.
2a GREENSHANK, summer
2b GREENSHANK, autumn
3a SPOTTED REDSHANK, autumn
3b SPOTTED REDSHANK, summer

1 COMMON SANDPIPER (*Tringa hypoleucos*). Nearly 8 ins. long, the smallest member of the *Tringa* group of waders is distinguished by its contrasting plumage of white underparts with more or less uniform dull brown upperparts. The white wing-bar and rounded tail with its dark centre and white edging show in flight. Juveniles are more barred than adults.

The 'summer snipe', as it is sometimes called, is a common summer visitor to the north and west of Britain and to Ireland, and a few winter in the south and west. It breeds beside sheets of fresh water, sea lochs, and fast-flowing rivers and streams, and is found on passage by fresh water of all types. The North American spotted sandpiper, often regarded as a separate species, has been recorded 16 times.

Its jerky action and repeated *kitty-wiper* call distinguish the common sandpiper from other small waders as it flies low over the water before settling on the bank or a stone, where it bobs its tail-end up and down like a wagtail; it also bobs its head as other *Tringa* waders do. It feeds largely on insects, which it wades after or picks off stones. It displays by special flights and chases on the ground, using its wings. The nest is not always near water and may be well hidden in vegetation or quite open. The four eggs are rather like small redshanks' eggs and are incubated by both sexes for 3 weeks. When the young fly, after 4 weeks, the families make their way to the coast or to the south. Large parties are unusual.

(1 2 3) 4 5 6 7 8 9 10 (11 12)

2 GREEN SANDPIPER (*Tringa ochropus*). Larger than the common sandpiper (about 9 ins. long) and much darker on the back, this species is unmistakable in flight when the almost black upperparts contrast with the white rump, tail (which has a dark tip), and belly. The dark underside to the wing is also distinctive. At close range in summer the light spotting on the upperparts can be seen.

The green sandpiper is best known as a passage visitor in autumn to much of Britain and Ireland but some also spend the winter in the south, and there is a recent breeding record from north Scotland, where birds have been seen many times in summer by wooded loch-sides. On passage they occur by lakes, reservoirs, pools, sewage farms, and marshes with ditches. The flashing black and white form and ringing *tit tlooet tlooet* call proclaim the green sandpiper as it flies up from a ditch or pool; it is usually much wilder than the common sandpiper, but in other respects resembles it in habits, though it may form small flocks of twenty or more. Like the jack snipe (p. 66) it shows an attachment to certain feeding places. It lays its four eggs in an old nest of some other bird up a tree, a habit shared by several other waders.

1 2 3 4 5 (6) 7 8 9 10 11 12

3 WOOD SANDPIPER (*Tringa glareola*). This rather less common species (about 8 ins. long), looks slightly more slender than the green sandpiper with a rathe round head and thin neck. Its upperparts are muc more mottled in summer and lighter at all seasons the white tail area is not so extensive, and the under side of the wing is grey. From the front, the light made by the meeting of stripes above the bill conspicuous.

The wood sandpiper is a passage visitor, chiefly t the south-east of England. It is much more frequer in autumn than in spring, but scarcer than the gree sandpiper, though it does occur in many other parts o the country as far north as Fair Isle. Small number now breed regularly in northern Scotland, usuall in moorland near trees. On passage, wood sandpiper haunt shallow pools and marshes, both inland and b the coast. Their habits in general resemble those of th green sandpiper, but they are less excitable and usuall do not fly so high when disturbed. The call *chiff-chif, chiff* is quite distinctive. They may be found alone c in quite large parties. They nest on the groun rather like common sandpipers.

. . . 4 5 (6) 7 8 9 10 11 . .

SOLITARY SANDPIPER (*Tringa solitaria*). Abou the size of a common sandpiper, this very rare visitc from North America has occurred about a doze times in the past 100 years. It looks like a small gree sandpiper, but without a white rump, though th spread tail is white at the sides.

MARSH SANDPIPER (*Tringa stagnatilis*). A ra visitor from eastern Europe and Asia which ha occurred about twenty times both in spring an autumn, mainly in south-east England. It is rath like a small greenshank with a conspicuously whit head, relatively long legs, and a very thin bill. Its upperparts become more mottled in summer.

TEREK SANDPIPER (*Tringa terek*). A very ra visitor from extreme eastern Europe and Asia, abou 9 ins. long, with a pale grey-brown plumage, mottle in summer with black above and whitish below. It ha bright yellow legs and a long up-turned bill. flight it shows white on the rump, outer tail feather and trailing edge of the wings. There have been fi records from England since 1951.

4 BROAD-BILLED SANDPIPER (*Limicola falcine lus*). A small sandpiper, only 6½ ins. long, with a da snipe-like plumage, though its stout body is more li a dunlin (p. 77). It has light stripes down its back li a jack snipe (p. 67), but in winter the white throat an pale stripe over the eye are distinctive. About thir have occurred, mostly down the east side of Englar and in autumn, no doubt on passage from Norther Scandinavia where they breed. They are rath solitary and skulking, tending to crouch whe alarmed.

1 COMMON SANDPIPER and chicks

3 WOOD SANDPIPER   2 GREEN SANDPIPER

4 BROAD-BILLED SANDPIPER

1 KNOT (*Calidris canutus*). At about 10 ins. long, this is the largest common wader of the stout-bodied 'dunlin' group. In winter (1a) it is grey above and white below, but not so pale as a sanderling or so dark as most dunlins (p. 77). Juveniles in autumn look scaly on the back and have pale buff breasts and underparts, which are rich chestnut in the adult summer plumage (1b), contrasting with the grey back. In flight a white wing-bar shows, and the rump and tail are uniform, rather lighter than the back.

Knots are winter visitors and passage migrants all round British coasts and occasionally inland; they are particularly numerous on sandy and muddy shores on the east coast, and on the west from the Solway Firth to the Cheshire Dee.

At a distance a pack of knots may look like a dark patch on the shore, so tightly do they keep together when feeding or resting. They move quickly over the mud searching for small animals of various kinds, and take flights together to perform the remarkable aerobatics for which waders of this group are famous, flashing now white, now dark as they turn over, each bird fractionally later than the one in front. They may mix with other waders and gather with them in vast numbers on the rocks at high tide. But knots also occur in ones and twos, especially inland, and a few remain through the summer in the beautiful breeding plumage. The usual call sounds like the name *knut* and becomes a chorus from a pack of birds; there is also a low-pitched *twit-wit* uttered in flight.

1 2 3 4 5 (6) 7 8 9 10 11 12

2 RUFF and **REEVE** (*Philomachus pugnax*). Males (ruffs) may be 1 ft. long and in spring have wattled faces, colourful ear-tufts, and ruffs unlike any other British bird. In autumn and winter (2c) they look like big females (reeves), with a prominent scaly back pattern, due to the pale margins of dark feathers. Juveniles have pale buff breasts. The bill looks rather short, for a wader, and the legs vary in colour from greenish yellow to red, causing confusion with redshanks (p. 71). The white crescents on each side of the dark tail and a narrow white wing-bar show in flight (2d).

Ruffs and reeves are mainly passage migrants, most common on grassy marshland on and near the east and south coasts; a few spend the winter and summer, and some now nest in East Anglia again.

The famous displays of the males at their mounds in spring are not likely to be seen in Britain, and the most usual view of a ruff or reeve is as it peers above the grass stems, elongating its neck like a rail (p. 59); then it stalks forward again, searching the vegetation or probing the mud for the various small animals on which it feeds. It generally flies without calling, quite unlike a redshank which in some ways it resembles. Parties up to twenty birds are found. The nest is like that of a redshank, but the four eggs resembl the snipe's.

(1 2 3) 4 5 (6) 7 8 9 10 (11 12)

3 PECTORAL SANDPIPER (*Calidris melanotos*) This is the American wader most often recorded i Britain. It is about 7½ ins. long and looks lik a small reeve, with its rather short bill, yellow legs and scaly back. Its spotted breast ends cleanly, no merging into the pale underparts, and the tail look pale grey in flight. Its habit of stretching its neck whe standing still increases its resemblance to a reeve. O taking wing, it has a double *trip trip* call, and ofte zigzags like a snipe. Most of the records are o juveniles from the coasts of England and south-wes Ireland in autumn; they feed on small animals i fresh-water marshes near the coast.

OTHER LARGE AMERICAN SANDPIPERS The **SHARP-TAILED SANDPIPER** (*Calidr acuminata*), or Siberian pectoral sandpiper, look much like the pectoral sandpiper but its spotte breast merges into the pale underparts. The tail i slightly wedge-shaped with projecting central feather Of eight British records, four are from Norfolk it breeds in Alaska as well as in Siberia. Th **STILT SANDPIPER** (*Micropalma himantopus* recorded nine times since 1954, is about 8 ins. long with long legs and a long, slightly-curved bill. It is gre in winter, with a streaked neck, but in summer becomes rich brown with prominent bars on its unde parts. The **BUFF-BREASTED SANDPIPER** (*Try gites subruficollis*) is now recorded annually, usuall from southern England in autumn. It is about 8 in long, and its scaly back pattern makes it look rathe like a small reeve; but it has a buff breast and unde parts and no rump and tail pattern. It is plover-lik and rather tame, crouching rather than flying, and prefers dry areas near the shore. **BARTRAM' SANDPIPER** (*Bartramia longicauda*), also called th upland plover, is about 11 ins. long with a noticeabl long tail, and a rather short bill for a wader. I plumage is buffish-brown with black markings and barred area under the wing, which shows up as th bird lands. It has occurred about two dozen times i Britain. The **LONG-BILLED DOWITCHER** (*Lir nodromus scolopaceus*), about the size and shape of redshank, has been definitely identified twenty-thre times usually in juvenile plumage, when it is buffisl grey above with whitish underparts, and a whit patch on its back and dark tail which shows up i flight. It has a prominent pale eye-stripe and a lon snipe-like bill. Its call is a long *keek*. Th **SHORT-BILLED DOWITCHER** (*Limnodrom griseus*) is very much alike but a little smaller an shorter-billed, and more buff when juvenile. The ca *kut kut kut*, is the best way of identifying it. There a about a dozen definite records, and more than fift which might refer to either species.

1a KNOT, winter
1b KNOT, summer
2b REEVE   2c RUFF autumn

2d RUFF, in flight
2a RUFFS, spring
3 PECTORAL SANDPIPER

1 DUNLIN (*Calidris alpina*). This is the commonest small shore-bird, stout-bodied, and about 7 ins. long. Its winter (1a), summer (1b), and juvenile plumages (1c) may be seen in the same flock. The bill, usually with a slight curve near the end, varies in length. A white wing-bar and white edges to the dark tail-area show in flight.

There are always dunlins to be seen, though the summer population, in fact, largely emigrates and is replaced in winter by birds from further north. They breed on moorland and coastal marshes from Dartmoor northward, and occur on passage inland round fresh water and on the sandy and muddy coasts where they winter.

Appearing singly or in large flocks the dunlin is the typical small wader. It is rather deliberate in its movements and is often remarkably tame. It feeds by tapping or probing the mud for small molluscs and other creatures, often accompanied by ringed plovers and other species. When disturbed, its trilling *schritt* call can be heard against wind and waves. This becomes a reeling song on the breeding grounds, where it nests in groups from sea level to 4,000 ft. The parents share the incubation of the four eggs, well hidden in a simple nest under a tuft and varying in colour but distinguished by reddish markings which have a pronounced twist. The young hatch in about 3 weeks and fly in another 3 weeks, after which families gather on the coast.

*1 2 3 **4 5 6** 7 8 9 10 11 12*

2 SANDERLING (*Crocethia alba*). .The very white winter plumage (2a) can be confused with that of a phalarope (p. 79), but as well as different habits, its body (about 8 ins. long) is stouter, and it has a dark shoulder-patch. In summer sanderlings become russet brown above (2b) but have much shorter bills than dunlins and no belly-patches; in flight they show a similar tail pattern but no white wing-bars. Juveniles have black flecks on their grey upperparts. They are passage migrants and winter visitors, preferring sandy shores and estuaries but also found inland by lake margins. They have quicker movements than dunlins, particularly their rapid run along the tide's edge, and they peck as they go, often darting into the surge to snatch up some small creature. Small parties are much tamer than large flocks, which fly up with a chorus of musical *wick wick* calls.

1 2 3 4 5 (6) 7 8 9 10 11 12

3 LITTLE STINT (*Calidris minuta*). Under 6 ins. long, this is the smallest of the commoner waders and looks like a little, straight-billed dunlin with a white breast. Its upperparts are browner in summer, greyer in winter, and mottled in the juvenile, which also shows a light, backward-pointing V on its back and has a light stripe over its eye. Little stints are passage migrants, varying in numbers, but most common in autumn and along the east and south coasts, on muddy and sandy shores; they come inland to the margins of freshwater lakes. They are often seen with dunlins and appear very active by comparison in their search for food. A feeding party may twitter pleasantly, and the flight call is a repeated *chit*.

(1 2) . (4 5) . (7) 8 9 10 (11 12)

4 TEMMINCK'S STINT (*Calidris temminckii*). A rarer wader, slightly smaller than the little stint, much more uniformly grey above, and with a greyish breast and greenish-black legs. Temminck's stint has attempted to breed in the Scottish Highlands and Yorkshire, but normally it is seen on passage in spring and autumn, generally in the south and east on freshwater marshes with good cover. Its habits resemble those of the dunlin, but it skulks more and flies up 'towering' like a snipe. It has a continuous tittering call, not a repeated note like the little stint's. The male makes song-flights over his territory before breeding. The nests in Britain were near shallow waters.

. . . (4) 5 6 7 8 9 10 (11 12)

5 CURLEW SANDPIPER (*Calidris testacea*). About the same size as a dunlin but rather slimmer looking, the curlew sandpiper has a curved bill and an unmistakable 'red' summer plumage (5b). In autumn or winter (5a) it can be distinguished from dunlins by its white rump. Curlew sandpipers are passage migrants, commoner in autumn and on the south and east coasts, where they frequent muddy and sandy shores and sometimes visit freshwater marshes. Their habits, as seen in Britain, resemble those of dunlins, but they do not form large flocks, and their call is less grating and penetrating.

SMALL AMERICAN SANDPIPERS. Five species have been recorded in Britain, though some of them only very rarely. The WHITE-RUMPED SANDPIPER (*Calidris fuscicollis*) occurs annually, usually in autumn in the south west. It can be told from a dunlin by its straight bill, a white bar above the black tip of the tail, and no black patch on its belly. The tiny LEAST SANDPIPER (*Calidris minutilla*) looks like a brown Temminck's stint but with pale legs and a fainter wing-bar. Since 1853 it has occurred at least sixteen times. BAIRD'S SANDPIPER (*Calidris bairdii*) has been recorded over thirty-five times. It is a difficult bird to identify, but its buff tints are cleaner than those on a juvenile dunlin, and it has longer wings with almost no wing-bar, and a rather long and slender bill. The SEMI-PALMATED SANDPIPER (*Calidris pusilla*), the commonest small shore-bird of eastern North America, resembles the little stint, but with a heavier, tapering bill and partial collar formed by the white on its throat. There are now eighteen records, all since 1953. The WESTERN SANDPIPER (*Calidris maura*), only recorded once from Fair Isle and twice from Ireland, has a longer, straighter bill than the two previous species, but in winter can hardly be told from the semi-palmated sandpiper.

5a CURLEW SANDPIPER, autumn
4 TEMMINCK'S STINT, autumn
3 LITTLE STINT, autumn

2a SANDERLING, winter   2b summer
1a DUNLIN, winter   1b summer   1c Juv.
5b CURLEW SANDPIPER, summer

1   PURPLE SANDPIPER (*Calidris maritima*). A stout little wader, about 8 ins. long, and distinguished from others of its size by its dark colouring at all seasons and its yellow legs. In winter (1b) its back is grey-brown with a slight purple gloss, and its face, neck, and breast are grey; in summer (1a) its upperparts look richer and more variegated. A white bar shows on the inner flight feathers. It is a winter visitor and passage migrant to rocky coasts, very seldom recorded inland. Some birds stay the summer in the north, and breeding has often been suspected. It nests as near as the Faeroe Islands.

Purple sandpipers, often found with turnstones, search sea-weed-covered rocks just above the water for small animals, which include fish and their eggs. Their plumage makes them hard to see, and they may allow an observer to approach them closely before flying off with a flash of white bellies and wing-bars, occasionally calling a quiet *wit wit*, which becomes a twitter from a flock. They are fond of the extreme end of a headland and may also haunt piers and breakwaters.

1 2 3 4 (5 6 7) 8 9 10 11 12

2   TURNSTONE (*Arenaria interpres*). A medium-sized wader, about 9 ins. long, with a short pointed bill and variegated plumage. In summer (2a) its upperparts are tortoiseshell patterned, its head whitish with black markings stretching up from the breast, and white underparts; the legs are bright yellow. The winter (2b) and juvenile plumages are much duller, but at all times turnstones look black and white in flight, due to the white wing-bar, white rump patch, and white tail with a black band at the end. They are mainly winter visitors, but there are some passage migrants, which occasionally appear inland. Some turnstones are to be seen throughout the year, and they are suspected to have bred several times in the north of Scotland or Shetland, but it has never been proved.

Larger than purple sandpipers, dumpier than redshanks (p. 71), and much smaller than oyster-catchers (p. 61), turnstones are one of the four common waders on rocky shores, sometimes in parties of several dozen, sometimes solitary. They run quickly, searching with their bills in crevices and under stones for invertebrate animals, and sometimes turning stones, as their name suggests. The usual call, uttered as they take flight, is a trilling *kitty-kitty-kitty*; they fly low and soon settle again.

1 2 3 4 5 6 7 8 9 10 11 12

3   GREY PHALAROPE (*Phalaropus fulicarius*). The phalaropes are a distinct group of waders, with lobed feet like those of coots (p. 59), and largely white winter plumages (3b). This species has a short straight bill and a rather uniform grey back and is about 8 ins. long. Its dark wings have white bars and markings, and the tail and rump have white edges. The summer plumage (3a) is unmistakable but seldom seen in Britain.

Grey phalaropes are passage migrants, far more common in autumn than spring, mainly to southern and eastern England, where they are usually found on or near the coast, but sometimes far out at sea and on shallow pools and lakes inland. Phalaropes are the only British waders which habitually swim; they have a remarkable twirling movement which stirs up the tiny animals on which they feed. They float well up on the water and fly swiftly but often erratically, calling a quiet *twit*.

(1 2 3 4 5 6) 7 8 9 10 11 12

4   RED-NECKED PHALAROPE (*Phalaropus lobatus*). This species resembles the grey phalarope closely but is smaller, only 6½ ins. long, and best distinguished in winter (4b) by the longer, very thin bill and the darker wings and markings on the back. In summer (4a) the two are quite unlike.

The red-necked phalarope is a rare summer visitor breeding in a few Northern and Hebridean Islands and in one mainland Irish locality. Elsewhere it is a passage migrant, less often seen than the grey phalarope, and mainly at sea or offshore in south and east England, though it occasionally appears inland in summer. The breeding habitat is bogland near shallow pools.

Its general habits resemble those of the grey phalarope, with a similar call-note. In breeding, the female occupies the territory and displays to the male as the dotterel does (p. 62). She helps build the nest but after laying the four small, pear-shaped, olive-brown eggs with dark markings, she leaves the male to incubate. The young hatch in just under 3 weeks, and the male usually looks after them until they fly about 2½ weeks.

*. . . . 5 **6** **7** 8 9 10 . .*

WILSON'S PHALAROPE (*Phalaropus tricolor*). This North American phalarope, the only other member of the family, was first recorded in Britain 1954 but has now occurred thirty-seven times in spring and autumn, and in widely separated places. It is about 9 ins. long, without a wing-bar but with a white rump; in winter it is more uniformly grey than its relatives. It spends more time on land, but has many of the typical phalarope characteristics.

4b RED-NECKED PHALAROPE, winter 4a summer
3b GREY PHALAROPE, winter 3a summer   2a TURNSTONE, summer 2b winter
1a PURPLE SANDPIPER, summer 1b winter

AVOCET, STILT, AND PRATINCOLES

1 AVOCET (*Recurvirostra avosetta*). An unmistakable large wader, about 14 ins. long, with its delicately up-turned bill making another 3 ins. The sexes are alike, and immature birds are browner. In flight a black bar shows on the white inner wing, and the whole tip is also black.

Avocets were lost to Britain, but they have now returned and are very carefully protected. They breed regularly in colonies on Havergate Island and Minsmere in Suffolk and occasionally elsewhere. They are also scarce passage migrants, and rare winter visitors to south-west England, Kent, and Co. Cork.

They are real waders, getting their food by walking through shallow water and skimming tiny animals from the surface by a side to side movement of their heads and fine bills; they also dip their heads or swim and up-end like dabbling ducks. They fly gracefully with necks rather bent and legs projecting beyond the tail, and often hold their wings open above their backs when landing. The typical call is *kloo-it*, repeated rapidly when the birds are alarmed. Display before mating takes place on the ground and consists of preening, bowing, and splashing in the water. Several scrapes are made and one, usually on a low hummock near the water, is selected for the nest. The four eggs are very like those of the lapwing. Both sexes share the incubation for about 3½ weeks, and have often been photographed changing over at the nest. Both attend the young, which fly at about 6 weeks, after which the birds gradually leave the area of the colony.

(*1 2*) **3 4 5 6** *7 8 9* (*10 11 12*)

2 BLACK-WINGED STILT (*Himantopus himantopus*). This unusual-looking bird is about 15 ins. long (of which 2½ ins. is bill), and has enormously long legs which project up to 7 ins. beyond the tail in flight. The amount of brown on the head varies with age, season, and sex. A few occur every year, usually during spring passage, but in 1945 two pairs bred near Nottingham, far to the north of their southern European breeding area. Their habitat at all times is the neighbourhood of shallow fresh or brackish water. Stilts can wade deeply, searching for small animals which they pick off the surface; on land they walk well, and in flight use their long legs in steering. The call, seldom heard in Britain, is *kik kik kik*. The nest may be quite substantial or an almost bare scrape in the open, and the four eggs are like large ringed plover's eggs.

3 PRATINCOLE (*Glareola pratincola*). Pratincoles have the characteristics of terns and plovers; this species is about 10 ins. long, of which the forked tail streamers account for 2½ ins. Most pratincoles occurring in Britain are chestnut under the wing, but the black-winged race, regarded by some authorities as a separate species, has also been recorded.

Pratincoles are most likely to be seen in Britain over open dune or marsh country near the sea; of about fifty recorded, most have been in the southern half of England, and in spring on passage. They breed in southern and eastern Europe.

In flight they are like large swallows, hawking their insect food on the wing; they also run well on the ground, like a plover. The call, a repeated *kikki kirrick*, is not likely to be heard in Britain.

3 (In flight) PRATINCOLES, black-winged form on right
2a BLACK-WINGED STILT, M.   2 b F.
3a PRATINCOLE, M.   3b F.   1a AVOCET, M.   1b F.

STONE CURLEW, BUSTARDS, COURSER

1 STONE CURLEW (*Burhinus oedicnemus*). Mainly desert birds, the stone curlews resemble bustards in their sandy plumage, but are quite distinctive at close range, when their large yellow eyes can be seen. The round head, short bill, and long legs suggest a plover, hence this species' local name of Norfolk plover; but it is larger than any British plover, being 16 ins. long. The prominent joint on the leg earns it another name: 'thick-knee.' In flight the black and white wing pattern distinguishes it from the true curlew, The sexes are alike, though some birds are darker than others, so the members of a pair can often be told apart. Juveniles resemble the adults.

Stone curlews are local summer visitors to England south and east of the line between the Wash and the Bristol Channel, though once they bred as far north as Yorkshire. Their habitat is bare open ground, such as chalk downs, flinty breckland in East Anglia, and shingle beaches in Kent and Sussex; they have now adapted themselves to nesting in arable farmland near their old haunts.

When disturbed stone curlews usually run away, crouching low, and finally take wing, often flying round behind the intruder to settle again. As the big eye suggests, they are active at dusk and in the night, when their wild, curlew-like calls may be heard some way from their usual habitats. They fly with rather slow wing-beats, extending their legs beyond the tail. They do not perch off the ground, and often rest on their shanks, looking as though they were sitting on a nest. They feed mainly on molluscs, insects, and worms, and sometimes catch and eat mice and voles. Both sexes display to each other, tilting their bodies till the bill touches the ground, and there are various actions when one relieves the other at the nest, which is a large scrape in the bare ground. Two rather round eggs, brown with darker spots and streaks, are incubated for nearly 4 weeks. Both parents also look after the young, which are beautifully camouflaged and lie flat on the ground to escape detection. They fledge in about 6 weeks, and parties build up before the autumn migration.

(1 2) <u>3 **4 5** 6</u> *7 8 9 10 (11)*

GREAT BUSTARD (*Otis tarda*). The magnificent male is about 40 ins. long, with light-brown upperparts barred with black, a grey head and neck with white feathers trailing below the bill, and pale underparts. The female is about 30 ins. long, less brightly coloured and without the 'moustache'. In flight the white wings with their black primary flight feathers change the whole appearance of the birds.

Once found on Salisbury Plain, the East Anglian breckland, and other open areas of England, resident great bustards were exterminated by 1850, and they are now very rare visitors indeed; they are also decreasing in Spain and in their central European haunts. A female was found dead in Norfolk in March 1963; two were seen in Kent, and one captured on Fair Isle in January 1970. An attempt is being made to reintroduce the bird in Wiltshire.

2 LITTLE BUSTARD (*Otis tetrax*). A rare visitor, about 17 ins. long, which looks rather like a long-legged partridge, but in flight is almost duck-like because of its extended neck. On the ground it appears to be a light brown bird, but in flight the white feathers of the wing are most conspicuous and distinctive. The amount of adornment on the male's head and neck varies, and in winter he resembles the duller female, as does the juvenile.

Little bustards are only occasionally recorded in Britain, usually in the eastern and southern counties of England, from October to January. Most of the birds definitely identified are of the eastern race, not, as might be expected, of the western race which breeds as near as central France. Their habitat is corn and other crop fields, and birds visiting England have been found feeding on turnip tops and other plants.

HOUBARA BUSTARD (*Chlamydotis undulata*). A very rare visitor from south-eastern Europe and Asia, recorded five times in the last 100 years, the most recent being a bird in Suffolk in 1963. It is about 2 ft. long and distinguished by long black and white feathers on the neck and a darkish wing pattern.

3 CREAM-COLOURED COURSER (*Cursorius cursor*). A sandy-coloured plover-like bird, related to the praticoles (p. 81), with a rather long curved and pointed bill, and a conspicuous amount of black on the wing; there are also black and white marks on the tail, and the male in summer has black and white stripes behind the eye. It is about 9 ins. long but looks bigger in flight. About thirty have been recorded in Britain, mainly in the south and east in autumn; they are most likely to be seen in open country near the coast.

3a CREAM-COLOURED COURSER. Ad. 3b Juv.
2a LITTLE BUSTARD, M., summer   2b F., in flight
1a STONE CURLEW, Ad.   1b Juv. (in hiding)

SKUAS

1 **ARCTIC SKUA** (*Stercorarius parasiticus*). The commonest species of skua in Britain is about 1½ ft. long, 3 ins. of which is the projection of the long central tail-feathers beyond the rest. The arctic skua is an outstanding example of 'dimorphism', that is, it shows distinct light and dark plumage phases, with many variations in between. The long central tail-feathers separate it from the pomarine skua, but are shorter than those of the smaller long-tailed skua. Young birds (1b) of all three species are almost impossible to tell apart; they do not get their full plumage until their third year.

The arctic skua is a summer visitor to the Northern Isles, Hebrides, and extreme north Scotland, nesting on boggy moorland, sometimes several miles from the sea. It occurs round all coasts on passage and may be numerous along the east coast.

Away from their breeding grounds, skuas are often seen pursuing another bird which has food in its bill. They follow its every move in a determined hawk-like manner until the victim drops the food it was carrying, whereupon the pirate swoops down to catch it in the air. Sometimes two skuas combine in the chase, one of the rare examples of co-operative feeding by birds. Arctic skuas spend much time on the sea, swimming buoyantly with tails raised; then they will suddenly rise to chase a tern or gull. Parties also sit on the shore and rise to 'buzz' human intruders; on their breeding grounds they are much fiercer, and some will strike with their feet at the end of their dive. Other birds throw themselves about on the ground when the nest is threatened. They have a display flight and dances as well. The breeding colony may be scattered over the moor, but the loud calling of the birds, which sound rather like kittiwakes (p. 90), reveals its presence. Other indications are the green hummocks on which the birds habitually sit in their territories. The two eggs are brown with darker markings, and both parents sit on them in an open nest-scrape for 3½ to 4 weeks. They feed the downy chicks, who soon move away and can fly after 3 weeks. As well as preying on other birds, arctic skuas eat fish, molluscs, crustaceans, insects, small mammals, birds and their eggs, carrion, and even plant leaves and berries.

$$. . . 4 \ \mathbf{5} \ \mathbf{6} \ \mathbf{7} \ \mathbf{8} \ \mathbf{9} \ 10 \ . \ .$$

2 **POMARINE SKUA** (*Stercorarius pomarinus*). About 1½ ft. long, with its blunt, curiously twisted central tail-feathers projecting another 2 ins. The pomarine is a stouter-looking bird than the arctic skua, but the difference between their tails is the best distinction.

The pomarine also has two plumage phases. It is a passage migrant, most regular down the east and along the south coasts in autumn, although odd birds have occurred in many parts and are blown inland after storms. A few stay all winter offshore, but spring visitors are rare. Its habits in Britain and also its food closely resemble those of the arctic skua. Its voice is unlikely to be heard on passage.

$$(1 \ 2 \ 3 \ 4 \ 5 \ 6) \ 7 \ 8 \ 9 \ 10 \ (11 \ 12)$$

3 **GREAT SKUA** (*Stercorarius skua*). Nearly 2 ft. long, this is a heavy-looking dark-brown bird at all seasons and ages, much bigger than other skuas and with a white patch at the base of the primary flight feathers. It is darker than any immature gull, and has a shorter bill and tail.

Great skuas breed as summer visitors on moorland in Shetland, Orkney, the Outer Hebrides, and very locally on the mainland. On passage they are seen off the east and outer west coasts, but are very rare inland.

They are very fierce and will attack anything from a tern to a gannet, but sometimes they fish for themselves or pick objects off the water. Skuas of the antarctic race are scavengers at penguin rookeries. Between attacks they spend much of their time on the wing, but may swim, or perch on the shore. They are usually silent, except during their display. when they call *hah hah hah* while raising their wings; and when attacking intruders at the nest they dive fearlessly, uttering a deep-toned double note. The nests, just hollows in the ground, are scattered over the moor; the two eggs are grey-brown with dark spots or blotches, and both parents sit on them for about 4 weeks; the female then broods the chicks, and the male feeds them. They fly in 6 weeks or so.

$$. . . 4 \ \mathbf{5} \ \mathbf{6} \ \mathbf{7} \ \mathbf{8} \ \mathbf{9} \ 10 \ . \ .$$

4 **LONG-TAILED SKUA** (*Stercorarius longicauda*). Smaller than an arctic skua, it is about 15 ins. long, but its central tail feathers may project 5 to 8 ins. beyond the rest. Birds with shorter streamers may be mistaken for arctic skuas, but their backs are greyer, their caps darker and more distinct, and they have no brown patch across the breast between the wings. Their legs are grey although their feet are black. Young birds tend to be greyer than young arctics and to show less white. This is the least common skua, occurring usually on autumn passage along the east coast, sometimes in numbers; it is rare in spring or summer. Its habits resemble those of the arctic skua, but it does more direct feeding and less piracy.

1a ARCTIC SKUA, Ad. dark phase
1b ARCTIC SKUA, 1st autumn
1c ARCTIC SKUA, Ad. light phase (chasing tern)

2 POMARINE SKUA, Ad. light phase
3 GREAT SKUA, Ad.
4 LONG-TAILED SKUA, Ad.

1 GREAT BLACK-BACKED GULL (*Larus marinus*). Up to 27 ins. in length, this is easily the largest of the commoner gulls. It is the only gull, except the Scandinavian race of the lesser black-back (2b), to have a very dark mantle, and its pale pink or greyish legs, when they can be seen, are also distinctive. Young and immature birds (1b) can be told from herring gulls and lesser black-backs by their whiter heads and underparts, the mantle becoming darker each year.

The great black-back nests at various points right up the west side of Britain and round the coasts of Ireland, but on the east side only as far south as Moray and Nairnshire, and in the south as far east as the Isle of Wight. Rocky islands and headlands are its main breeding habitat, but it sometimes joins other gulls on bogs inland in the north. In winter it is found more widely, often far inland and even right into the London area. There are probably many visitors from the north.

Great black-backs are quite a familiar sight among flocks of gulls, when they stand out by their size, or in parties on their own on sandbanks, beaches, refuse tips, and docks. On the wing their beat is slower than the lesser black-back's, and their deep *aw aw* can be picked out among the cries of other gulls. They usually win a tussle for offal with their relatives and are also merciless killers in seabird colonies, leaving the skins of their victims inside out. They will eat anything, varying in size from new-born seals to insects, and groups can be seen either hawking flying ants in the air or waiting hopefully for carrion at the breeding stations of grey seals. They like high perches on rocks and walk slowly with almost a waddle. There is, as with most gulls, a complicated series of displays between the males and also between members of a pair, which often occupy a territory without nesting. An isolated pair may nest on the top of a rocky pinnacle, but colonies may spread out over lower ground. The nest is a large saucer of dry grass and feathers. The usual clutch of three rather greasy-looking light olive-brown eggs with dark spots is incubated by both parents for nearly 4 weeks, and they look after the downy young for about 7 weeks. Long after they are fledged, the juveniles go on begging for food.

1 2 3 **4 5 6** *7 8 9 10 11 12*

2 LESSER BLACK-BACKED GULL (*Larus fuscus*). This species, about 21 ins. long, is closely related to and the same size as a herring gull (p. 89), but it has a darker mantle and yellow legs. Mediterranean herring gulls also have bright yellow legs, and those from eastern Scandinavia have pale yellow legs. The Scandinavian race of the lesser black-back (2b) has a mantle as dark as a greater black-back; but in the British race only the wingtips are really dark. Young birds are very hard to tell from herring gulls, but they become more distinct each year, though they do not achieve full adult plumage until their fourth spring.

The British lesser black-backed gull is resident in small numbers, but is chiefly a summer visitor; the Scandinavian race is a passage migrant, chiefly in the east and south, though some stay the winter. Lesser black-backs breed all up the west side of Britain, round the Irish coasts and down the east side to Yorkshire, and occasionally on the south coast east of Devon, and there are a number of inland colonies in moorland bogs. In winter the residents are concentrated in areas where there are large rubbish tips near towns and ports.

Although they resemble herring gulls in many ways, the lesser black-backs have some distinctive habits: in certain areas they, rather than herring gulls, follow steamers; their nesting preferences may be different; and their call notes are deeper. They take much the same great variety of food. They sometimes nest among herring gulls and even interbreed; but usually they form separate groups in deeper cover — heather, bracken, bluebells — away from the cliffs and often on the tops of islands. The nest and eggs are indistinguishable from those of herring gulls. Both parents sit for nearly 4 weeks, but the female does most of the care of the young, which fly after 5 weeks.

1 2 3 4 **5 6** *7 8 9 10 11 12*

1b GREAT BLACK-BACKED GULL. 1st year
1a GREAT BLACK-BACKED GULL. Ad.
2c LESSER BLACK-BACKED GULL. 1st year

2b LESSER BLACK-BACKED GULL.
    Ad., winter, Scandinavian race
2a LESSER BLACK-BACKED GULL. Ad.

1 HERRING GULL (*Larus argentatus*). The best-known gull over the country as a whole, about 22 ins. long, the herring gull is much larger than the common gull (p. 91) and also has a more powerful yellow bill marked with a red spot, pinkish legs, and a different pattern of black and white 'mirrors' at the wing-tips. In winter (1d) the adult has light-brown flecks on the head and neck, and the immature birds, at first darker, gradually get lighter for 3 years (1b, 1c) and are difficult to tell from lesser black-backed gulls (p. 87).

Herring gulls are resident right round the coasts of Britain, though they do not normally breed where there are no cliffs. Abroad they nest in sand dunes, as they now do in Anglesey and elsewhere. Recently they have begun to build on the roofs of houses in coastal towns, and for some years they have bred with lesser black-backs on factories in South Wales; a few pairs breed in central London. In winter they flock to ports and towns, but some remain even on the wildest shores.

Herring gulls often float in the air behind a steamer, taking advantage of every eddy of wind; then, with a few powerful beats, they catch up to land on a mast or flagstaff. Like their relatives, they also soar and circle for long periods on fine days, but at other times they beat purposefully low over the water to gather food. The variety of their diet is enormous, and consequently they profit in winter from the profusion of edible rubbish now put out by man near large towns. The herring gull's laughing call is one of the best known of all bird cries, but it has many others, most of them used in its displays. These are of great interest in the study of bird behaviour because the plumage of the sexes is alike, and the birds can be watched comparatively easily in their large colonies. Intensive observation has shown that it takes a long time for the members of a pair to overcome suspicion of each other. This is achieved gradually by a series of calls and movements, mainly of the head and neck. Herring gulls also fight to establish their breeding territories and the pairs in a big colony may be widely spaced, each defending its own area. The saucer nest of grass, feathers, and seaweed is usually quite exposed, and the clutch of two or three olive-brown or green, brown-marked eggs is incubated by both parents, the female taking the larger share, for up to 4 weeks. The male does most of the feeding of the young chicks, which fly when about 6 weeks old but continue begging for food long afterwards.

1   2   3 **4 5 6** *7 8 9 10 11 12*

2 ICELAND GULL (*Larus glaucoides*). Although on average the same size as a herring gull, some individuals are as big as small glaucous gulls, but the distinction between them is described under 'glaucous gull'. When at rest, the longer wingtips of the Iceland gull extend beyond the tail and are often crossed.

This gull is a scarcer winter visitor than the glaucous gull and, in spite of its name, only known to breed in Greenland. It occurs mainly in the extreme north of Britain, though odd birds may be found all round the coast and may stay for long periods. Its long wings give the Iceland gull a more graceful appearance on the wing than most large gulls. Its habits in Britain resemble those of its relatives.

1   2   3   (4   5   6   7   8   9)   10   11   12

3 GLAUCOUS GULL (*Larus hyperboreus*). As big as a great black-backed gull, the glaucous gull has a pale mantle and white wingtips; in plumage it is much like an Iceland gull, but larger, with a longer and more powerful bill, relatively shorter wings, which barely reach the tip of the tail when it is at rest, and a yellow ring round its eye, which is red in the Iceland gull. In winter it has light-brown flecks on the head. Young and immature birds of both species (2a, 3b) are very hard to separate; they are both much paler than other large gulls at all stages. The length of wing is probably the best distinguishing feature. Not only are these two big gulls very hard to tell apart, but the situation is made confused by the occurrence of albino or semi-albino herring gulls, and this possibility must be taken into account when a large gull with white wing tips is seen.

Glaucous gulls are winter visitors from the sub-arctic, mainly to the Northern Isles and north Scotland, but immature birds are found at times all round the coast, often associating with native gulls; they are very rare inland. Their habits in Britain are like those of the great black-backed gull, though they are less active and are even fonder of carrion. Single birds or parties may occur, and occasionally large numbers appear in Shetland.

1   2   3   4   (5   6   7   8)   9   10   11   12

1c HERRING GULL. 2nd winter   1d Ad., winter 1a Ad., summer, and chick
1b HERRING GULL. 1st winter   2a ICELAND GULL. 2nd winter 2b Ad., winter
3a GLAUCOUS GULL. Ad., winter 3b 2nd winter

1 **COMMON GULL** (*Larus canus*). Rather like a small herring gull, this gull is about 16 ins. long, and has different coloured legs, bill, and eyes, and a different pattern of the wing-tip 'mirror' of black and white (1c). It differs from the kittiwake also in the colour of its legs and the 'mirror'. Juveniles (1b) resemble those of herring and lesser black-backed gulls, but have paler tails with a dark band across them (1d); later they moult into adult plumage (1a), except for the tail and brownish wings. Second-year birds look like adults, but have more black on their wing-coverts.

A 'common' gull in the south in the winter only, this species breeds from south-west Scotland northwards, and in Ireland; a few nest in Kent and Anglesey. Islands in freshwater or sheltered sea-lochs and the surrounding moorland are favoured; not sea cliffs or exposed coasts. In winter common gulls are widely distributed over farmland and on parks and playing fields near towns, roosting on reservoirs or estuaries; flocks include visitors from the north.

They are often seen with black-headed and other gulls, but in some areas they may be the only gull in winter, following the plough or searching for worms and grubs in grassland. Others are found on the coast, eating small animals, carrion, and refuse. Towards evening they fly off, sometimes in formation, to their roost. They are rather silent in winter, but have a call similar to but higher-pitched than that of the herring gull (p. 88). In early spring they begin to move northward, pausing by day in the fields; they begin to display at their colonies by the end of March. Their actions, though having a general resemblance to the displays of the herring gull, differ in many details. The nest, also, is like a herring gull's but smaller, and so are the two or three brown or green eggs with dark markings. Both parents sit, for about $3\frac{1}{2}$ weeks, and then look after the young, which begin to fly at 4 weeks. British common gulls scatter or move into Ireland, and birds from the north pass southwards, often in parties of adults, the juveniles following. Immature birds may spend their first and second summers on the coast.

1 2 3 4 5 6 7 8 9 10 11 12

2 **KITTIWAKE** (*Rissa tridactyla*). A gull with a remarkably clean-looking grey and white plumage, about 16 ins. long. It has dark eyes and legs, with no hind toes, and a pale yellow bill. The long wings are held crossed beyond the tail. The juvenile or immature 'tarrock' (2b) is like an adult but with a black band at the base of the neck behind, and black bands on the wings and tail, which is slightly forked. The black wing-tip distinguishes it from the common gull in flight.

The kittiwake breeds on sea cliffs at many points along the west side of the British Isles and round the north to Yorkshire on the east coast; it has tried to nest on the sand in Norfolk. In winter kittiwakes scatter over the sea, and some birds reach North America; visitors also enter British waters.

A visit to a kittiwake colony will fix the *kittiwa-ak* call in the memory for ever, as it is uttered incessantly by the birds while they bicker on their nest-sites. Intruders keep flying up, and the members of a pair have to greet each other every time one arrives, even when they are feeding young. But away from the nesting cliff they tend to be silent. The nests of seaweed are built on small ledges and brackets, often on an overhanging cliff, or in several places the birds nest on buildings, sometimes using window-ledges. The parents take it in turns to incubate the two or three eggs which are paler than those of other gulls. The young hatch in about 3 weeks and crouch in the precarious nest for at least 4 weeks before they can fly down to the sea below. The parents feed them on a variety of small fish; but kittiwakes will also follow boats to pick up edible rubbish, and they take offal like other gulls. They often gather in the autumn on sandy shores with terns before flying out to fish. Their action is quicker and more graceful than that of the bigger gulls. In stormy weather they may be driven inland and stay for some time if they survive.

1 2 3 4 5 6 7 8 9 10 11 12

ROSS'S GULL (*Rhodostethia rosea*). Just over a foot long, this beautiful gull from the far Arctic has been recorded eight times in Britain; five of these birds were after 1960, when one was found dead in Northumberland on 30 April. The 1960 bird was in spring plumage: white with grey wings and a thin black collar, a black bill, and red legs. It did not show the famous rosy tinge seen in illustrations, but this may have been due to lack of the right food.

3 **IVORY GULL** (*Pagophila eburnea*). This rare visitor from the Arctic has an appropriate plumage, snowy white with black legs and a bill shading from black through yellow to a red tip. Immature birds have some grey on the upperparts, and black spots and a black band on the tail. The length is $1\frac{1}{2}$ ft., about the same as a common gull. About seventy-five have occurred, mostly in Orkney and Shetland in the winter months. Beautiful on the wing, it looks somewhat awkward on the ground, and seldom swims; it feeds on droppings, carrion, and some small water creatures. Visitors to Britain join in the scavenging crowds of gulls at fishing ports.

1a COMMON GULL. Ad., summer   1b 1st winter
1c Ad., winter   1d Juv.   3 IVORY GULL
2a KITTIWAKE, Ad., summer   2b Juv.   2c Ad., winter

1 BLACK-HEADED GULL (*Larus ridibundus*). Although nearly the same length as a common gull (up to 15 ins.) this is a much slenderer bird, with a smaller head and neck and narrower wings. At all seasons it can be distinguished by its red legs and bill, by the dark markings on its head, and by the white front edge to its wings. The chocolate mask of summer (1a) is moulted, and many intermediate stages are seen. Juveniles (1b) have brown upperparts, and immature birds (1c) show some brown and have paler legs and bill than adults.

The breeding colonies of black-headed gulls are concentrated in the west and north of Britain and in Ireland, though there are odd ones in the south and east; they may be by moorland pools, on sand-dunes, coastal marshes and mudflats, or on the old type of sewage farm. Outside the breeding season the black-headed gull is the commonest gull inland almost everywhere except in the south-west; this is the gull seen circling over London in wintertime. Its numbers are increased by visitors from Europe, and British birds may migrate as far as Africa. Non-breeding birds occur on the shore all the year.

Its behaviour resembles in general that of the bigger gulls, but it is more like a tern in its graceful flapping flight. Black-headed gulls spend more time searching for insects in the fields or the air, and they often accompany lapwings and other birds and try to rob them of their food. Their laughing call, which gives them their scientific name *ridibundus*, becomes a fierce cackle when they are defending their nests. They have complicated displays in which the black mask plays an important part. The nest is often a large saucer of water-weeds built on very boggy ground, and the three eggs are more pointed and darker than those of the bigger gulls. Both parents incubate them for about 3½ weeks, and the downy young soon leave the nest and begin to swim about in the pool; they fly after 5 weeks.

*1   2   3   **4   5   6   7**   8   9   10   11   12*

MEDITERRANEAN BLACK-HEADED GULL (*Larus melanocephalus*). This rare visitor from southern Europe has a slightly larger summer black mask than the black-headed gull and no black on its wings; the juvenile has a brown front edge to its wings. In recent years it has become an annual visitor in autumn or spring, especially to the English south coast where a few pairs were found breeding among black-headed gulls in 1968.

SLENDER-BILLED GULL (*Larus genei*). The two British records of this southern gull are of immature birds in Sussex in June 1960 and April 1963. It differs from the black-headed gull in having a longer bill and neck, grey marks on the neck, and a longer-looking tail. The adult has no dark mask in summer. In spite of its name, its bill is relatively stout.

2 LITTLE GULL (*Larus minutus*). Under a foot long, this is the smallest British gull, but it is sometimes hard to tell from immature black-headed gulls. The adults (2c) have a more extensive black cap and are dark under the wings, which have no black tips. The juvenile (2a) has dark markings on the upperparts, a black bar across the wings, and a black bill, which the adult also has in winter (2b).

A passage and winter visitor mainly to the east side of Britain and along the south coast, the little gull sometimes occurs in large parties, but usually only in ones and twos; it is rare in Ireland. The winter habitat is much the same as that of black-headed gulls.

Its rather fluttery flight and its feeding habits are between those of black terns and black-headed gulls. It often hawks over open water after insects, taking them on the wing or off the surface. The call note is lower pitched than the black-headed gull's cackle.

1   2   3   4   5   (6)   7   8   9   10   11   12

GREAT BLACK-HEADED GULL (*Larus ichthyaëtys*). As big as a great black-backed gull, with an orange bill and black hood, this very rare visitor from south Russia and Asia has been recorded seven times between 1859 and 1967. In winter its head becomes white with dark streaks; the juvenile and immature birds are brownish with a black band on the white tail and dark bills and legs.

BONAPARTE'S GULL (*Larus philadelphia*). This North American species, just over a foot long, has a black bill and slate-coloured hood in summer, and is otherwise very like a black-headed gull, except that at all seasons the underside of the primary flight feathers is white instead of greyish. There have been over twenty British records, mostly from the south, and in winter. FRANKLIN'S GULL (*Larus pipixcan*). One record from Hampshire, one from Sussex 1970 (possibly same bird). This gull, from mid and western North America, is smaller than a black-headed gull and has a short black bill and dark red legs; a distinctive white trailing edge to the wings extends as a bar across the primary flight feathers. LAUGHING GULL (*Larus atricilla*). A North American species recorded six times since 1923. About the size of a common gull, it is distinguished by its dark mantle and black wing-tips with a conspicuous white trailing edge to the wings. In winter the adult's head is white with dark markings, but in summer it is black; the legs and rather large bill are deep red, becoming darker in winter.

3 SABINE'S GULL (*Xema sabini*). This is one of the American birds which visits Britain most often. It can be told in all plumages by its slightly forked tail and black, white and grey wing pattern, the grey being brownish in the juvenile. The whole effect in flight is of three narrow triangles, with black at the tip (3a). In summer (3b) the hood is slate-grey, the bill black with a yellow tip, and the legs greyish.

Visitors, mostly juveniles, arrive in autumn in the south-west, and also quite often on the east coast up to Yorkshire, but they are rare in Scotland and Ireland, and in spring and summer. A few stay over winter. Sabine's gull has a tern-like flight and hawks for small flying creatures over water, or picks food off the surface; its call is also harsh and like a tern's.

1a BLACK-HEADED GULL, Ad., summer 1b Juv. 1c 1st winter 1d Ad., winter
2a LITTLE GULL, 1st winter 2b Ad., winter 3a SABINE'S GULL, 1st winter
2c LITTLE GULL, summer 3b SABINE'S GULL, summer

MARSH TERNS

1 BLACK TERN (*Chlidonias niger*). About 9½ ins. long, the adult black tern in breeding plumage (1b) is distinctive, but juvenile and winter plumages are very difficult to separate from other marsh terns. The adult (1a) has a dark patch on the sides of its breast and a fairly definite black cap, while the rump is pale grey, and the bill longer than that of the white-winged black tern; it is also of slimmer build.

A passage migrant, it is often more numerous in spring than autumn, and in the east of England than in the west, though it occurs regularly in Somerset and Cheshire. It is much rarer in Scotland and Ireland where a pair bred in 1967. Others have nested recently in East Anglia on shallow fresh water — their usual habitat; they may be seen offshore on migration.

They look smaller than the commoner sea terns (p. 97); their tails in flight seem almost square, not forked, and their wing-beats are quicker than those of the rare white-winged black tern. They are usually seen beating against the wind and dropping to the surface from time to time to pick up a floating insect or other small animals. Occasionally they tower upwards and then rapidly fly with the wind to begin another series of tacks. At other times they hawk insects in the air like a big swallow. Sometimes large parties pass through in spring, and there will be a movement over the country as a whole, often lasting only a day or two; in the south this very often happens in the second week of May. The black tern's voice is seldom heard in Britain, but the call is a repeated *kik kik kik*.

. . . (4) 5 6 7 8 9 10 (11)

2 WHITE-WINGED BLACK TERN (*Chlidonias leucopterus*). The adult is easily told from the black tern in summer by its whitish wings and tail and red bill and legs. It is a little smaller. Juveniles (2c) and birds in winter plumage do not show dark patches on the sides of the breast, and the dark mantle looks like a saddle bounded by the white collar and rump. The dark cap is flecked with white. At all seasons this species looks stouter in build than a black tern, and its bill is shorter.

It is a rare passage migrant, usually occurring at the same time as the black tern and, like it, commoner in spring, though this may partly be due to the difficulty of identifying it in autumn. It is found in the same sort of places, and its habits on migration are similar; but it has a less vigorous wing-beat.

3 WHISKERED TERN (*Chlidonias hybrida*). The rarest and largest (11 ins. long) of the marsh or freshwater terns, this species in spring looks more like a very dark-breasted sea tern with white sides to its face and neck. But the tail is less forked than those of sea terns, and the legs and bill a darker red. Juveniles and adults in autumn and winter are generally pale grey above, though the juvenile has a dark mantle and inner wing. They have more forked tails than other marsh terns, and can most easily be confused with a plumage phase of the arctic tern (p. 97) called '*Sterna portlandica*'. The whiskered tern comes from southern Europe and has occurred over forty times, mainly in south and east England, usually in spring and autumn; it behaves much like a black tern but flies more like a sea tern.

SOOTY TERN (*Sterna fuscata*). This rare visitor from the tropics, about 15 ins. long, has occurred in Britain about twenty times, in spring, summer and autumn. Its underparts, cheeks, and forehead are white; its upperparts and eye stripes are sooty brown; and its legs and bill are dark. The juvenile is a lighter sooty brown all over except under the tail but has numerous whitish flecks on its back and wings. Sooty terns feed on small fish and, outside the breeding season, spend most of their lives on the wing, often far out at sea.

BRIDLED TERN (*Sterna anaethetus*). A very rare visitor whose nearest breeding area is the Red Sea. All the four birds which have been recorded between 1931 and 1958 were found dead. It looks rather like a sooty tern but is about an inch shorter, has a more definite black cap, and the upperparts are a lighter brown, both in the adult and juvenile. Its habits resemble those of the sooty tern, but it can swim, although it does not often do so.

2c WHITE-WINGED BLACK TERN, 1st autumn
2b WHITE-WINGED BLACK TERN, Ad., autumn
2a WHITE-WINGED BLACK TERN, spring

1a BLACK TERN, autumn
1b BLACK TERN, spring
3 WHISKERED TERN, spring

1 ARCTIC TERN (*Sterna paradisea*). This species and the common tern are remarkably alike. The arctic tern has rather longer tail 'streamers' — as the long outer feathers are called — and may be up to 15 ins. in total length; but it can be told apart from the common tern with certainty in spring only by its blood-red bill with no black tip; its legs are shorter, but this character is only of use for identification when the two species perch near each other. Juvenile and winter plumages cannot usually be distinguished, though in winter the adult arctic tern has a black or blackish bill and legs, features which can be seen only at close range.

As summer visitors arctic terns are usually seen in the more northerly regions of the British Isles. There are colonies on the Farne Islands off the coast of Northumberland, in Anglesey, and in north-west England, and many in Scotland and Ireland, where the birds sometimes nest inland by fresh water. On the coast they breed both on sand and shingle beaches and on rocky islands. They are to be seen inland on migration in spring and autumn, but are much more common along the coast.

The loud *kee-rah* call soon announces the arrival of the graceful, swallow-like terns. It is possible with practice to distinguish the two species by their voices, for the call of the arctic is less drawn-out than that of the common tern. The males fly over the colony carrying small fish crosswise in their bills to attract the females; they chase each other in the air, uttering the *kee-rah* call, and have elaborate displays on the ground, using their heads and necks. Terns fish by flying slowly 20 ft. or more above the water, perhaps hovering with lowered tail, then plunging just under the surface. Their nests, which are shallow scrapes lined with grass, may be close together, scattered, or even isolated. The usual clutch is two or three brown, green, or blue eggs, blotched with dark brown, in shape between a gull's and a typical wader's. Sometimes only a single egg is laid. Both parents take it in turn to sit for about 3 weeks; the downy chicks are brown above, speckled with black, and have white underparts with a black throat. They are fed on sand eels and other small fish, often carried for miles, and swallow them head-first. The parents are more aggressive in defence of the young than other terns, and often strike human intruders. The young fly when about 4 weeks old. Arctic terns carry out the longest migratory flight of any bird; some travel from the arctic circle almost to the antarctic.

Some birds in their first summer show what looks like a winter plumage, and even breed in it; this phase was once thought to be a distinct species and was named *Sterna portlandica*.

. . . *4* **5** *6* **7** *8* *9* *10* (*11 12*)

2 ROSEATE TERN (*Sterna dougallii*). About the same length as the arctic and common terns, this species can be distinguished from them, especially in summer, by its almost black bill, white or pinkish breast, and very long tail streamers. The juvenile is more boldly marked on the back than common or arctic juveniles, and the chick resembles a Sandwich tern chick (p. 99) in its curiously spiky appearance.

Roseate terns are rare summer visitors, with scattered colonies in the Scillies, Farne Islands, North Wales, southern Scotland, and the east coast of Ireland; a few pairs occasionally nest elsewhere in colonies of other terns. They are seldom seen on passage and are very rare inland.

The call and alarm note, a drawn-out *aagh aagh*, can be picked out in a cloud of terns over a mixed colony. The nest site is often hidden in a recess or under a tussock, and the clutch is one or two eggs, scribbled rather than blotched. In other respects the food and general habits of the roseate tern are like those of its relatives, though the display differs in details, and the birds are less aggressive against intruders. They have a faster wing-beat than common terns.

. . . *4* **5** *6* **7** *8* *9* . . .

3 COMMON TERN (*Sterna hirundo*). An adult with long tail streamers measures about 14 ins. and can be distinguished from the arctic tern by its light red bill with a black tip; it also has longer legs, which helps when identifying the chicks. Juveniles and winter plumages are very difficult to distinguish from arctic terns, though the legs and bill of this species in winter are generally more red.

Common terns are summer visitors breeding in colonies all round British coasts, also inland up rivers and by lochs in Scotland and Ireland, and in a few places in England. They nest on beaches, sand-dunes, and low rocky islands, and on river gravel and moorland. They are often seen inland when on migration; some are passage visitors.

The common tern has a long drawn-out *kee-rah* call, and also a loud *kik-kik-kik* which is uttered at all times — during the breeding season, when fishing, and on migration. The birds have many other notes as well. In general their behaviour is similar to that of arctic terns, though their displays differ in details. The nest and eggs cannot be told apart, but the common tern usually lays a clutch of three. The incubation and fledging periods are the same, but in some colonies where both species occur, they tend to feed in different areas, the common terns close to shore, taking some insects as well as small fish, and the arctic terns out to sea. Common terns migrate in autumn as far as South Africa.

. (*2 3*) *4* **5** *6* **7** *8* *9* *10* (*11*) .

1a ARCTIC TERN. Ad., summer
2b ROSEATE TERN. winter
1b ARCTIC TERN. winter

2a ROSEATE TERN. Ad., summer
3a COMMON TERN. Ad., summer
3b COMMON TERN. winter 3c Juv.

1 SANDWICH TERN (*Sterna sandvicensis*). Named after Sandwich in Kent, though it is no longer found there, this largest tern to breed in Britain is 15 to 17 ins. long and can be distinguished from other British nesting terns by its size, the tufted appearance of its crest, and its black legs and black, yellow-tipped bill. It is generally whiter-looking and has a less forked tail than the terns shown on p. 96. In winter its head, like that of the Caspian tern, is flecked with white and it often begins to show this change of plumage while still at the breeding ground. The juveniles have mottled backs and look brown at a distance.

Sandwich terns are summer visitors, breeding in scattered colonies, mainly in eastern England, southern and eastern Scotland, and Ireland, where they sometimes nest by fresh water; elsewhere they breed on coastal beaches and islands. They are seen on migration in many other places, and sometimes inland.

This rather heavy-looking tern is a forceful diver, flying higher, plunging harder, and submerging deeper than its relatives. It dives for sand eels and other small fish, and also picks up marine worms and shellfish. Its loud call note *kirrick* can be heard a long way off over the sea and is often the first sign of the bird's presence. Sandwich terns have many other calls when in their colonies, where they display in the air and on the ground like their relatives. They often droop their wings, as shown in the picture. They make their shallow nest scrapes, which may be lined with a little dry grass, very close together in dense groups, and the whole area becomes 'white-washed' with droppings. The usual clutch of one or two creamy-coloured eggs, covered with spots and scribbles, is incubated for $3\frac{1}{2}$ weeks. The chicks, which have a light, spiky down at first, fly after 5 weeks, and then often form closely-packed herds. British Sandwich terns migrate down the west coast of Africa to winter in South Africa.

. . *3 4 5 6 7 8 9 10 (11 12)*

2 LITTLE TERN (*Sterna albifrons*). This smallest of the sea terns is about 9 ins. long and is distinguished from the others in summer by the white on its forehead and by its black-tipped yellow bill and yellow legs. Juveniles and adults in winter look like small common terns, except that the bill and leg colour remains yellow, though much duller in the juvenile.

Little terns are summer visitors, with colonies all round the British coasts, some of them many miles apart; they are most numerous along the east coast up to the Moray Firth. They nest on beaches of sand, shingle, or mud, and several pairs of ringed plovers (*see* p. 65) are sometimes found breeding among or close to a little tern colony. During migration they may appear inland on lakes and rivers.

Their small size, narrow wings, and quick fluttering flight, punctuated by sudden dives to take a small fish, make little terns conspicuous shore birds in summer. Their flying and ground displays are similar to those of other British terns. They mob a human intruder coming near a colony, uttering a variety of angry *kik kik kik* notes, sharper and higher-pitched than those of the common tern; but as soon as the intruder moves away, they hover over and finally drop straight on to their nests again. These are just small scrapes in the sand or shingle, holding two or three fawn or green eggs with dark spots. Both parents share the incubation of about 3 weeks, and the young, which are covered with sandy down when hatched, fly at about 4 weeks old. Little terns often lose their nests in storms and high tides, and may lay several times in a season before rearing any young; sometimes they fail altogether.

. . . *4 5 6 7 8 9 (10 11)*

3 GULL-BILLED TERN (*Gelochelidon nilotica*). One or two gull-billed terns appear in Britain every year, mainly in spring, and a pair have nested once, on a reservoir in Essex in 1951. There are colonies on the coasts of Germany and Denmark. They look like short-tailed Sandwich terns, but have no crest and black bills with a marked gonys, the ridge where the two halves of the lower jaw meet. They resemble the commoner terns in general habits, except that they hunt a great deal over land, like gulls, catching large insects and animals as big as lizards and mice. They nest both inland and by the sea on shallow lagoons, often with other terns.

4 CASPIAN TERN (*Sterna caspia*). One or two of these big terns (about 20 ins. long) visit Britain almost every year, mostly in summer. One ringed bird came from North America, where many of the European terns are also found; but the nearest breeding colonies of the Caspian tern are on islands in the Baltic. It looks like a huge common tern with a powerful red bill, black legs, and a slightly forked tail. The juvenile has a mottled back and paler bill, and in winter both it and the adult have white-flecked caps; the adult, like some other terns, has a rather less bright red bill during the winter months.

ROYAL TERN (*Sterna maxima*). A dead bird of this American species, which is very similar in appearance to the Caspian tern, was washed up on the coast of Ireland near Dublin in 1954 and one was seen in Kent in 1965. It has less black on the primary flight feathers, a paler bill, and a more forked tail. In autumn and winter it has a pure white forehead.

1b SANDWICH TERN, winter
3a GULL-BILLED TERN   3b winter
1a SANDWICH TERN, summer   1c nest

4   CASPIAN TERN, summer
2a LITTLE TERN, Ad., summer   2b Juv.

AUKS

1 PUFFIN (*Fratercula arctica*). Often called 'comical' in its breeding plumage, the puffin is not possible to mistake for any other British bird. It is about a foot long. Its bill is duller in winter, and juveniles and first-winter birds have quite thin, black bills. Puffins breed mainly round the western and northern coasts and islands of Britain and Ireland. The colonies are placed on headlands or on islands with a rocky scree or earth cap. In winter the birds usually go well out to sea, but may be carried inland by storms.

Most puffins arrive at their colonies already paired after carrying out their group displays at sea; but many 'parties' take place on land, the pairs shaking their bills and nibbling each other's faces. The nest is at the end of a tunnel made by rabbits or shearwaters or excavated by the puffins themselves, or sometimes under a boulder. The single white, faintly speckled egg soon becomes covered with dirt. The female does most or all the incubation of 6 weeks, and the chick, attended by both parents, leaves the nest by itself when it is about 7 weeks old.

1 2 3 4 5 6 7 8 9 10 11 12

2 BLACK GUILLEMOT (*Cepphus grylle*). About 13 ins. long, the black guillemot is unmistakable in summer plumage, but in winter it may be confused either with a grebe (p. 3) or with a common guillemot at long range; but the red legs are always distinctive, and so is the red gape which shows when it opens its mouth.

Black guillemots are resident round northern and Irish coasts, and a few breed in North Wales and in Cumberland. They prefer sheltered sea-lochs and bays, and in winter are found much nearer the shore than others of this family.

Though in general their habits resemble those of other auks, black guillemots are more active on land, and use their legs more when diving. The usual call in the breeding season is a rather feeble whistle. They nest in small groups. Two chalky white eggs with dark markings are laid in a deep crevice or under a boulder on a rocky island or near the foot of a cliff. Both parents incubate them for about 3 weeks, and the chicks remain in the nest hole for another 5 weeks, not leaving it until they are fully fledged.

1 2 3 4 5 6 7 8 9 10 11 12

GREAT AUK (*Alca impennis*). This is the only British bird to become extinct in historic times; the last British one was killed on St. Kilda about 1840, and the last nesting attempt may have been in Orkney about 1812. The great auk was like a huge flightless razorbill; it laid a single egg on an exposed site.

3 RAZORBILL (*Alca torda*). Adult razorbills, which are about 16 ins. long, are easily distinguished from guillemots by their deep bills with a white mark. First-winter birds, which do not have this mark, can be confused with the northern race of guillemot which has dark upperparts.

The razorbill is a resident, breeding in colonies round the coast and dispersing offshore in winter, but it does not nest between Yorkshire and the Isle of Wight. It occurs inland only when storm-driven.

Razorbills take some time to settle into colonies, beginning to land on the cliffs in March after group displays on the sea. On the site of the colony the pairs nibble and peck each other and rattle their bills. Their call is a growling *kaarr*. There is a continual passage to and from the cliffs of birds going out to feed and returning with their catch to the nesting crevice. The single egg is laid without a nest and is incubated by both parents for at least 4 weeks. Both feed the chick for about 2 weeks, and then it takes to the sea, still attended by one parent.

1 2 3 4 5 6 7 8 9 10 11 12

4 GUILLEMOT (*Uria aalge*). Guillemots are about the same size as razorbills. In Britain they are divided into two races, the northern race having upperparts almost as dark as a razorbill, while those of the southern (shown in the picture) are much more chocolate. In winter the adults have more white on the face, and the juveniles look scaly. There is a variety known as the bridled guillemot which has a white ring round the eye and a line extending backwards from it.

Like razorbills, guillemots do not breed between Yorkshire and the Isle of Wight; otherwise they breed on suitable cliffs with ledges all round the British coasts, and birds of the northern race winter in the seas round Britain. Like other sea-birds, they may be driven inland by storms, or birds which have become contaminated with oil may land on the shore.

In general their habits resemble those of razorbills, except that the one large, pointed, very variable egg is laid on an open ledge, and the incubating birds stand upright in rows, almost touching their neighbours, holding their eggs between their feet.

1 2 3 4 5 6 7 8 9 10 11 12

BRÜNNICH'S GUILLEMOT (*Uria lomvia*). This guillemot of the far north has occurred only six times in Britain. It is distinguished from the dark northern race of common guillemot by its shorter, heavier bill, which has a white line along the upper mandible; there is more black on the head in winter.

LITTLE AUK (*Plautus alle*). This smallest of the auks, shown in winter plumage at the top of the picture, is only 8 ins. long. It can be confused with young guillemots or razorbills, though both are bigger by the time they leave the cliffs. It is usually seen in winter plumage when the side of the neck and throat are white; in summer the upperparts are dark all over. The short, stout bill is distinctive at all times.

Little auks breed in the far north, and are most common as winter visitors on northern and eastern coasts, though they may be seen all round the British Isles and are sometimes driven inland in large numbers by storms. Their habits are like those of other auks, but, being so small, they cannot take many fish and feed mainly on the plankton, the tiny floating life of the sea.

1 2 3 (4 5 6 7 8 9) 10 11 12

Winter Plumages: RAZORBILL, PUFFIN, LITTLE AUK, BLACK GUILLEMOT, GUILLEMOT

4 GUILLEMOTS

1 PUFFIN   2 BLACK GUILLEMOT   3 RAZORBILL

PIGEONS AND DOVES. 1

1 WOODPIGEON (*Columba palumbus*). This is the biggest and heaviest pigeon or dove (the names are interchangeable), being about 16 ins. long. It is easily distinguished by its white collar (hence the name 'ring dove') and broad white bars on the wings. Juveniles, which have no collars, may be confused with stock doves until they fly.

Woodpigeons are found everywhere in Britain, from the centre of London to Shetland and the Outer Hebrides; they are probably most numerous in the farming areas of southern and eastern England and eastern Scotland. Some British birds apparently cross the Channel in winter, but there is no evidence of a big immigration which it has been suggested comes from abroad in autumn. The huge flocks seen in winter are mainly of home-bred birds.

They roost in woods and scrub of all kinds, but prefer thick firwoods. They leave cover in the morning and wait in hedgerow trees for the ground to dry before descending into the fields to feed, often in company with stock doves, lapwings, rooks, jackdaws, starlings, and smaller birds. Their appetite is enormous, and they eat seeds and grain, berries and nuts, including acorns and beechmast, and the green stems and leaves of many plants from grasses to brassicas. In consequence, they are the farmer's worst bird pest, and a great deal of research has been done into ways of keeping their numbers down. Hard winters like 1947 and 1963 kill more woodpigeons than any human devices, but in two breeding seasons their numbers are up again. Typical farming countryside, with its tall hedges lined with trees, shelterbelts, and spinneys, is ideal habitat for them, giving protection close to their main sources of food. Woodpigeons also drink greedily, not in a series of sips like most other birds.

In the country woodpigeons are always on the lookout and will take wing with noisy flaps when danger is a long way off. But in London and other cities they are quite tame, and even a country bird will usually sit tight on its nest. The normal flight is fast and regular with occasional glides, but a woodpigeon displaying rises steeply, claps its wings loudly once or twice, then glides downwards, often to repeat the performance. On the ground or in a tree two birds bow their prominent breasts towards each other, raising and spreading their tails. These displays and the famous song, which sounds like *Two coos, Taffy, take* repeated several times, continue for much of the year for there is a very long breeding season. The peak is in late summer when seeds and fruits are most plentiful, and several broods may be reared. The two white eggs are laid in a flimsy nest in a tree or bush, though nests used several times become quite solid. The parents share incubation, which lasts $2\frac{1}{2}$ weeks, and the young fly in about $3\frac{1}{2}$ weeks. Flocks of tens or even hundreds of birds are seen throughout the breeding season, and build up to thousands in winter.

1 **2 3 4 5 6 7 8 9 10 11** *12*

2 STOCK DOVE (*Columba oenas*). Smaller (13 ins. long), darker, and bluer than the woodpigeon, the stock dove is more likely to be confused with the rock dove, and in some districts it is called the 'blue rock'. But it is grey under the wing and lacks the broad black wing-bars and white rump of the rock dove. The juvenile is like the adult but duller.

Stock doves are less numerous and widely distributed than woodpigeons and are not found in most highland areas and islands, though they do inhabit sea cliffs and sand-dunes where there are no woodpigeons. They are resident and move about very little, but form flocks of several hundred birds in winter.

The coo, a coughing *oo-hoo*, is quite distinct from the song of the woodpigeon, and the flight is faster, more like that of a rock dove or racing pigeon. The display flight and bowing performance are similar, and are often combined with curious fights in which the birds slap each other with their wings. Like woodpigeons, stock doves have a long breeding season; they nest in holes of trees, buildings and cliffs, down rabbit burrows, and in nestboxes, several pairs often nesting close together. The clutch of two white eggs and incubation and fledging periods are similar to those of the woodpigeon.

1 **2 3 4 5 6 7 8 9 10** *11* *12*

3 ROCK DOVE (*Columba livia*). This ancestor of the domestic pigeons is the same size as the stock dove. In its pure form it has a white rump, rather pale blue upperparts, and two black bars on the wing, the underside of which is white. Juveniles are duller. But almost everywhere, except in the Scottish islands and in Ireland, the wild population is mixed with escaped domestic pigeons, and all sorts of colours occur.

Only along the western coasts of Scotland and of Ireland and in the Hebrides are pure strains of rock doves now to be found. They are resident and seldom go far inland; 'blue rock doves' reported inland are either stock doves or escaped domestic pigeons. Large numbers of the latter now live perfectly free in big cities. Flocks of true rock doves seldom number more than 250.

Rock doves have a faster flight than either woodpigeons or stock doves, and parties may be mistaken for waders as they approach. They feed on fields inland from their homes in the cliffs. They build on ledges in caves and crevices and have displays, a long breeding season, and nesting habits like other doves.

1 2 3 4 5 6 7 8 9 10 11 12

3 ROCK DOVE

1 WOODPIGEONS

2 STOCK DOVE

1 COLLARED DOVE (*Streptopelia decaocto*). This comparatively new British resident is just over a foot long and has a rather uniform and drab grey-brown plumage with blackish primary flight feathers, a black and white pattern underneath the tail, and a narrow black and white half collar. The male is slightly larger and greyer than the female, and the collar hardly shows in the juvenile plumage, which has pale edges to the feathers. The domesticated Barbary dove (*Streptopelia risoria*) (1d), which sometimes escapes or is kept at large, is easy to confuse with collared doves, but is, in fact, smaller, shorter-tailed, and more brightly coloured, with dark brown rather than black primaries, and a quite distinct voice. In flight, the difference in the shape and pattern of the tails of collared and turtle doves shows clearly (1c, 2b).

Collared doves have spread right across Europe since about 1930. They first bred in Britain, in Norfolk, in 1955, and in the next 5 or 6 years they spread right over Britain to the Outer Hebrides and Ireland, first colonising certain areas and leaving whole counties unoccupied. Where they breed, they remain as residents. Collared doves are close associates of man, feeding in chicken runs and nesting in ornamental fir trees, so that residential areas and the suburbs of towns, as well as villages and farms, make suitable habitats for them. They live in the centre of many European cities.

Often the first sign that collared doves have arrived is the triple call *coo-cooo-ook*, distinct from the Barbary dove's call *coo-crroo-oo*. When excited, the collared dove utters a short harsh *cwurr*, while the Barbary has a laughing *kek-kek-kek*. The cooing call often accompanies the bowing display which is characteristic of all doves. Small parties perch prominently on roof-ridges or television aerials and perform to each other. But, in spite of their dependence on man, they are often not easy to approach or even to see in places where they are nesting. They feed on grain and other seeds, fruit, and berries. They usually build close to the trunk of a tree or bush from 6 ft. to over 50 ft. above the ground. The nest of sticks, at first flimsy, becomes more substantial when it is used throughout the long breeding season, for as many as five broods are hatched, and may be hatched in any month in the year. The male sits on the two white eggs by night and the female by day; the eggs hatch in about 2 weeks, and the young, though often only one is reared, fly after 2 or 3 weeks. Flocks of many hundreds have been seen in the autumn in England.

1   2   3   4   5   6   7   8   9   10   11   12

2 TURTLE DOVE (*Streptopelia turtur*). About 11 ins. long, the turtle dove has much more variegated upper-parts than the collared dove, much less white on the fan-shaped tail, and the black and white neck patch has a different pattern. The sexes are alike, but the juvenile has no neck patch.

The turtle dove is a summer visitor to England and Wales and the extreme south of Scotland, though it occurs on migration much more widely, even on remote islands. Its breeding habitat is in bushy country and farm land with tall hedges and thickets, and it often colonises young fir plantations. It does not breed in highland areas or in extensive woodland.

The continuous rhythmic purr of the turtle dove is a typical sound of the English summer; the birds often fly up from the roadside where they have been getting grit for their gizzards, and show their fanned black and white tails. Their wings are more sharply angled in flight, and they move more jerkily than their bigger relatives. They feed mainly on seeds and leaves, but are not considered to be pests, though large parties form at the end of the breeding season and may be seen perched on wires running over a cornfield. They perform a display flight and also a bowing ceremony between members of a pair. The female lays a clutch of two white eggs in a small nest of sticks, well hidden in a bush a few feet above ground, and both parents incubate them for 2 weeks. The young fly after 3 weeks, and there are usually two broods.

.   .   .   *4*   **5   6   7   8**   *9   10*   *(11)*   .

RUFOUS TURTLE DOVE (*Streptopelia orientalis*). This very rare visitor from Asia has occurred three times in England, in May 1889, in 1946 when an immature female was shot in Norfolk, and in 1960 when one spent several days with migrating turtle doves on St. Agnes in the Isles of Scilly. It is larger and darker than the common turtle dove, and its tail has a grey, not a white, edge.

3 PALLAS'S SAND GROUSE (*Syrrhaptes paradoxus*). Sand grouse are related to the pigeons, though they behave like game birds of open country, especially on steppes and deserts, where they live in flocks. This species, from Russia and central Asia, has invaded western Europe several times, reaching Britain in numbers in 1863 and 1888, when some tried to breed. Four have been recorded since 1909. Pallas's sand grouse is about a foot long, with central tail feathers up to $3\frac{1}{2}$ ins. longer, coloured rather like a partridge (p. 57) but with pointed wings. It lays two to four eggs, buff-coloured with dark markings, in a bare scrape on the ground.

2a TURTLE DOVE   2b in flight   1a   COLLARED DOVE. M.   1b in flight
        1c Juv.   1d   BARBARY DOVE
      3a PALLAS'S SAND GROUSE F. 3b M.

1 **BARN OWL** (*Tyto alba*). The only common white owl in Britain is about 13½ ins. long. Close to, its upperparts are seen to be a beautiful mixture of pale buff-brown and grey (more prominent in the female) with dark and light flecks and bars. It is much smaller than the rare snowy owl. Some dark-breasted Continental birds (1b) sometimes appear in Britain, and there are also intermediate forms. Young birds are like the adults.

Barn owls are resident throughout the British Isles, except on some of the islands, and do not move about much. They do not inhabit the centres of towns like tawny owls (p. 109), but are found in villages, farms, old quarries and wooded country, on sea cliffs, and even small rocky islands. They do not like thick woods or the wilder moorland. They roost in buildings, holes in trees, and rocks.

The barn owl is most often seen nowadays as an upright white shape on a fence-post caught in the head-lights of a car. But at some times of year — in early spring when food is scarce, or in late summer when it is feeding big young ones — it hunts by daylight, flapping along roadside verges or over open fields, then dropping suddenly on a mouse or vole, snapping up a flying insect. Its hunting speed has been timed at about 14 miles per hour. It takes mainly small mammals, insects, and birds, particularly starlings and sparrows in farmyards. But birds do not mob it as they do other owls. The barn owl throws up two pellets every day; they are black and shiny, quite distinct from those of other birds of prey. The male displays by clapping his wings and by presenting food to the female in the future nest-hole, which is usually occupied long before egg-laying begins. The nest-site is in a similar place to the day-roost, often in a dark loft or other large cavity. The female lays four to six (more when food is plentiful) white eggs and incubates them for 4 to 5 weeks. The owlets may hatch at intervals of a day or two or all together, and stay in the nest for about 7 weeks, making a snoring noise which becomes very loud as they grow up and sit at dusk outside the nest-hole, waiting to be fed. The adults also snore, but the best-known call is a piercing shriek, often uttered in flight. Barn owls seem to suffer worse than other owls in hard winters, and many died in the cold spell of 1963.

*1 2 3 **4 5 6** 7 **8 9** 10 11 12*

2 **SNOWY OWL** (*Nyctea scandiaca*). Much larger than a barn owl, the snowy owl is from 21 to 24 ins. long, females being bigger than males. Its white, lightly barred plumage (the markings are heavier on the female), and yellow eyes also distinguish it from the barn owl. It is found exclusively in open country where it preys on mammals, birds up to partridge size, insects, and spiders. It breeds in northern Scandinavia and used to be a fairly regular winter visitor in very small numbers to the north of Scotland; since 1967 a pair has bred successfully on Fetlar, one of the northern isles of Shetland. It is very rarely seen in the south of Britain.

A snowy owl is most likely to be seen during a spell of hard weather, quartering moorland or rough fields in daylight, rather like a harrier (p. 45) or a short-eared owl (p. 111). But it sometimes chases and strikes down birds as falcons do. When it perches on a prominent stone or post, it leans forward more like a hawk than an owl.

HAWK OWL (*Surnia ulula*). This is a very rare visitor from northern Europe or America, which has been recorded only ten times between 1830 and 1966 when one occurred in August in Cornwall. It is about 15 ins. long, and its pointed wings, long tail, and incomplete facial disk suggest a hawk rather than an owl. Its plumage is white, barred with brown and black; its white face is edged with black; and its eyes are yellow.

2 SNOWY OWL

1b BARN OWL, dark breasted

1a BARN OWL and young

1 TAWNY OWL (*Strix aluco*). The largest common British owl is about 15 ins. long, with a relatively big head even for an owl, and a stout body. The plumage is richly mottled, the facial disk being greyer than the rest, but a grey plumage form (shown in flight) sometimes occurs. The fluffy young birds are often seen away from the nest, but after the first winter moult they cannot easily be told from the adult.

The tawny or brown owl is resident throughout Britain, but is not found on many of the Scottish islands, the Isle of Man, or Ireland. It may be seen right into the heart of cities, but its real habitat is well-wooded country.

It is best known by its voice, the popular 'tu-whit tu-whoo'; but this is really a mixture of the loud hunting call *kee-vit* and the 'song': *too-whoo, ooo, whoooo*, prolonged and quavering, to which the female may answer *kee-vit*. Young birds have a similar call. Tawny owls are active entirely by night and only fly by day when disturbed, though they appear to enjoy sunlight, and tame birds often sunbathe. They hunt mainly by means of their acute hearing and take many kinds of mammals and roosting birds, and also fish, frogs, insects, and earthworms. The pellets are large and grey. When threatening, tawny owls stretch out their wings, lower and bring forward their heads and raise their back feathers. The male claps his wings in his display flight. Tawny owls nest in holes in trees, especially with an entrance above, in buildings, rocks, and on the ground; they will use nest-boxes of chimney type and often occupy disused chimneys in towns. Two to four white eggs are laid at intervals and incubated by the female, hatching in about 4 weeks each. The male then brings food, and the young fly in about 5 weeks but leave the nest-hole earlier. They are often found apparently wandering about, but really the adult is not far off, ready to look after them, and they should be left. A tame owl cannot hunt for itself — it must learn from the parents; so it is no kindness to rear one by hand and then release it.

1   2   3   4   5   6   7   8   9   10   11   12

2 TENGMALM'S OWL (*Aegolius funereus*). A rare visitor from the Continent, which is slightly larger than a little owl (about 10 ins. long), with a rounder facial disk, and legs feathered to the toes. It has occurred in Britain about forty times, mainly in winter and in northern and eastern England, though it has been recorded very seldom in recent years. In general appearance it resembles a little owl, but the plumage appears whiter.

3 LITTLE OWL (*Athene noctua*). This is the most commonly seen owl in Britain. It is about 9 ins. long, and its size, as well as its liver-brown and white mottled plumage which shows when the light is good enough, make it distinctive. The downy young soon resemble the adults after moulting.

The little owl was successfully introduced to Northants in 1889 and to Kent in 1896; it is now found all over England and Wales and just into Scotland, though it is thought to have decreased in recent years. It is native across the Channel, and birds have fairly certainly crossed as occasional visitors too. Its favourite habitat is farming country with buildings and old trees, but it is also found on some bare Welsh islands.

The little owl is usually seen at dusk as a squat figure on a post or telegraph pole, bobbing up and down when alarmed, then flying off low, its rounded wings and short tail being conspicuous. It is often out in daylight when it can be confused momentarily with a mistle thrush (p. 137). It has a variety of calls, but the most common is a repeated, rather sad *quew quew*, a little like the beginning of the curlew's call (p. 69). It hunts by pouncing from its perch and by hovering for short periods. It can run fast but looks comical when doing so. Its food varies from small mammals and birds to insects, which are its main prey, and other invertebrate animals, including earthworms. Its pellets are grey, resembling those of the kestrel (p. 49). The male flies in display over the nest site, which may be a hole in a tree, building, or cliff, or in the ground. The clutch of three to five eggs is incubated by the female and hatch in about 4 weeks, when the male brings the food to the nest. Later, both parents feed the young, and they fly in 5 or 6 weeks.

1   2   3   4   5   6   7   8   9   10   11   12

4 SCOPS OWL (*Otus scops*). A very small owl, 7½ ins. long, much slimmer than the little owl, and distinguished by its ear tufts. It has a grey plumage, though a reddish form occurs. It is a rare visitor from the Mediterranean, where it lives in the towns, and it has been recorded about 70 times in Britain, as far north as Shetland, but some may have been escapes.

1a TAWNY OWL   1b TAWNY OWL (grey form) in flight
4 SCOPS OWL   3 LITTLE OWL   2 TENGMALM'S OWL

1 LONG-EARED OWL (*Asio otus*). About 13½ ins. long, this owl is smaller, much more slender, and has longer wings and tail than the tawny owl (p. 109), and at reasonably close range a perched bird is distinguished by its yellowish-red eyes and long ear tufts. In flight the tufts are hidden, but the bird looks greyer than a short-eared owl and its wings are more rounded.

The long-eared owl is now scarce and local over most of England and Wales, but is rather more common in the north and in south and central Scotland, and is the most common owl in Ireland. In Britain it is the most woodland of the owls and is particularly associated with conifers. There are some winter visitors from Europe.

The typical call has been described as 'a cooing moan rather than a hoot', but there is a barking call in the breeding season, and various other cries are given by the young and when alarmed. As well as by its voice, this owl may be located by a circle of droppings and pellets below a favourite roosting tree, where the bird may be seen, pressed against the trunk, its eyes closed. If small birds find a long-eared owl, they will mob it furiously. It hunts by night, chasing small mammals, birds, and insects. Its display includes flying through the trees and wing-clapping, and young birds defying an intruder spread their wings round their heads, snap their bills, and hiss. The female lays three to six white eggs, usually in the old nest of another bird in a tree, but sometimes on the ground, and she incubates them for about 4 weeks; the young leave the nest after 3½ weeks. Small parties may be seen in winter.

1   2   3   4   5   6   7   8   9   10   11   12

2 SHORT-EARED OWL (*Asio flammeus*). This is a rather larger bird than the long-eared owl (about 14½ ins. long), and distinguished from it in flight by its relatively longer wings and pale brown appearance; there are conspicuous dark brown marks on the underside of the wing. Even at close range the ear tufts can hardly be seen, but the plumage is heavily streaked, and the feathers round the yellow eye are dark.

The short-eared owl is both a resident and a winter visitor; it breeds very locally in East Anglia, Wales, the north of England, and parts of Scotland, and in winter may be quite common in open areas in the south. During vole plagues, especially in newly afforested moors and heaths, a great many short-eared owls may appear. This regular association with treeless habitats distinguishes it from other British owls.

When first seen quartering over open ground, this owl may be mistaken for a hawk or harrier, for it is active in daytime, hunting principally small mammals, though it takes some small birds and insects. In winter a number of birds may occupy quite a small area of good hunting ground, and an observer may see a dozen at a time. The short-eared owl is usually silent away from the nest, but has an attractive hooting 'song' uttered during the display flight, which is elaborate and includes wing-clapping. It walks on the ground, where it makes its nest hidden by long grass or low bushes. The female lays four to eight eggs (more during vole plagues when food is plentiful), which she incubates for about 4 weeks; the young fly when nearly 4 weeks old. There may be two broods in a vole-plague season. The short-eared owl is the best British example of a bird of prey which responds quickly to a peak population of its favourite food animal.

1   2   3   4   5   6   7   8   9   10   11   12

EAGLE OWL (*Bubo bubo*). This is the largest European owl, 25 to 28 ins. long, the females being bigger than the males. The upperparts are mottled blackish and rich brown, the underparts are paler, and the wings and tail are barred. But the big ear-tufts and orange eyes are the distinctive features of the eagle owl. As a very rare visitor, it has occurred all over Britain, but some records are considered doubtful and may have been captive birds, for eagle owls are often kept in captivity. A pair which haunted a craggy hillside in south-west Scotland in the spring of 1941 behaved as if they were nesting. In Britain eagle owls have taken rabbits and water voles, and in Europe they kill a great variety of birds and mammals up to a roe deer in size. They sit upright like tawny owls (p. 109) and have a surprisingly feeble *oo* call, as well as a loud *keck keck*.

1   LONG-EARED OWLS
2a SHORT-EARED OWL, Ad. 2b Juv.

NEAR-PASSERINES

1 KINGFISHER (*Alcedo atthis*). This short-tailed, long-billed, brilliantly coloured little bird, about 6½ ins. long, is quite unmistakable. Males, females, and juveniles look more or less alike.

The kingfisher is resident and generally distributed over most of England and Wales, becoming scarcer in the north as far as central Scotland; it is local in Ireland. It is found along slower-moving rivers and streams with banks high enough for it to nest in safety; it has spread to gravel pits in southern England. In autumn some move to tidal waters, particularly estuaries and sheltered bays, and to the shores of lakes and reservoirs.

The first sight of a kingfisher is usually a blue streak darting away along a stream or over a lake, its short rounded wings beating rapidly, and uttering its sharp *cheee* call as it goes. When it is at rest on a perch over the water it is much more difficult to see because the darker wings cover the brilliant back and rump, and the chestnut breast blends with the background, especially with autumn leaves. It feeds mainly on small fish which it catches by dropping on them from above, either from a perch or from hovering. It also takes water beetles and dragonfly larvae, and small crustaceans on the coast. Chases in the air, sometimes accompanied by a whistling song, are an important part of its display. The kingfisher excavates a nest-hole in a bank, usually over water, and sloping slightly upward for about 2 feet to the nest chamber. The female lays five to seven round, glossy-white eggs, through which the yolk shines pink when they are fresh. Both parents incubate the eggs which take about 3 weeks to hatch. They then feed the young on fish, the bones of which accumulate around them in the nest. After 3½ weeks the young ones come out of the hole and fly; and soon a second brood follows, sometimes in the same hole.

1 2 3 4 5 6 7 8 9 10 11 12

2 HOOPOE (*Upupa epops*). Whether its crest is fanned or compressed, the pinkish-brown hoopoe, with its black and white wings and tail, can hardly be confused with any other British bird, except perhaps with a jay when in flight, though it is smaller than a jay, being less than 1 ft. long, of which the bill may be 2¼ ins. Juveniles look like adults with smaller crests.

The hoopoe is now a regular spring and autumn visitor in small numbers, mainly to southern England and Ireland. A pair probably breeds somewhere almost every year, and odd birds have occurred in most parts of the country, usually in autumn. Migrants may be seen in bare coastal areas, but the birds breed in well-wooded country with old trees and buildings.

In flight (top right on plate), with its very round wings, the hoopoe looks like a big black and white moth. On the ground it walks easily over a lawn or rubbish heap, probing for insect grubs. It gets its name from the call—a repeated *hoo hoo hoo*, soft and musical, but carrying a long way. Hoopoes nest in holes in trees or buildings, laying up to ten whitish eggs. The female incubates for about 2½ weeks, and both parents feed the young for some 4 weeks before they fly.

. (2) 3 4 5 (6 7) 8 9 10 11 .

3 ROLLER (*Coracias garrulus*). A brilliantly blue bird about a foot long, the adult roller is quite unmistakable, if seen clearly; in shape it looks rather like a big thrush. The juvenile is paler and lacks the black spots at the tips of the tail. In flight, the brown, black, and turquoise-blue wing is particularly striking.

The roller is a rare and irregular passage migrant, though it has been seen in England at other times; most records come from the eastern counties. It likes a prominent perch, from which to drop on the insects which are its chief food, but it also feeds on the ground, where it hops like a crow. It flies mainly with continuous wing-beats, but can glide for short distances. The call is a harsh crow, and the name 'roller' comes from its tumbling display flight; but neither call nor display are likely to be observed in Britain.

4 BEE-EATER (*Merops apiaster*). The brilliant plumage of the bee-eater only shows up in a good light, but its long central tail-feathers, rather pointed wings, and long, thin bill (1½ ins. of its total length of 11 ins.) are distinctive. The juveniles are duller than the adults and do not have the long tail-feathers.

They are irregular visitors on passage, usually in spring, and sometimes appearing in small parties, mainly in the south and east of England. In 1920 a pair tried to nest near Edinburgh, and in 1955 two out of three pairs nested successfully in a sand-pit in Sussex; a pair nested in 1956 in Alderney. Bee-eaters may appear in open wooded country with good perching places, often near water.

Bee-eaters' flight is rather swallow-like, with quick wing-beats; the birds soar in circles, swooping on insects, bees, wasps, dragonflies, beetles, and flies. They also spend long periods on prominent perches, especially on telegraph wires. The usual call note *qui-ick qui-ick* is uttered constantly, at all seasons. They usually nest in groups: the three nests in Sussex were close together; they burrow a hole of varying length into a bank or flat ground, and lay four to eight roundish white eggs.

BLUE-CHEEKED BEE-EATER (*Merops superciliosus*). Single birds of this North African and Asiatic species were recorded in the Scillies, 1921 and 1951. In size and shape it resembles the European bee-eater but is bright green above, with a yellow throat shading to copper, and copper-coloured underwings.

4 BEE-EATERS   3 ROLLERS

1 KINGFISHERS   2 HOOPOES

WOODPECKERS

1 **GREEN WOODPECKER** (*Picus viridis*). Like other colourful birds, the biggest British woodpecker (about 12½ ins. long) can look quite dull in poor light; only in good sunlight does the green of the wings and upper back look really bright. The yellowish rump, however, seen as the bird flies away, is conspicuous and leads to reports of 'golden orioles' (*see* p. 173). The female has a black cheek stripe, while that of the male is crimson-red bordered with black. Juveniles have light markings above, with dark streaks and bars below and on the wings.

The green woodpecker is a resident, generally distributed in England and Wales and now also found in southern Scotland; there are no recent records for Ireland. Its main habitat is well-wooded country, but it does not go far into continuous woodland.

The laugh or 'yaffle': *whee whee whee whee* . . . with several variations, often announces the presence of a green woodpecker before it is seen; the *quip quip* of alarm is also well-known and is often uttered while the bird is making its slow, undulating flight, which is rather like that of the mistle thrush (*see* p. 137). Green woodpeckers are frequently seen on the ground, where they go to hunt ants, probing with their bills, then catching them with their immensely long tongues. They sit rather upright, supporting themselves on their tails, and move in big hops. They climb trees also by a series of hops, and can 'reverse' but not move head-downwards. The display includes spiral chases round tree-trunks. They chip out grubs from bark or dead wood with their powerful bills, and can bore through several inches of live wood when excavating the nest-hole, which is over 2 ins. in diameter, and may go down over a foot from the round entrance on the side of the tree. Five to seven white eggs, soon stained, are laid in a bare 'chamber', and both parents incubate them for over 2½ weeks. They feed the noisy young by regurgitating a paste of insect food. Fledging takes up to 3 weeks. Woodpeckers remain alone or in pairs after nesting.

1   2   3   4 5   6 7   8 9   10   11   12

2 **GREAT SPOTTED WOODPECKER** (*Dendrocopus major*). The 'pied' woodpecker, as it is sometimes called, is about 9 ins. long and can usually be told from the lesser spotted woodpecker by size alone; it is also differently marked on the shoulders and back and has a brilliant crimson patch under the tail. The female has no crimson on her head; the male has a small patch at the nape of the neck, and the juveniles have crimson crowns.

Great spotted woodpeckers are normally residents, but there are also periodical invasions of the race from northern Europe in autumn — these occurred, for example, in 1962 and 1968 — and some of these birds reached Ireland. They now breed all over England and Wales and far into the Highlands of Scotland; and they have also reached some of the Inner Hebrides. They are more woodland birds than green woodpeckers and are found in old coniferous forests; but they also haunt open wooded country, and

European visitors are found on bare islands and coasts.

Even against the sky, the. undulating flight and repeated *pic pic* call make this woodpecker easy to recognise. It behaves in typical woodpecker fashion on trees, and has also taken in recent years to visiting bird tables, where it takes all sorts of scraps and robs other birds near the table; it also takes seeds of many kinds, including those from fir cones, and will attack nestboxes to get at broods of young birds. It will ring trees, especially limes, with rows of holes through which it sucks the sap. In spring both sexes drum on a chosen 'sounding board', striking a series of very rapid blows with their strong beaks; they will drum on other materials as well as wood, for example, on the metal cap of a telegraph pole. Chases in the air and round tree-trunks and a special quivering flight also form part of the display, all accompanied by calls. The nest hole is nearly as large as a green woodpecker's, and the central shaft is about a foot deep. The female lays four to seven white eggs and does most of their incubation, which lasts over 2 weeks. Both parents feed the young with bills full of insects. The nestlings are very noisy and put their heads out of the hole as they get near to fledging, which takes place in about 3 weeks. Like other woodpeckers, the great spotted woodpecker is solitary outside the breeding season.

1   2   3   4 5   6   7   8   9   10   11   12

3 **LESSER SPOTTED WOODPECKER** (*Dendrocopus minor*). The 'barred' woodpecker looks little bigger than a chaffinch, being under 6 ins. in length. Its wings and back are barred black and white. The male's crown is crimson, the female's white, and juveniles of both sexes have some crimson.

This woodpecker is resident south from Lancashire and Northumberland, and is always rather local in distribution. It is found in much the same habitats as the great spotted woodpecker, except that it avoids conifers.

It is probably one of the least known and least often seen of the commoner birds. In spring its ringing call: *pee pee pee pee*, very like that of the wryneck (*see* p. 117), and its drumming can be heard, the latter being surprisingly powerful but more rapid than that of the great spotted; it also has a similar *pic* call, but less loud. If the call or drumming is heard, the bird may be tracked and finally seen high among the small branches and twigs, often perching across them or fluttering from branch to branch with round, moth-like wings. The male's display includes a slow flight. The lesser spotted feeds typically like a woodpecker, but does not visit bird tables and seldom lands on the ground. The nest hole is about 1½ ins. wide, usually in a dead side branch at heights from a few to 70 feet; the shaft is about 8 ins. The usual clutch is four to six white eggs, which both sexes incubate for about 2 weeks. The young are fledged in about 3 weeks. Lesser spotted woodpeckers often join up with roving parties of titmice in the winter.

1   2   3   4 5   6   7   8   9   10   11   12

2a   GREAT SPOTTED WOODPECKER, M.   3a LESSER SPOTTED WOODPECKER, M.
   2b F., and young   3b F.
       1a GREEN WOODPECKER, M.   1b Juv.

CUCKOOS AND WRYNECK

1 C U C K O O (*Cuculus canorus*). An adult cuckoo has a superficial resemblance to a hawk, but its thin bill, small head, fanned tail with white spots, and way of flying are distinctive among British birds. Cuckoos are about 13 ins. long. The female is rather browner than the male, and there is a red-brown variety (in flight, top left of picture). The juvenile (1c) is dark brown above, barred with black and flecked with white, and has a white patch on the back of its neck.

The cuckoo is a summer visitor all over the British Isles, both in bare habitats and in wooded areas. No British bird is so well known and so little seen. The male only calls its famous *cuck-oo* for about 2 months, up to the end of June, when the adults seem to disappear, though juveniles may be seen until the end of August. The female has a bubbling call, and both sexes may utter an angry *kow kow kow*, sometimes combined with the *cuck-oo*. Cuckoos call on the wing or from perches, often moving their heads and tails. They fly with rapid beats and glides, and are rather clumsy on the ground, whether walking or hopping. They eat insects, especially hairy and other caterpillars, and also small animals. The male often combines his display with the cuckoo call, and he may show off his spread tail to a female, competing with another male.

It is possible one male may have several mates, each of which has a fixed territory where she lays from 6 to 18 eggs in the nests of small birds such as hedge sparrows, usually one to a nest. She lays the egg direct into the nest, either sitting on it or projecting the egg from just outside. She usually removes one of the host's eggs to make room for hers. She chooses a nest of newly laid eggs so that the young cuckoo hatches at the same time or just before the host's brood; the incubation period is 12½ days — about the same as that of the principal hosts. When the young cuckoo hatches, it gets below the other chicks or eggs and throws them out one by one; then it remains for 3 to 3½ weeks to be fed by the hosts, who continue to look after it even when it has left the nest. Its constant cries and wide red gape often attract strange birds to feed it.

Most British cuckoo's eggs are speckled greyish-brown; they resemble but are larger than the eggs of the meadow pipit, one of its chief hosts; but are quite unlike the eggs of the hedge sparrow, its most popular host in lowland wooded habitats. Other frequent hosts are reed warblers, pied wagtails, robins, tree pipits, and sedge warblers. About fifty different species have been victimized in Britain, but in most cases accidentally and unsuccessfully.

. . (3) *4 5 6 7 8 9 (10 11)* .

GREAT SPOTTED CUCKOO (*Clamator glandarius*). The French name of this rare visitor means 'cuckoo-jay', though in some ways it looks more like a mixture of cuckoo and magpie, with its long white-edged tail. But it has a grey crown and crest, brown upperparts boldly spotted, and pale underparts; it is about 16 ins. long, half of which is tail. It nests in southern Europe, and has occurred 13 times in the British Isles, in spring or autumn.

YELLOW-BILLED CUCKOO (*Coccyzus americanus*). Two American cuckoos have occurred in Britain, this one the more frequently. It is about 11 ins. long, dark above, and pale below, and distinguished by the reddish flight feathers which show up on the wing and by black tail feathers with white tips. At close range the yellow on the mandible can be seen. Over twenty have been recorded, all in autumn and mostly on the west side of Britain or in Ireland.

BLACK-BILLED CUCKOO (*Coccyzus erythropthalmus*). Another American cuckoo, very like the previous species, but without the reddish patch on the wings, and with no black and less white on the tail. At close range the red rim to the eye and the all-black bill are conspicuous. Six have been recorded in Britain and Ireland, all in autumn. Both these species build their own nests, lay greenish-blue eggs, and incubate them.

2 W R Y N E C K (*Jynx torquilla*). The wryneck has two toes pointing each way, and is grouped with the woodpeckers (p. 115), although it is much less specialised in its habits. It is 6½ ins. long, and looks not unlike a thrush at a distance; but at closer range the beautifully mottled and variegated plumage of greys and browns is quite distinctive. Juveniles resemble the adults.

Wrynecks are now very rare summer visitors to the east and south-east of England, where a few pairs breed each year in well-wooded country and orchards. They are seen on passage as far north as the central Highlands of Scotland where three pairs bred in 1969. They feed mainly on ants and beetles, with some other insects, and they are among those species which have become much rarer in Britain in recent years possibly because the cold summers have made it difficult for them to catch their prey.

On arrival, the male begins to call, usually from a high perch and with head pointing upward, a penetrating *quee quee quee quee*... rather like the calls of some falcons and also of the lesser spotted woodpecker. At other times it is not an easy bird to see, though it does much of its feeding on the ground, hopping agilely. It uses its tail as a prop, as does a woodpecker, but cannot bore into timber either in search of food or to make a nest-hole. It breeds in natural holes, usually in trees but sometimes in banks, and will take to nestboxes. It makes no nest and lays seven to ten dull white eggs. The female does most of the incubation which lasts 12 to 14 days; both parents feed the young until they fly after about 3 weeks. There is occasionally a second brood.

. (2 3) *4 5 6 7 8 9 (10 11)* .

1a CUCKOO. M.   1d CUCKOO. F. (red-brown variety)
                1b CUCKOO. F.
2 WRYNECK   1c CUCKOO, Juv.

SWIFTS AND NIGHTJARS

1 SWIFT (*Apus apus*). Its stout body, about 6½ ins. long, rather short forked tail, and very long curved and pointed wings distinguish the swift in silhouette from the swallows and martins (p. 121). It is very dark brown all over except for its pale throat, and it has a pronounced brow over the big black eye. Juveniles look scaly owing to the pale margins to their feathers. Swifts have tiny bills but wide mouths, in which they resemble the nightjars.

These summer visitors are widely distributed over most of Britain and Ireland, except the northern Highlands and most of the islands, though they may be seen there also on migration. The breeding colonies are almost all in buildings of some kind, though there are a few in cliffs in Wales; but the birds hunt for great distances over all types of country, to the tops of the highest hills and far over the sea. They are a familiar sight in the spring and summer sky over towns and villages.

The swift is one of the most remarkable of British birds. It spends most of its time on the wing, non-breeding birds even roosting in flight; it mates in the air after wild flights in which parties of screaming birds take part. If a swift lands, it cannot very easily take off again, but it can cling to walls and crawl about. It takes all its insect food in flight, and collects its nesting material of airborne feathers, grass stems, and other plant fragments without landing on the ground. It carries these materials into a hole or crevice, and there moulds them into a saucer with saliva. The clutch of two or three pointed white eggs is incubated by both parents in turn, and both spend the night in the nest-hole. The eggs hatch in about 20 days, and the young take a long and variable time to fledge, from 5 to 8 weeks. They have the ability to lower their body temperatures and survive in a dormant condition, rather like reptiles. There is only one brood.

. . (3) 4 **5 6 7** 8 9 (10) . . .

2 ALPINE SWIFT (*Apus melba*). This is a much larger bird than the common swift, over 8 ins. long. It is paler brown above and has a white underside, visible a long way off. Alpine swifts nest in France and Switzerland, and over 110 have been recorded in Britain, mostly in southern counties. In general habits they resemble the common swift.

LITTLE OR HOUSE SWIFT (*Apus affinis*). A single bird of this species from Asia and Africa (now nesting in south Spain) was recorded at Cape Clear, Co. Cork in June 1967. This is one of several small, white-rumped swifts and is distinguished by its almost square tail.

NEEDLE-TAILED SWIFT (*Chaetura caudacuta*). This big swift from eastern Asia, about 7½ ins. long, has been seen about three times in the British Isles, the last being in Co. Cork in 1964. It has mainly dark underparts, including a conspicuous patch on each flank. The spiny tail feathers can be seen only at close quarters.

3 NIGHTJAR (*Caprimulgus europaeus*). This is a long-tailed, long-winged, flat-headed bird, with big black eyes and a very small bill. It is about 10½ ins. long and its plumage is soft like that of an owl and mottled in shades of brown and grey, which give it a perfect camouflage among the dead twigs and stems in which it often sits. The male is distinguished by white spots on the wing and tail which the female and juvenile do not have. The nightjar has bristles round its big mouth which help it to entrap insects in flight. The 'comb' on the middle of the three front claws is probably used to clean these bristles.

Nightjars are summer visitors, still widely distributed throughout Britain and Ireland, though absent from most of the islands and decreasing almost everywhere. Their habitat is dry heaths, felled woods, and newly forested areas. Odd birds may appear almost anywhere on migration. Often the first sign that nightjars have arrived in spring is the sight of a male bird's prolonged reeling (or 'jarring' — hence the name), now rising, now falling, and going on for several minutes. A bird may reel from the ground, but usually when sitting along a branch or high perch of some kind. In between bouts of reeling the male flies round clapping his wings and gliding with raised wings and tails spread like a huge moth, and making the flight call *kew-ick*. Nightjars catch most of their insect food on the wing. They make no nest, but lay the two round-ended marbled eggs side by side on the ground; these are incubated mainly by the female for 2½ weeks. Both parents feed the young at first, but later the male takes over, while the female lays her second brood. The fledglings can fly after about 2½ weeks.

. . . 4 **5 6 7 8** 9 (10 11)

RED-NECKED NIGHTJAR (*Caprimulgus ruficollis*). This very rare visitor from the Mediterranean region is about a foot long and is distinguished from the common nightjar by its reddish collar and large white patch on the throat. It has only been recorded once, in Northumberland in 1856.

EGYPTIAN NIGHTJAR (*Caprimulgus egyptius*). A single specimen of this North African species was recorded in Nottinghamshire in 1883. It is about the same size as the common nightjar but much paler and without the white spots on the wing.

AMERICAN NIGHTHAWK (*Chordeiles minor*). Three American nighthawks have been recorded in Britain, all in the Isles of Scilly in autumn: one in 1927 and two in 1957. They are rather smaller than common nightjars, but with relatively longer wings and slightly forked tails. They also have a white bar across the wings and a white patch on the throat and their underparts are barred. They hunt by day and in modern America they nest on the flat tops of buildings in towns.

2 ALPINE SWIFT

1 SWIFT

3b NIGHTJAR M.

3a NIGHTJAR F.

SWALLOWS AND MARTINS

1 **HOUSE MARTIN** (*Delichon urbica*). Its white rump, white-feathered legs, and shorter less forked tail distinguish the house martin from the swallow, and it is smaller — only about 5 ins. long. Juvenile house martins are rather like sand martins but without the brown band across the breast.

House martins are common summer visitors over most of Britain, though less widely distributed than swallows. Colonies are found at isolated farms, but they also penetrate further into cities than swallows, some nesting on the edge of central London. Like swallows, they flock near water before they migrate in autumn, when they travel as far as South Africa.

In general habits they resemble swallows, but house martins are less dashing in their movements. Their call is a rather hard 'gritty' chirrup, and the song, though sweet, is less musical and more twittery than that of swallows. They catch small insects on the wing, as swallows do, but they may hunt higher up in the air. House martins nest in colonies, up to 500 pairs in England, typically under the eaves of houses and buildings, but the largest gatherings are under bridges. Many also nest on cliffs by the sea and in-land. Groups of martins collect mud from puddles and pools to build their deep mud cups, deeper than a swallow's nest, with only a small entrance at the top. They line the cup with grass and feathers, and they lay a clutch in it, usually of four to five pointed white eggs. Both parents incubate them for about 2 weeks and feed the young, which fledge at about 3 weeks. Older juveniles often help to feed the young of the second and third broods.

(1 2) 3 **4 5 6 7 8 9** 10 *11* *(12)*

2 **SAND MARTIN** (*Riparia riparia*). Slightly smaller (under 5 ins. long) and much slimmer than the house martin, the sand martin is dark brown above, with a brown band across the breast. The juveniles are rather scaly-looking owing to the pale margins of their feathers.

Sand martins are more local summer visitors than their relatives, but they are found all over Britain, and they are commoner than house martins in Ireland. They make their colonies mainly in sandy riverbanks, in sand and gravel pits, and on soft sea-cliffs; but birds fly a long way from where they nest in search of food.

Sand martins are usually seen over or near water, except where they are nesting in a dry pit or cutting. They fly about in a cloud, like huge insects, uttering an even harsher chirrup than the house martin, mixed with a sharp alarm note: *zit zit*. The song is an elaboration of the chirruping call. They feed on the wing and collect straws and feathers for their nests which are built at the end of tunnels up to 3 ft. long which the birds excavate. The four or five white eggs are incubated by both sexes for about 2 weeks;

and the young are fed in the nest for 19 days. The are generally two broods.

. . *3* **4 5 6 7 8** 9 *10* *(11 12)*

3 **SWALLOW** (*Hirundo rustica*). This typical bird summer can be told from its relatives by its long pointed wings, very long outer feathers of the ta which has white spots, buff underparts, and dark r on the head; it is about 7 ins. long. The juveniles a duller, with much shorter tail streamers, and silhouette can be mistaken for house martins.

The swallow is a widespread summer visitor, foun on many islands and quite high in the hills. In Britai it is now always associated with human habitation and domestic animals, though hunting birds may l met miles from houses. Birds on migration ofte gather by lakes and shallow waters, especially near tl sea, and about October they fly southwards, many them as far as South Africa.

A twittering musical song and flashing, almc butterfly-like flight announce the first swallows spring. They sweep into sheds where they may hav nested before, out over a river or pond to dip rapid and flutter just above the water, then up to soar an circle high against the sky, all the time hawking f small insects. Their display consists of chases an fights on the wing, accompanied by loud song. The also spend much time perched, nowadays usually o telephone wires; but, particularly in the autum they use branches and twigs, sometimes whole parti descending on a tree and almost covering it. Thes flocks may roost in hundreds, often choosing reec beds. Several pairs may nest close together in all typ of buildings from concrete cowsheds to boathouse The nest is a bracket of small pieces of mud, eac moulded round a fragment of grass; these are built u in layers and lined with grass stems and feather The nest usually has some support, if only a nail a wall. The nest cups last a long time and may l built up and used over several years. Swallows la four to six elongated white eggs with red spots, whic are incubated by the female for about 2 weeks. Bot parents feed the young from their throats until the fledge in about 3 weeks. There is a second, sometim even a third brood, and the juveniles of the first broc often help to feed the second brood.

. *(2)* *3* **4 5 6 7 8 9** 10 *11* *(12)*

RED-RUMPED SWALLOW (*Hirundo daurica* This very rare visitor from the Mediterranean regio is about the same size as the common swallow, an may be told from it by the pale underparts extendin right to the bill and over the rump. Both the rump an the nape are light chestnut red, and there are n white spots on the tail. More than twenty-five hav been recorded in Britain between 1906 and 197 when two occurred.

1 HOUSE MARTIN

2 SAND MARTIN

3a SWALLOW, Ad. 3b Juv.

LARKS

1 WOODLARK (*Lullula arborea*). About 6 ins. long, the woodlark is distinguished by its short tail, by the prominent pale stripes over the eyes which meet behind the head, and by a dark brown and white mark on the edge of the wing. The crest is often flattened, but when raised is more pronounced than the skylark's. Juveniles look more mottled than adults.

The woodlark is a local resident in the southern half of England, extending into mid and south Wales; it is an occasional visitor elsewhere but does not appear to move about much. Its habitat is open ground with scattered trees: heaths, felled woodland, downs and breckland, and industrial wasteland, often in places where skylarks are absent.

Woodlarks may allow a human being to come quite close before flying up with their musical call *titlooit*; their rounded wings and a very short tail are then obvious. The male sings either from a perch or circling in the sky; it is one of the most beautiful songs of any British bird, made up of rising and falling sequences of notes: *lu lu lu lu*. Woodlarks feed mainly on insects and grubs and do not frequent crop fields. They usually make a very open nest in bare ground or low cover; the three or four eggs show more white than those of the skylark. The female incubates them for about 2 weeks, and both parents feed the young, which leave the nest before they can fly. There are generally two broods.

1 2 3 4 5 6 7 8 9 10 11 12

2 SKYLARK (*Alauda arvensis*). This famous songster is about 7 ins. long, a little larger than the woodlark, and with a longer tail; it is larger than any of the pipits (pp. 163 - 165), and, like them, has conspicuous white outer tail feathers; it has a crest, though this often lies flat. The crest, white tail feathers, and thinner bill distinguish it from the corn bunting (p. 191) which often shares the same habitat. Short-tailed, bright-coloured juveniles may be confused with woodlarks.

Skylarks are to be found throughout the British Isles, wherever there is a large area of open ground: heath, moor, pastures, arable land, dunes, and coastal shingle. Most of the birds which have nested in Britain migrate southwards in winter and are replaced by visitors from northern Europe.

A fluttering speck in the sky pouring out an apparently endless warbling song is how people generally think of skylarks; also at any time of year larks will fly up from the roadside in farming or moorland country, showing their white tail feathers and streaky brown plumage at close range, and calling a pleasant *chirrup*. In winter great flocks may pass over during spells of hard weather, and birds land in city parks looking for food. They search the ground busily for the small animals and seeds on which they feed; though they take some corn, they are not considered pests and probably prefer smaller weed seeds. The male displays by his song flight, descending with wings stretched before a final drop to land. Skylarks also often sing from posts or

from the ground. The nest is a cup of grass, usual fairly open but sometimes well hidden, in a crop fiel pasture, or rough ground. The female builds t nest, and she alone incubates the three or fou occasionally five, rather glossy-brown speckled egg The eggs hatch in 11 days, and both parents brin food in the bill. The young, at first covered wit yellowish, rather hairy-looking down, move out the nest after a week or more, but do not fly fc 3 weeks. There may be two or three broods in season.

1 2 3 4 5 6 7 8 9 10 11 12

3 CRESTED LARK (*Galerida cristata*). A littl smaller than a skylark and distinguished by its longe crest and bill, shorter tail, and very round wings wit orange undersides. Though it is resident in Norther Europe, the crested lark has only been recorded abou fifteen times, all except one in southern England.

4 SHORT-TOED LARK (*Calandrella brachydactyla* A small sandy-looking lark, with very pale unde parts. In flight the tail looks very dark, with a whit border. This is a Mediterranean species, which ha occurred over a hundred times, mostly in autumn.

The LESSER SHORT-TOED LARK (*Caland rella rufescens*) is about the same size (5½ ins.) but look more like a very small skylark, with a distinctl streaked breast and dull brown upperparts. Abou forty were seen in small flocks in southern and wester Ireland in 1956 and 1958.

5 SHORELARK (*Eremophila alpestris*). The black an yellow head pattern distinguishes all plumages of th scarce winter visitor from other larks and pipits Small parties haunt shingle beds and waste groun near the coast, feeding on seeds and small inverte brates at the high tide line. The call note is a shri *tseep*. It is a regular visitor only on the English ea and south-east coasts.

1 2 3 (4 5) . . . (9) 10 11 12

RARE LARKS Three closely related larks hav been recorded occasionally in Britain. They are th WHITE-WINGED LARK (*Melanocorypha leucop tera*) from southern Russia, recorded six time the latest in 1955; the CALANDRA LARK (*M calandra*) from the Mediterranean, seen for the firs time at Portland, Dorset, in 1961; and the ver similar BIMACULATED LARK (*M. bimaculata* from south-west Asia, also seen only once, in 1962 on Lundy, Devon.

The white-winged lark, about the size of a skylark but heavier looking with a thicker bill and no crest has white wing-bars and chestnut on its wing an tail. The calandra lark is rather larger. and its rounde wings with thin white trailing edge look blackish i flight. It has white outer tail feathers and a blac patch at the side of the neck.

1 WOODLARK   2 SKYLARKS

3 CRESTED LARK

4 SHORT-TOED LARK   5a SHORELARK, M.   5b F.

LARGER CROWS

1 **R O O K** (*Corvus frugilegus*). About 18 ins. long and slightly smaller than a crow, the rook has a less massive head and more pointed bill, at the base of which the adult has a bare white patch (1a). Juvenile rooks (1b) can easily be mistaken for crows because they are feathered to the bill in the same way. Rooks are also distinguished by the appearance of the thigh feathers which look like baggy breeches, and the blue gloss of the plumage, which in the crow tends to be greenish.

Rooks are birds of wooded agricultural land; they are therefore local or absent in highland areas and from many islands and do not nest in large cities. Some British rooks leave their breeding areas in winter, and some also immigrate.

A great flock of rooks, spread over grass fields with jackdaws or following the plough with gulls, is a familiar sight of the countryside. Walking or hopping, they search for insect grubs, which they probe from the ground. But as they also take corn and green crops, their value or otherwise to the farmer has been the subject of argument for years. When a rook caws, its whole body jerks; but rooks also have a variety of other calls, some quite musical. They have the same bowing display that other crows have. They nest in colonies of all sizes from a few to hundreds of pairs, sometimes straggling for a mile in a line among the upper branches of tall trees. Some rookeries persist for years; others only last for a season or two, and the birds often dismantle outlying nests. Outside the breeding season they may roost at their rookery or in a different wood not used for nesting. The nest is rather less rounded than a crow's nest and is lined with leaves, grass, and moss, but not with wool. The four to six eggs are more pointed than those of crows; the female, fed by the male, incubates them for about 17 days. At first she feeds the young herself, but later the male helps. They fly in just over 4 weeks.

1 2 3 4 5 6 7 8 9 10 11 12

2 **CARRION AND HOODED CROWS** (*Corvus corone*). The 'hoodie' of Ireland and the Scottish Highlands is now considered to be the same species as the black carrion crow, with which it interbreeds freely. It has a grey body which looks almost pink in certain lights. Hybrids (2b) are generally less grey, sometimes with only a grey collar. Crows are 18½ ins. long, considerably smaller than ravens; they have rounder wings and a straighter edge to the tail (*see* flying birds in the plate); and the bill is noticeably less powerful.

Crows of one or the other race are found all over the British Isles, from the centre of London to the remotest islands. The 'hoodie' occupies Ireland, the Isle of Man, and north-western Scotland. Hybrids occur mainly in the southern and central Highlands of Scotland. Some hooded crows are winter visitors to the east side of Britain, but are much less numerous than formerly. Crows are found in all habitats up to

3,000 ft. above sea level and are common along mu of the coastline.

It is not safe to believe that crows are alwa solitary and rooks always in parties; crows may som times gather in tens or hundreds at roosts or favour feeding places, for example on muddy shores and v fields. They take almost anything that is edible a often fight with gulls at rubbish tips; they drop shellf from a height to break them; they rob nests and su the eggs, usually near water. On the other ha crows often are solitary, calling their deep *caw* fr high in a tree. In display the male bows to the fema wings lowered and tail spread. Usually they do r build as high as rooks and often use an isolated tr they may occupy bushes in hill country and ro ledges on the coast. They line the stick, heather, even bone foundation of the nest first with moss a earth, then with wool and plant fibres, and make deep cup in which the sitting female can hardly seen. She incubates the three to five eggs, which a greenish-blue with brown markings, for about 19 day both parents feed the young in the nest for 4 5 weeks.

1 2 3 4 5 6 7 8 9 10 11 12

3 **R A V E N** (*Corvus corax*). The raven, over 2 ft. lor is easily the biggest British passerine (perching bir It is much larger than the carrion crow and also has more wedge-shaped tail, a relatively much bigger b longer neck and wings (*see* flying birds in the plat

Ravens are more or less confined as residents to west and north of Britain and Ireland, inhabiti moorland and mountainous country and sea cli and rocky islands; but in some parts of Wa and elsewhere they also occur on farmland with t trees. They are rarely seen in south-eastern Englan

The deep *cronk cronk* call attracts attention to raven flying purposefully high overhead, looki relatively much longer in the wings and body th other crows, which may sometimes mob it. Rave also perch on prominent rocks and tree-tops, wh their pointed throat feathers stand out. They land the ground to eat carrion, which is their princip food; they also take live birds and eggs, sm mammals and large insects, and some fruit and see At times large parties collect and wheel and soar the air together, and they may form roosts containi dozens of birds. Wonderful aerobatics take place the spring as part of the courtship display. and the are ceremonies on the ground as well. But rave perform flying tricks throughout the year, accom panied by a variety of calls, some remarkably music One of the earliest nesters, they build a foundation sticks or heather stems, lined with wool or hair, on ledge in a cliff or quarry, often overhung, or in a b tree. The three to six eggs are rather more elongate than crow's eggs but similar in colour, and they a incubated mainly by the female for about 3 week The young remain in the nest for 5 or 6 weeks.

1 2 3 4 5 6 7 8 9 10 11 12

1a ROOK. Ads. 1b Juv. 2b HYBRID CROW
2a CARRION CROW 2c HOODED CROW
3a RAVEN. Ad. 3b Juv.

SMALLER CROWS

1 JACKDAW (*Corvus monedula*). Jackdaws usually associate with rooks (p. 125) but are distinctly smaller than rooks, being 13 ins. long. They also have rather short bills, light-coloured eyes, and grey on the back of the neck, or nape. Juveniles are browner and have no grey on the nape.

Though local in the Scottish Highlands and Islands, jackdaws are widespread and often abundant residents throughout the British Isles; also a few Scandinavian birds, which have paler napes, have been recorded. Jackdaw colonies live in habitats of all kinds, from large towns to sea-cliffs, but most of them are near farmland.

The jackdaw's chuckling call sounds above the cawing of the rooks as they fly together to feed or to roost. They feed on grubs and other small invertebrate animals and on fruits and seeds. They haunt chicken runs and chaff heaps, and they take food scraps from bird-tables and rubbish tips. Jackdaws are well-known for their curiosity, 'stealing' brightly coloured objects. They tame easily when young and can be taught to 'talk'. They have a repeated laughing *chacck* call and a quite musical *kyow*. A flock often flies round, calling and chasing, though within the flock the birds are in pairs. They display by bowing to each other, as crows and rooks do. Jackdaws build untidy nests of sticks, lined with wool and paper, in any sort of hole, from a rabbit burrow to a church tower, and the nest may be a foot or more deep or simply a pad of lining. The normal clutch is four to six light blue eggs with fewer dark spots than crow's or rook's eggs. The female incubates for about 17 days; then both parents feed the young, which fledge in about 4½ weeks.

1 2 3 4 5 6 7 8 9 10 11 12

2 CHOUGH (*Pyrrhocorax pyrrhocorax*). Though easy to distinguish on the ground or at close range, a chough on the wing might be taken for a jackdaw if its slender curved bill cannot be seen; but it usually spreads its primary feathers when soaring. It is about 15 ins. long, of which 2 ins. is bill. The young have orange bills.

The chough is a very local resident, no longer in Cornwall, but scattered along the coast of Wales, in the hills of Snowdonia, on the Isle of Man, and in the Inner Hebrides where it may be increasing. In the west of Ireland it is almost common in some areas.

Choughs are usually seen soaring or diving in the up-currents of air along a cliff, their twanging calls sounding above the waves. They feed on grassy slopes or pastures inland, mainly on insect grubs or worms, running or hopping as they search. Pairs nest separately, usually in a cave or old building, or in a wide crevice on a cliff. The nest resembles a jackdaw's, but the three to six eggs are yellowish green with brown markings. The female incubates the clutch for about 18 days; then both parents feed the young, which fledge after about 5 weeks.

1 2 3 4 5 6 7 8 9 10 11 12

3 JAY (*Garrulus glandarius*). Another distinctive bird, about 13½ ins. long, with a conspicuous black tail and white rump, and a black and blue barred speculum (patch) on the wing.

Jays are common residents throughout Englan and Wales but are very local in Scotland; in Irelan they are widespread in eastern counties, and are con sidered to be a distinct race. Continental jays some times arrive in large numbers in autumn. Jays ai woodland birds, originally living in oak forests, bu now in all types, including conifers.

A harsh scolding scream and a catlike mew ai the calls most often heard, but jays have a variety c notes, including a definite song for a short time i spring, and like jackdaws, they are good mimic Their typical food is acorns, but they eat man fruits and seeds and some invertebrate animals, an they attack nests and young of other birds. They sta mainly well hidden in trees and bushes, but hop o the ground, flirting their tails. Their flight is heav and flapping, which is more marked when they ai displaying; there are also noisy spring gathering The light but strong nest of sticks lined with ro hairs is built in a thin tree or bush. The three to s greeny-brown eggs scrawled with black hair-lines a incubated by both parents for 16 days, and tl young are fed for about 3 weeks.

1 2 3 4 5 6 7 8 9 10 11 12

4 MAGPIE (*Pica pica*). Without its distinctive ta which may be up to 10 ins. long, the magpie is quite small bird, about 9 ins. long. Juveniles have short ta at first, but their pied plumage is like the adult's.

The magpie is a common resident througho England and Wales. It is local in Scotland but commo in Ireland, where it first appeared in the 17th centur Its favourite habitat is probably well-wooded farn land; it is often particularly common near towns where there are many tall hedges.

The harsh chatter, the unique long-tailed, broa winged outline and black and white colouring mal the magpie easy to recognise. Though often seen alo or in a pair, they form parties and small flocks, a larger numbers may roost together. Magpies fe mainly on insect grubs but, like other crows, will e a great variety of food and are dangerous to you birds and eggs. On the ground they may take b hops, though they normally walk. They have soc displays, when they make a variety of calls. Magp nest in trees or bushes and build an unmistakal dome of sticks; they line the cup with mud and th with fine root hairs. The female lays five to nine ratl shiny greenish eggs with brown markings and s for 17 to 18 days. The young, fed by both paren fledge in about 3½ weeks.

1 2 3 4 5 6 7 8 9 10 11 12

NUTCRACKER (*Nucifraga caryocatactes*). T races of this rare crow-shaped visitor from Europe conifer forests have occurred in Britain, mostly in t south-east in autumn. It has a long bill, a brown bo spotted with white, black wings, and a black a white tail. There was an unprecedented invasion autumn 1968, involving at least 315 birds of t thin-billed eastern race; some stayed into 1969.

4 MAGPIE
1 JACKDAWS.

3 JAY
2 CHOUGHS

BLACK-HEADED TITS (TITMICE)

1   COAL TIT (*Parus ater*). The smallest of the black-capped tits, under 4½ ins. long, is distinguished from the others by a white patch running up the nape into the cap. The wings have two narrow white bars, and the black bib is prominent against the white cheeks. Juveniles and some Irish birds (1b) are tinged yellow. The coal tit is almost as widely distributed as the great tit but less numerous, except in conifer and highland scrub woods where it is the commonest tit; and there may be one or two wherever there is a clump of firs or even a single large tree. The coal tits of western and southern Ireland are regarded as a distinct race and so are those from the Continent, which occasionally visit Britain.

A thin call-note *zee* and a more powerful song *cher-tee cher-tee*, usually reveal the presence of coal tits; and then they can be seen flitting among the needles of a fir tree. They come to the ground more than other tits and also search trunks for pupae and spiders. They take nuts and conifer seeds and come to bird-tables for them. The nest is a characteristic tit's nest with wool or rabbit fur prominent. It is often built in a mouse run in a bank, among tree roots, or in stone walls. The seven to twelve tiny eggs are of usual tit type; the male feeds the incubating female for about 2 weeks, and both feed the young, which fledge in about 16 days. There is occasionally a second brood.

1   2   3   4   5   6   7   8   9   10   11   12

2   GREAT TIT (*Parus major*). The largest of the British tits is about 5½ ins. long, and can be told from the other black-capped species not only by size but by its greenish upperparts and yellow underparts divided by a black band, which is broader in the male (2a) and expands to cover the belly. Juveniles look duller, with pale yellow cheeks and a dark smoky-brown cap.

The great tit is found throughout wooded districts of Britain and Ireland, and on many of the smaller islands. It is chiefly a bird of broad-leaved woods and a typical garden bird, but does not penetrate as far into cities as the blue tit (p. 131). Birds from the Continent visit Britain in autumn in certain years.

A party of tits, searching twigs and bark and occasionally dropping to the ground, brings the winter woodland to life; among them the ringing calls of the great tits are prominent, or the rapid tapping as they attack an oak gall or nut. They have a great vocabulary of notes, varying in different areas, but the *teacher* or saw-sharpening song is general, and so is a loud call like the chaffinch's *pink*. Great tits eat a variety of insect food, nuts, and buds. In display, the male shows his breast to advantage. Both parents build the nest, a deep cup of moss and wool with vegetable fibres but no feathers, which is placed in a hole in a tree, stump, wall, nestbox, and many odd sites. Up to fifteen white eggs with red spots are laid and covered with moss until the clutch is complete. The female, fed by the male, incubates them for about 2 weeks; then both feed the young, which fledge in about 2½ weeks. There are occasional second broods.

1   2   3   4   5   6   7   8   9   10   11   12

3   WILLOW TIT (*Parus montanus*). It is not safe to distinguish this species from the marsh tit on plumage alone, though usually it has a rather more extensive dark smoky-brown (not shiny black) cap, a less neat bib, and a pale area on the secondary flight feathers. But juvenile marsh tits also have smoky-brown caps and look rather 'untidy'. The most certain way to identify the willow tit is by its squeezed out *tcha, tchay tchay* call, much harsher than the *tchee* call of the marsh tit, and often introduced by a quiet *zi-zit*. The usual song is a drawn out *tew tew tew*, but sometimes birds utter a rich, continuous warbling song.

Willow tits are found locally through England and Wales and in southern Scotland, and occasionally in the Highlands; they are unknown in Ireland. Their main habitats are wettish ground with alders and birches and also quite dry woods on downland with old elder bushes.

Willow tits usually forage alone or in pairs and dive into thick cover, quite unlike other tits. They take the natural food of tits but rarely come to bird-tables. They excavate their nest-holes usually in stumps or dead trees, making an oval entrance and leaving the chips below. The nest is a small pad of moss and fur in which six to ten typical tit eggs are laid and incubated by the female for 13 days. The young are fed by both parents and fly in about 18 days.

1   2   3   4   5   6   7   8   9   10   11   12

4   MARSH TIT (*Parus palustris*). This neat little bird, about 4½ ins. long, is easily told from great and coal tits, but not at all easily from the willow tit.

Marsh tits are well distributed throughout England and Wales, but only reach the extreme south of Scotland and are unknown in Ireland. They avoid fir woods, and seem to be most numerous in woods with ash trees. Though they join in parties of other species they are seldom found in numbers; often a pair will forage alone, perhaps attacking the heads of the tall marsh thistles in late summer. Their food is much the same as that of other tits, and they will come to bird-tables, often flying off with a morsel to store it in a crevice. The typical calls are *pitchoo* and a scolding *tchee tchee tchee tchee*; the song, often uttered high in a tree, is *tschuppi tschuppi tschuppi*. The male flutters his wings in display. The nest is built in a cavity of a tree, preferably with a very small entrance and is lined with moss, wool, and fur. Seven to ten white eggs with red spots are the usual clutch, which the female incubates for about 13 days. Both parents feed the young, which fly after about 16 days.

1   2   3   4   5   6   7   8   9   10   11   12

1a COAL TIT
2a GREAT TIT, M.
3   WILLOW TIT

1b COAL TIT, Irish race
2b GREAT TIT, F.
4   MARSH TIT.

OTHER TITS (TITMICE)

1 BLUE TIT (*Parus caeruleus*). This familiar garden bird is about 4½ ins. long and easily distinguished from any other tit by its blue crown and generally blue and yellow plumage. The female (1b) is rather less bright than the male (1c) and has greener secondary flight feathers; the young birds (1a) have yellowish cheeks.

Blue tits are even more widely distributed residents than great tits (p. 128), because they go further into cities; but they are scarce in pure conifer woods. Birds of the Continental race sometimes invade Britain in autumn. Tits freely visit the bird-table, especially where coconuts, fat, or nuts are hung up. They are acrobatic little birds, as happy upside down as upright, searching for food in cracks and crannies. Both blue and great tits have learned to prise off milk bottle lids, and blue tits sometimes enter houses to attack paper and cloth.

The usual call is a rather scolding *tsee tsee tsit*, which is the basis of the spring song. In display both sexes raise their crown feathers and wings, and the male makes slow 'butterfly' or dancing 'gnat' flights. Blue tits eat a variety of small creatures, seeds, and fruits, as well as scraps. Like great tits, they take readily to nest boxes as an alternative to natural tree holes; in some areas they seem to prefer stone walls, and they have nested in many odd sites. Up to sixteen rather round eggs of tit type are laid in a nest often lined with feathers on a foundation of moss and plant fibres. The female incubates them for about 2 weeks, and both parents feed the young which fly in about 2½ weeks.

*1 2 3 **4 5 6** 7 8 9 10 11 12*

2 CRESTED TIT (*Parus cristatus*). About the same size as a blue tit, the adult is distinguished by its crest, which is shorter and darker in young birds. The resident Scottish race is confined to the old native pine and some new conifer forests in the north central Highlands, chiefly in Strathspey. Occasional birds reported elsewhere may have wandered from the Continent.

The purring call, rendered *pturr-ree-ree-ree*, is the best evidence that crested tits are hunting food in a fir wood. They search like other tits, feeding in summer mainly on insects, in autumn and winter on pine seeds as well. They also have a sharp *zee zee zee* call and a trilling song, which the male uses when chasing the female on courtship. The female excavates a hole for the nest, of moss and other soft material, the male accompanying her. The five to seven eggs usually have a zone of red spots, and the female, fed by the male, hatches them in about 2 weeks. She also feeds the young, which fledge in 16 to 18 days.

*1 2 3 **4 5 6** 7 8 9 10 11 12*

PENDULINE TIT (*Remiz pendulinus*). Now usually regarded as a member of the family *Remizidae*, this species from the wetlands of central and southern Europe has occurred once, in Yorkshire in 1966. The adult, 4½ ins. long, is distinguished by its grey head and thick black mask; the back is chestnut, the underparts pale buff, and the juvenile is pale grey-brown all over.

3 LONG-TAILED TIT (*Aegithalos caudatus*). With out the 3 in. tail, this tit is one of the smallest British birds, with a 2½ in. body. Young birds are duller and have shorter tails. The long-tailed tit is widely distributed in the British Isles, in woodland and scrub of all types, though rare in dense conifer forest. The white-headed race from northern Europe (3a) has been recorded in Britain.

A party of long-tailed tits, uttering their shrill mouse-like *zee zee zee* and more distinctive *zup* calls, bob up and down in flight like small balls with tails attached, then swarm all over a tree. They feed almost entirely on insects and other small creatures and suffer disastrously in hard winters. While other tits roost singly in holes, they sit huddled together on a branch. Their display consists of chases and butterfly flights. The nest is unique in Britain: an oval ball of moss covered with lichen, with a small hole near the top, placed in the fork of a tree or bush or hanging in brambles and briars. It may be lined with as many as 2,000 feathers. The female lays up to twelve rather round whitish eggs zoned with tiny red spots, and both sexes usually share the incubation for about 2 weeks. The male brings food for the female to pass to the young, which fly after about 15 days.

*1 2 **3** 4 **5 6** 7 8 9 10 11 12*

4 BEARDED TIT (*Panarus biarmicus*). Larger and rather different from other tits, the bearded tit is about 6½ ins. long, of which 3 ins. is tail. The male (4a) has a remarkable head pattern, which the female (4b) lacks. The young birds resemble her, but are darker on the back and tail, and the males show a small black eye stripe.

Bearded tits now nest in the reed-beds of East Anglia, Essex and Kent and have bred recently in Anglesey (1967), and at least four other English counties after autumn irruptions.

When moving through the reeds, bearded tits can be recognised by their call, a rather penetrating *ping ping — tick*. They may appear for a moment then drop out of sight again. They are dependent in winter on the reed seeds, but feed their young on caterpillars and insects. Males and females show off their plumage when courting and make display flights. The open nest, low down in the reeds, is built of reeds, lined by the male with flowering heads. Five to seven white eggs with brown streaks and spots are laid, and are incubated for 12 to 13 days by both parents; both also feed the young, which may leave the nest in less than 10 days and clamber about the reeds. There are two, sometimes three, broods in a season.

*1 2 3 **4 5 6** 7 8 9 10 11 12*

1a BLUE TIT, Juv.   1b F.   1c M.   3a LONG-TAILED TIT. Northern   3b British, and nest

2 CRESTED TIT

4a BEARDED TIT, M.   4b F.

CREEPERS AND NUTHATCH

1 TREECREEPER (*Certhia familiaris*). The tree-creeper is about 5 ins. long and has dark-brown mottled plumage with paler spots above and pure white below. There is a pale stripe over the eye, and the rump, seen in flight, is reddish; the wings look rounded and transparent; the stiff tail is fan-shaped; and the bill is long, thin, and curved. The sexes are alike but young birds are more spotted and yellowish.

Although confined to woodland or well-wooded country, the treecreeper is a generally distributed resident in the British Isles. A few individuals of the northern European race have occurred in Scotland.

Running up a treetrunk or along the underside of a branch the creeper is more likely to be mistaken for a mouse than for any other bird. Having worked up to a certain height, it then flutters down and starts again, or flits off to another tree. Like nuthatches, a pair may join a tit flock, but parties of treecreepers are exceptional.

The shrill call can be confused with those of the coal tit (p. 128), the long-tailed tit (p. 130) and the gold-crest (p. 158), but the rather explosive song phrase is distinctive once it has been heard several times; the bird seldom utters it twice in the same place. The food, winkled out of cracks in the bark, is almost entirely eggs, pupae, larvae, and adults of insects and spiders. Treecreepers seem better able to survive hard winters than goldcrests and long-tailed tits; they roost in hollows excavated in rotten wood or the soft bark of Wellingtonia trees. The display includes chases, often spirally round tree trunks. The nest is unique among British birds' nests; it has an oval cup and is typically wedged behind loose bark on a foundation of rotten wood and sticks, and is lined with moss and feathers. Four to seven eggs, marked like tits' eggs, are incubated mainly by the female for about 2 weeks, but both parents feed the young, which fledge after about 2 weeks. A second brood often follows, sometimes in the same nest.

1 2 3 4 5 6 7 8 9 10 11 12

SHORT-TOED TREECREEPER (*Certhia brachy-dactyla*). This is not strictly a British bird because it is resident in the Channel Isles and has never been recorded in Britain. It may easily have been over-looked because it is so like the common species. The shorter hind claw can, in fact, seldom be seen, but it has a rather longer bill and buff on the flanks. The call-note is louder, the song is a much louder but shorter phrase, and the male often sings from the top of a tree, holding his head upward and bill wide open. In general habits this species resembles the common treecreeper, which it replaces in much of Western Europe

2 WALLCREEPER (*Tichodroma muraria*). Seven of these beautifully coloured grey, black, and crimson birds from the mountains of Europe have been seen in England. They are 6½ ins. long, with thin curved bills, and are most likely to be seen, living up to their name, on a rock or building. In flight white spots show on the rounded wings.

3 NUTHATCH (*Sitta europaea*). No other British bird has the same squat form, short tail, and long bill, together with a pleasing combination of colours. It is about 5½ ins. long. The female is paler on the flanks than the male, the young are duller.

The nuthatch is a resident, widespread in southern England and Wales, but becoming local in the north and only known in Scotland as a very rare visitor, though there have been attempts to introduce it there and in Ireland. It is a bird of oak and beech woods or gardens where these trees grow, and is a ready visitor to the bird-table.

Its loud *wit wit wit* call or alternative songs, a repeated *chuchuch chuchuch* or ringing *pee pee pee* rather like the cries of kestrels, wrynecks, and lesser spotted woodpeckers, identify the nuthatch when the foliage is thick. As a climber it is superior even to woodpeckers because it can not only go up but also down a trunk head first, and does not use its tail for support. It takes insects in summer, especially for its young, but feeds on tree-fruits of many kinds, wedging hard nuts in cracks and hammering them open. Although pairs may join tit flocks, nuthatches do not form parties on their own. The white spots on the tail, seldom seen, are used in the display, which includes a 'floating' flight and chases; and there are special calls in the breeding season. Nuthatches have the habit, unique in Britain, of reducing the diameter of their nest-hole by applying wet mud, worked in with the bill; the nest is a loose collection of dead leaves and bark in which the five to nine white eggs, boldly marked with red-brown, are hidden when the female is not sitting. The naked young hatch in 2 weeks and are fed by both parents; they fly after 3½ weeks.

1 2 3 4 5 6 7 8 9 10 11 12

1 TREECREEPER   3 NUTHATCH
2 WALLCREEPER

WRENS AND DIPPERS

1 **WREN** (*Troglodytes troglodytes*). This round little bird, under 4 ins. long, is easy to recognise, especially by the upright tilt of its tail; but when their tails are lowered, wrens can be mistaken for the short-tailed juveniles of other species. The sexes are alike, and the juveniles are similar to the adults, though more mottled.

Wrens are among the most widely distributed of common British residents. They live from the outskirts of towns to the tops of the hills at 3,000 ft., and on sea-cliffs and bare, rocky islands. Besides the distinct island races (2), there are passage migrants from Europe along the east coast.

The perky wren, with its loud song bursts and scolding chatter, flitting with a whirr of short, round wings about the garden, is almost as well known as the robin. It feeds mainly on insects and spiders at all stages of their development and is therefore a difficult bird to help in hard winters, when many die, sometimes clustered together in a roosting hole. But in a few years its numbers are up again. Wrens have many calls, from the *tic tic tic* of alarm to the thin wheezing food-cry of the juveniles just out of the nest. The male sings his explosive, rattling song all through the year and combines it when displaying with movements of tail and wings. He builds several rough domed nests of leaves, grass or straw, moss or bracken, and the female selects one and lines it with feathers. Sites vary from the fork of a bush to a hole in the wall and the old nests of other birds. The female sits on five to seven white eggs with faint dark markings for about 2 weeks; both parents usually feed the young, which are fledged in up to 2½ weeks. The female has two broods, and males often have more than one mate.

*1 2 3 **4 5 6** 7 **8** 9 10 11 12*

2 **ST. KILDA WREN** (*Troglodytes troglodytes hirtensis*). This is not a separate species but a distinct island race of the common wren on St. Kilda in the Outer Hebrides. It is larger, greyer, and rather paler above. In habits it is like the common wren but has an even louder song. Besides the St. Kilda wren, the wrens of Shetland, Fair Isle, and the Hebrides are considered to form distinct races.

3 **DIPPER** (*Cinclus cinclus*). A stout black and white bird which might be described as a thrush with the shape of a wren. It is about 7 ins. long. The British race is distinguished by a chestnut band between the dark belly and the white breast. This is lacking in Continental dippers (3c) and less marked in Irish birds, which are darker above. Juveniles (3a) look dark grey above and scaly in their first winter, due to the pale tips to the feathers.

Typically a bird of fast-flowing water, the dipper is resident throughout the highland parts of the British Isles, though sometimes very local; elsewhere it is an occasional visitor. Outside the breeding season it visits the shores of lochs and lakes and sheltered coasts near the mouths of rivers.

Its bobbing action on a stone, followed by rapid whirring flight usually over the water, is as characteristic as the dipper's shape and plumage. Alone of British passerines (perching birds) it habitually swims and dives (its method of progress underwater has been the subject of much argument), because it feeds mainly on the larvae of water insects and small fishes. It has a loud call in flight, rendered *clink clink* and an attractive warbling song which can sometimes only just be heard above the accompanying water-music, and is uttered by both sexes, often in winter. There is a mutual bobbing display, and the male repeatedly brings his white eyelid over his eye. The nest, built by both sexes of wet moss, is like a big wren's nest, domed and tucked into a crevice or hollow over the water. A favourite site is under a bridge, supported by a beam or girder. Occasionally nests are built on exposed stones or tree branches. The nest has a cup of grasses and lining of dead leaves, on which four to six pointed white eggs are laid. The female incubates them for up to 2½ weeks, and both parents feed the young, which fly after about 3 weeks. There are two broods in the season. Dippers do not flock and stick strictly to territories. Continental black-bellied dippers are rare visitors in winter.

*1 2 **3 4 5 6** 7 8 **9 10** 11 12*

1 WREN
3a DIPPER, Juv. swimming

2 ST. KILDA WREN
3b DIPPER, Ad.
3c DIPPER, Black-bellied

1 FIELDFARE (*Turdus pilaris*). A common winter visitor, nearly as big as a mistle thrush (about 10 ins. long), but easy to separate in a good light because of its brighter colours, especially the grey rump and dark tail, which show up in flight. It is generally distributed in open wooded country from the outskirts of towns to the edge of the moors.

Fieldfares often mix with redwings, whose sharper notes mingle with the loud *chack chack* of the bigger birds as they fly over in loose flocks. They feed together in the fields, landing first in a hedge and working outwards, running a few steps, then standing up to look round. They take grubs and worms, and clean the berries from the hawthorns and other bushes. In hard weather they suffer severely. They roost with other thrushes in thick cover. Towards spring fieldfares become restless, moving about locally before departing to their breeding areas in Scandinavia and eastern Europe. Since 1967 fieldfares have nested in Orkney, Shetland, Inverness and one English county.

1 2 3 4 5 (6) . (8) 9 10 11 12

2 REDWING (*Turdus iliacus*). This common winter visitor, rather smaller than a song thrush (about 8¼ ins. long), has grey-brown upperparts, a pale stripe over the eye, and a 'red' (orange-chestnut) patch on the flanks and under the wings.

Early in October redwings can be heard overhead at night, and can be recognised by their *tseep* notes, similar to but more drawn-out than the song thrush's flight call. Their general feeding habits resemble those of fieldfares, but they come more readily to gardens, even entering central London in hard weather. Early in spring flocks sit in trees or bushes, twittering musically, with occasional phrases of the true song: *cher cher cher*. Many pairs now breed in northern Scotland; their nests and eggs are similar to but slightly smaller than those of the blackbird (p. 138). Some Scottish nests have been in bushes near houses, but in Scandinavia birches and firs are typical sites.

1 2 3 4 (5 6 7 8) 9 10 11 12

3 MISTLE THRUSH (*Turdus viscivorus*). This is the biggest thrush, 10½ ins. long. Its bounding flight is like that of the green woodpecker or little owl. Its upperparts are more uniform grey-brown than those of the fieldfare or song thrush. It has a longer tail than the song thrush, with pale outer feathers, a paler, more densely spotted breast, and white underwings (see bird in flight opposite). Young birds (3b) have pale markings on their upperparts.

The mistle thrush is a common resident, migrating locally in winter. Its habitats range from cities to bare uplands. Its rattling cries often warn the garden that a cat is about, and birds with young will dive-bomb enemies fiercely. Mistle thrushes feed in the fields, and take berries in autumn, and they seldom come to bird-tables. Their song, delivered from a high perch, is a ringing phrase, similar to but less fluting than the blackbird's. They begin to pair in autumn, and hop from branch to branch as though trying out possible nest-sites. The nest may be from 5 to 50 ft. high in a tree, often on a horizontal bough, sometimes on a building or rocky ledge. The female incubates 3 to 5 buff or pale blue eggs, spotted with red-brown, for 13 to 14 days; both parents feed the young, which fly in about 2 weeks. There are usually two broods in a season.

1 2 3 4 5 6 7 8 9 10 11 12

4 SONG THRUSH (*Turdus philomelos*). One of the most familiar garden birds, smaller than the mistle thrush (about 9 ins. long), with warmer brown upperparts and yellowish upper breast with more scattered spots. It has an orange patch on the flanks and underwing (see bird in flight opposite), and no stripe over the eye, as the redwing has. Young birds (4a) have light spots on their upperparts.

Song thrushes are residents, summer and winter visitors, and passage migrants. They breed anywhere from remote islands to city parks. They sing for most of the year, and for longer periods than blackbirds, often repeating phrases like *katydid katydid katydid*, or mimicking other birds. The call-note is a sharp *tsip*. They eat insects, worms, and berries, but their special diet is snails, which they hammer on chosen stones or bits of metal, leaving a mass of broken shells. They are noted for persistent fights and chases during the breeding season, chattering and screaming as they fly. They build in a variety of trees and bushes, in ivy on walls and banks, and sometimes on the ground; they make a foundation of moss or stems, and plaster the cup with a hard lining of mud, wood chips, or dung. Their blue eggs with black spots are like no other eggs. The female sits on the clutch of three to five eggs for 13 to 14 days. Both parents feed the young and defend them fiercely until they fly after about 2 weeks. They rear two or three broods a year. Parties seen in winter are probably visitors from Europe.

1 2 3 4 5 6 7 8 9 10 11 12

1 FIELDFARES
3a MISTLE THRUSH, Ad. 3b in flight 3c Juv.

2 REDWINGS
4a SONG THRUSH, Juv. 4b Ad. 4c in flight

THRUSHES. 2

1 R I N G O U S E L (*Turdus torquatus*). The 'mountain blackbird' is 9½ ins. long. The male is dark grey rather than black and has a distinctive white half-collar in front, and the wings when closed look paler than the body. The female is browner, rather scaly-looking, and has a duller half-collar. The juveniles are like grey young blackbirds. A partly albino blackbird can easily be mistaken for a ring ousel.

Ring ousels are summer residents in highland areas from south-west England to northern Scotland, probably being most numerous in the north of England and parts of Scotland. They are very local in Ireland and the Inner Hebrides. Passage migrants occur elsewhere in spring and autumn.

A flurry of wings along a heathery hillside and a loud clacking call are often the first signs of a ring ousel. They are not easy birds to approach, but at a distance a male will perch on a rock or cliff-top to sing his ringing *tew tew tew*. Ring ousels feed on small creatures from the soil and feast on moorland berries later in the season. Several pairs often occupy an area of steep banks or low rock faces, where they build their nests, often well hidden by long heather or woodrush. Elsewhere they use old buildings and walls. The nest is like a blackbird's, usually with a peat layer, and the three to five eggs are like well-marked blackbirds' eggs. Both sexes incubate them for about 2 weeks and feed the young, which fledge in another 2 weeks. There are usually two broods, after which family parties move about the hills and valleys; passage birds are seen in the south, often on downland, feeding in the hedges.

(1 2) 3 4 5 6 7 8 9 10 (11 12)

2 B L A C K B I R D (*Turdus merula*). The commonest of the British thrushes is a little larger than a ring ousel, 10 ins. long. It has an unmistakable adult male plumage (2d), but young males (2a) have dark bills and brown patches on the wings. The dark brown females (2c) are variable, some having quite light, speckled breasts. Juveniles (2b) are rusty-brown on the head, breast, and upper back, and there is a confusing stage when young males have black bodies and light heads. Males in particular tend to have some white feathers, and piebald or completely albino birds are not rare.

Blackbirds are residents or summer visitors throughout the British Isles; and many winter visitors and passage migrants occur along the east coast in autumn. They breed in almost all habitats, with or without trees, from city centres to the edge of the moors at 2,000 ft.

A blackbird hopping on the lawn and 'listening' for worms is a familiar sight; few gardens are without a pair. They feed on the same variety of foods as other thrushes, eat scraps freely, and even rob song thrushes of their snails, though they do not break the shells themselves. Among many call notes the *tchook*, uttered at dusk and repeated to make a chattering alarm, is the best known. The song, heard mainly at dawn and dusk is simple, mellow, and fluting, but individual birds have their own variations. Males and females as well as birds of the same sex often have

fights, and in autumn there are early morning gatherings of both sexes. The large nest, of moss or grass stems and other materials, has a thick mud cup and inner lining of fine grass. It is built in a great variety of sites from ground level to 40 ft. high and is often used twice. The female incubates the three to five greenish eggs with brown markings, which hatch in about 13 days; both parents feed the young, which fly in about the same time. Two or three broods are raised but many pairs lose several clutches and may easily build half a dozen nests in a season. Blackbirds do not flock but parties gather in autumn where food is plentiful, for example fallen apples in an orchard.

1 2 3 4 5 6 7 8 9 10 11 12

T H R U S H E S F R O M A S I A . There have been occasional visits from four species from Asia. The biggest, W H I T E ' S T H R U S H (*Turdus dauma*), has occurred about thirty times, mostly in winter in England. It looks rather like a juvenile mistle thrush but has a distinctive black and white pattern under the wing. The D U S K Y T H R U S H (*Turdus eunomus*) about the size of a song thrush, has a white stripe over the eye, a white throat, dark scaly upperparts and chestnut on the wing. Five have occurred in England and Scotland, two of which were recorded in 1961. The B L A C K - T H R O A T E D T H R U S H (*Turdus ruficollis*) is like a small fieldfare in shape and has a black or densely spotted throat and uniform brown upperparts. There are English records in 1868 and 1879 and a male appeared on Fair Isle, Shetland, in 1957. A male S I B E R I A N T H R U S H (*Turdus sibiricus*) occurred on the Isle of May, Fife, in 1954; it is about 9 ins. long, and is distinctively dark slate grey with white stripe over the eye; the female looks rather like a scaly song thrush. E Y E - B R O W E D T H R U S H (*Turdus obscurus*). There are now three records of this Asiatic species, all in autumn 1964. Its upperparts are olive brown, the crown is grey, there is a white stripe above the eye and a white patch on the chin. The grey upper breast contrasts with buff on the sides and flank.

A M E R I C A N T H R U S H E S . Three species have been recorded in recent years. In spite of its name, the A M E R I C A N R O B I N (*Turdus migratorius*) is the North American counterpart of the blackbird. Its upperparts are dark grey, and the male's head almost black; both sexes have white throats, streaked with black, and brick-red breasts. One was caught on Lundy in the British Channel in 1952 and eleven more have been recorded since then, three in Ireland, five in England and three in Scotland. The G R E Y - C H E E K E D T H R U S H (*Hylocichla minima*) has been reported seven times since 1953, four in Scotland, two in Wales and one in England. It is about 7 ins. long and looks like a small song thrush, with grey cheeks and a narrow buff ring round the eye. The O L I V E - B A C K E D T H R U S H (*Hylocichla ustulata*) has occurred three times, twice in Ireland (1958, 1968) and once in Wales (1967). It is very like the previous species but has a broader eye-ring.

1a RING OUSEL, M.

2a BLACKBIRD, M., first winter

2c BLACKBIRD, F., and young

1b F.   1c Juv.

2b BLACKBIRD, Juv.

2d BLACKBIRD, M.

WHEATEARS AND CHATS

ROCKTHRUSH (*Monticola saxatilis*). About 7½ ins. long, the colourful male has a grey-blue head, white patch on the lower back, and orange-red underparts and tail. The female has the same bright tail, but is otherwise scaly brown, and the male in winter resembles her. Rockthrushes inhabit rocky areas of central Europe. Ten have now occurred in Britain, one each in 1969 and 1970.

1 **WHEATEAR** (*Oenanthe oenanthe*). A plump passerine, about 6 ins. long, with distinct male and female spring plumages. The male looks like the female in autumn (1c), and juveniles are spotted; but in all plumages the black and white tail distinguishes wheatears from whinchats or stonechats.

The wheatear is a summer visitor which nests very locally in south-eastern England, but is commoner in the west and north. Its habitat is uncultivated open country of all kinds, and on passage it also appears on ploughed fields and fallows. Some of the passage birds are of a bigger race which breeds in Greenland and Iceland.

Passage birds are usually silent, but in their breeding haunts wheatears constantly utter their *whip cluck cluck* calls and in spring their wheezy but rather attractive song, as they flirt their black and white tails or perform their dancing display flights. They feed mainly on insects, carrying them from the richer grassland to their nests in the rocks. These are built in holes or crevices at varying depths, and are made of grass stems, wool, and fur. The four to six pale blue eggs are incubated, chiefly by the female, for up to 2 weeks. Both parents feed the young, which fly in just over 2 weeks. There is sometimes a second brood.

(1 2) 3 **4 5 6** *7 8 9 10 (11)* .

MEDITERRANEAN WHEATEARS. Five species are rare visitors to Britain. Two races of the **BLACK-EARED WHEATEAR** (*Oenanthe hispanica*) have been recorded twenty-one times. The males either have black throats or broad black stripes through the eye; both races have bright brown and white upperparts, black wings, and more white on their tails than the common wheatear. The female has no black on her head and much lighter upperparts than a common wheatear. The sandy-coloured **DESERT WHEATEAR** (*Oenanthe deserti*), now recorded eighteen times, mainly on the east coast in autumn, has more black and very little white on its tail; both sexes have dark wings, and the male has a black throat. Four **PIED WHEATEARS** (*Oenanthe leucomela*) from south-eastern Europe and Asia have occurred in autumn, the last in 1968. The male has a black throat and both sexes have more black on the tail than the common wheatear, but in autumn are very much like the black-eared wheatear. A single **ISABELLINE WHEATEAR** (*Oenanthe isabellina*) occurred in Cumberland in 1887. It is about 6½ ins.

long, pale, and sandy, with lighter wings than a desert wheatear and much more white on its rump. The **BLACK WHEATEAR** (*Oenanthe leucura*), about 7 ins. long, is black or very dark brown all over, except for the white rump and part of the tail. There are five records between 1912 and 1964, two on Fair Isle.

2 **WHINCHAT** (*Saxicola rubetra*). The adults are lighter in colour, both above and below, than stonechats; and they have pale stripes over the eye and white on the sides of the tail. Both species have white on the wing and are about 5 ins. long. In autumn male whinchats are more like the duller female (2a). Juveniles, which show less eye stripe, can be confused with stonechats, but their breasts are brighter.

Whinchats are summer visitors, commonest in the west and north of Britain, and local in Ireland; birds on passage may be seen in other areas. Their favourite habitat is heath or rough grassland with bracken and low bushes; they are often plentiful in new plantations, along railway embankments, and on the uncultivated edges of farmland.

Both small chats perch typically on the topmost spray of a bush or plant, flicking tail and wings. The whinchat's call-note is *tcha*; if young are about, the parents also call *tick tick* or *tu-tick*. The song is a brief rather wheezing phrase, which often includes some mimicry of other birds. They feed on insects, worms, and spiders, sometimes catching prey on the wing. The nest is usually well-hidden in a grass tussock and made largely of grass by the female. She lays five or six blue-green eggs and incubates them for 13 days, being called off by the male when danger threatens. Both parents feed the young, which leave the nest before they can fly properly; there is sometimes a second brood.

. . *(3)* **4 5 6** *7 8 9 10 (11)*

3 **STONECHAT** (*Saxicola torquata*). Stonechats are more round-headed than whinchats; the differences in plumage is described under 'Whinchat'. The severe winters of the 1940's caused resident stonechats to disappear from many inland areas where they used to nest, and many died in the winter of 1962-3. But they are still found all along the west coast of Britain and in Ireland. They are more generally distributed in winter and on passage. Heaths and moorland with heather and gorse are their breeding habitat; at other times they haunt open rough ground and waste places, often near water.

In general behaviour, food, and nesting habits stonechats resemble whinchats, but they have a louder alarm note, like pebbles knocking together, and the male often sings during the dancing display flight. The grass nest has a soft lining, and the eggs are paler than whinchats', with a zone of small reddish spots. Two broods are usual.

1 2 **3 4 5 6** *7 8 9 10 11 12*

3a STONECHAT, M.   3b F.   3c Juv.   2c WHINCHAT, Juv. 2b M. 2a F.

1b WHEATEAR, F.   1c WHEATEAR, M., autumn

                        1a WHEATEAR, M., spring

1 BLACK REDSTART (*Phoenicurus obscurus*). All plumages of this species are some shade of grey or black, which distinguishes them from the common redstart, though both have similar chestnut-red tails, and are the same size, about 5½ ins. long. Males in full plumage (1b) have white wing-bars and occasionally some white on the forehead; but they often breed in 'immature' dress (1c).

Although there had been occasional breeding records for many years, it was only during the 1940's that black redstarts, which are numerous across the Channel, began to colonise England as summer visitors, using the many nest-sites provided by bombed buildings. Odd birds or pairs reached South Wales, and the North of England, but more recently, apart from a nest in Northumberland in 1962, breeding has been confined to the south-east and the Midlands. Black redstarts are much more widespread as winter visitors and on passage, and are found in Ireland and south-west Scotland, as well as in Wales and along the south coast of England, usually in open rocky areas.

In general behaviour they resemble the common redstart, but spend more time on the ground; abroad they are the typical bird of towns, villages, and farms, and often appear in such places in Britain, hunting for insects on walls and in odd corners. They also eat berries. The call-note is less plaintive but the alarm notes much the same as common redstarts'; the song has a short, loud phrase, followed by a curious rattle, which is sometimes left out. The male begins to sing very early in the morning, above the sound of early morning traffic. The nest, similar to the common redstart's, is built in a hole in a wall or building or on a ledge in a shed; the hen incubates the four to six white eggs for about 13 days; then both parents feed the young, which fledge in about 16 days. There are usually two broods.

1 2 3 **4 5 6** *7 8 9 10 11 12*

2 REDSTART (*Phoenicurus phoenicurus*). About 5½ ins. long, the male redstart's plumage (2b) is distinctive. The female (2a) is much browner than the female black redstart, and the juvenile is spotted, very like a young robin but with a chestnut-red tail. Some females in spring resemble the duller autumn males (2c).

A summer visitor of general distribution, the common redstart is local or scarce in south-eastern England and most numerous in highland districts of the west, Wales, the north of England, and Scotland; it sometimes nests in Ireland. It occurs more widely on passage. Its breeding habitats are various, including old trees or buildings with holes; in the south it is found along rivers with pollard willows, and is common in western and northern scrubwoods and round farms.

In spring a male redstart in good light, with his tail quivering as he perches between fly-catching flights, is a beautiful bird. With their long legs, redstarts are as much at home on the ground as in trees, though they prefer to be aloft. They feed mainly on insects, taking larvae to their young, and they eat berries in late summer. The call is a long *wheet* like one note of the chaffinch (p. 184); the alarm is a loud *whee-tuck* or *whee-tuck-tuck*, while the rather short song begins strongly and tails off; some males are good mimics. In display the male chases the female, then courts her, flirting his tail. The female builds the nest in a hole in an old tree or stonework, in a bank, on a ledge, in nestboxes, and in the old nests of other birds; in some districts redstarts make tunnels in the grass, as chats do (p. 140). The nest has a foundation of moss, grasses, and bark, and is lined with hair and feathers. The female incubates the clutch of five to eight rather pointed greeny-blue eggs for 13 days, and both parents feed the young, which fledge in 14 to 15 days. There is sometimes a second brood, for which the birds may re-mate.

. . (*3*) **4 5 6** *7 8 9 10* (*11*) .

RED-FLANKED BLUETAIL (*Tarsiger cyanurus*). There are four British records of this Asiatic species, which seems to be moving westward into Europe. The male has blue upperparts, white underparts, and orange-red flank patches; females and immature males have the bright flank patches but dull blue tails and brown upperparts. The blue tail is the same size and shape as a redstart's tail.

3 BLUETHROAT (*Cyanosylvia svecica*). A robin-like bird, about 5½ ins. long, usually seen in Britain in varying autumn plumages (3c), but always with a darkish back and a reddish base to the dark tail. Only the males of the two races which occur, the white-spotted northern (3a) and red-spotted southern (3b), can be told apart, and then only in spring dress. But bluethroats can be recognised by their generally pale underparts with more or less blue, black, and chestnut on the throat and upper breast.

The red-spotted race is a regular autumn visitor on passage to the east coast of Britain, more occasional on the south coast, and rare elsewhere. About half a dozen certain records of the white-spotted males have been made. A pair, race unknown, attempted to breed in Inverness-shire in 1968. In Britain, the bluethroat is a shy bird, keeping to thick coastal cover. It feeds on insects, small molluscs, worms, and berries, and hops and flies like a robin. The call notes resemble those of redstarts, a harsh *tack* and piping *wheet*.

. . . (*4*) 5 (6 . 8) 9 *10* . .

1a BLACK REDSTART, F.   1b M., summer   1c M., Imm.
2a REDSTART, F.   2b M., spring   2c M., autumn
3a WHITE-SPOTTED BLUETHROAT, M., Imm.   3b RED-SPOTTED BLUETHROAT, M.   3c F., autumn

1 R O B I N (*Erithacus rubecula*). Although the plump, long-legged robin is so well known, the spotted juvenile (1a) is not always recognised, nor is the moulting bird when only the lower part of the breast is red. The sexes are alike, but the amount of red on the breast varies in individual birds.

Robins are residents throughout Britain and Ireland, though also many emigrate, and visitors arrive on the east coast in autumn, some staying the winter. Originally a woodland bird, the robin is now particularly associated with gardens in Britain.

Although they take berries from bushes, robins feed largely on the ground, searching soil and leaf litter for worms and grubs. They take big hops and have a rather fluttering flight over short distances. The usual call is a hard *tick tick*; in the breeding season there is drawn-out *tseee*. The song, uttered by both sexes in winter, is a simple phrase which changes in quality after the summer moult. Robins keep to their territories, except in hard weather, and fights and displays along the edges are common, the birds spreading their breasts and swaying from side to side as they face each other. The nest, usually with a frontage of dead leaves, is made of moss and lined with hair, and is placed in some sort of hollow: in a bank, wall, tree-stump, old tin, and in many curious places, even in occupied houses. The four to six eggs are white with light red spots; the female, fed at times by the male, sits on them for 13 to 14 days, and the young, fed by both parents, fly in about the same time. There are two or three broods.

1 2 3 4 5 6 7 8 9 10 11 12

2 N I G H T I N G A L E (*Luscinia megarhyncha*). This most celebrated of all song-birds is 6½ ins. long and looks like a big robin from behind, though it has brighter brown upperparts and a conspicuously reddish tail. The sexes are alike.

Nightingales are summer visitors to England south and east of a line between the Severn and the Humber. Odd birds appear outside this line and may sing for a time, and some may travel on passage along the east coast. The breeding habitat is thick cover of brambles and nettles, in or near broad-leaved woodland or scrub.

The famous song is often unrecognised in day-time, and almost any bird singing at night is reported as a 'nightingale'; but it is unmistakable once heard: a mixture of *jug jug* sequences, croaks, and long drawn-out notes which have led poets to think of it as 'sad'; it is delivered in sudden loud bursts. The call-notes are of the *wheet* and *tack* type common in the family, and there is a loud scolding note. Nightingales are hard to see, for they keep to thick cover in which they feed on berries and insects and worms from the ground. The tail is used in display. The foundation of the nest is of dead leaves, with a cup of grasses and hair; it is placed on or near the ground under cover. The female incubates the four to six eggs, which are glossy brown all over, and hatch in 13 or 14 days; then both parents feed the brood, which fledges in 10 to 12 days.

. . (3) 4 5 6 7 8 9 (10) . .

T H R U S H N I G H T I N G A L E or Sprosser (*Luscinia luscinia*). The northern counterpart of the nightingale has been recorded sixteen times, mainly in Scotland, but as it and the common nightingale are almost indistinguishable, there may have been others. This species has faint streaks on the breast and a greyer back. Its song is louder than the nightingale's but not so musical.

3 D U N N O C K Hedge Sparrow, or Hedge Accentor (*Prunella modularis*). One alternative name comes from its streaky-brown back and wings, but the grey head and breast and thin bill distinguish it from real sparrows; it is also much slimmer though about the same length (5¾ ins.). The sexes are alike, but juveniles are more spotted, and brown on the head.

The dunnock is resident all over the British Isles from town gardens and parks to heathland and moorland up to 1,500 ft., but its habitats always have thick, low cover. Continental birds are passage migrants to the east coast, and British birds move locally in autumn.

The shy dunnock only becomes noticeable when a party of three chase each other with much flicking of wings in and out of a hedge, calling sharply. But they feed on the ground in the open, taking insects in summer and seeds in winter, and sometimes visiting bird-tables. The song is a simple phrase, uttered in rather a burst, sometimes at night. The beautiful nest, a mossy cup on a foundation of twigs and lined with fur and wool, is well hidden in a hedge or bush, and the three to five eggs are pure blue. The female hatches them in 12 to 14 days; both parents feed the young, which fly from 11 days onwards. There are two and sometimes three broods; from May onward they are often victimised by cuckoos.

1 2 3 4 5 6 7 8 9 10 11 12

4 A L P I N E A C C E N T O R (*Prunella collaris*). About 7 ins. long, this big accentor is like a brightly coloured dunnock with bold black markings and a pale throat spotted black. It is a bird of the mountains of central Europe and has occurred in Britain about thirty times, mainly in autumn and winter and in the south

1a ROBIN, Juv.   1b Ad.
2 NIGHTINGALE   3a DUNNOCK (Hedge Sparrow), Ad.
4 ALPINE ACCENTOR   3b DUNNOCK, fledgling

WARBLERS. 1

RUFOUS WARBLER (*Erythropygia galactotes*). A light-brown bird, some 6 ins. long, with a rounded chestnut-red tail, black and white spotted along the fan-shaped edge. It is sometimes included with the thrushes. Nine have been recorded in autumn either in the south of England or Ireland; its nearest breeding area is in Spain and Portugal.

1 GRASSHOPPER WARBLER (*Locustella naevia*). About 5 ins. long, it has dark-brown upperparts streaked with black, in contrast to the larger and rare Savi's warbler. The tail is long and fan-shaped, and the underparts may be whitish or yellowish.

The grasshopper warbler, a widely distributed summer visitor, reaches the northern Scottish Highlands and many parts of Ireland. Birds on passage occur away from their breeding habitat, which is usually sedgy ground near water, though they also like very young fir plantations where the cover is thick.

The thin reeling song is generally the first sign that grasshopper warblers are about. Sometimes the male sings and displays in full view, his whole body shaking with the effort. Normally they are shy, scuttling mouse-like through the grasses or flying a short way with rounded wings, uttering their sharp call-note. Their food consists of small invertebrate animals. The nest of grasses is usually very well hidden under a tussock or at the end of a tunnel. Both parents incubate the six pink-spotted eggs for about 2 weeks and feed the young, which fledge in 10 to 11 days. There are two broods in the south of England.

. . . . 4 5 6 7 8 9 (10) . .

RARE GRASSHOPPER WARBLERS. The central European RIVER WARBLER (*Locustella fluviatilis*), about 5 ins. long, which has now occurred three times since September 1961, has no streaks on its upperparts, light-brown streaks on its underparts, and a bright brown tail. The smaller LANCEOLATED WARBLER (*Locustella lanceolata*) from northern Russia resembles a drab common grasshopper warbler, but with a densely streaked breast. Of the twelve which have occurred in Britain since 1908, ten have been on Fair Isle. PALLAS'S GRASSHOPPER WARBLER (*Locustella certhiola*), also from Asia and recorded three times in Britain since 1908, is about 5¼ ins. long and has a reddish-brown rump marked with streaks, which contrasts in flight with its very dark tail. Its underparts are noticeably pale.

THICK-BILLED WARBLER (*Phragmaticola aedon*). This very big (nearly 8 ins. long) Asiatic warbler occurred on Fair Isle in 1955. It has a shorter bill than the great reed warbler (p. 149) and no stripe over the eye.

CETTI'S WARBLER (*Cettia cetti*). A dark reddish-brown warbler, about 5½ ins. long, which nests in southern Europe and has appeared six times in southern England and Ireland since 1961. It has a whitish stripe over the eye, rather grey underparts, and a fan-shaped tail which shows in flight.

2 AQUATIC WARBLER (*Acrocephalus paludicola*). This streaky 'reed' warbler is distinguished from the sedge warbler by a creamy-buff stripe down the centre of the crown. The rump, and in summer also the breast and flanks, are streaked. Its general habits are like those of the sedge warbler; it breeds as near as Holland and is a rather rare and irregular autumn visitor, mainly to south and east England, where it frequents reed-beds and marshy areas near the coast.

3 SEDGE WARBLER (*Acrocephalus schoenobaenus*). About 5¼ ins. long this common warbler has a rather olive mantle, a rufous rump, and a light brown crown with a creamy stripe over the eye, which distinguish it from the reed warbler (p. 149). Juveniles are a brighter, yellow-brown, sometimes with a faint pale line on the crown.

The sedge warbler is a widely distributed summer visitor, reaching to the Outer Hebrides and many parts of Ireland. It is usually found in bushy ground near water, but also breeds in dry habitats with thick cover.

The dancing display flight and loud, jazzy song proclaim its arrival; after mating it is more often heard than seen, uttering a scolding *tuck tuck tuck* from thick cover. In flight it spreads its rounded tail. Its food consists of insects in all stages. The substantial nest is made of dead grasses and moss, with a finer lining. The female incubates the five or six dark-brown eggs, with thin black 'hairstreaks', which hatch in about 2 weeks; both parents feed the young, which may leave the nest after 9 days but do not fly for about 2 weeks. There is sometimes a second brood.

. . (3) 4 5 6 7 8 9 10 . .

4 MOUSTACHED WARBLER (*Lusciniola melanopogon*). This rarity from southern Europe is like a sedge warbler but slightly smaller, with more rufous upperparts, an almost black crown, and a white instead of creamy thick stripe over the eye. A pair actually bred successfully in Cambridgeshire in 1946, and there have been three records since.

5 SAVI'S WARBLER (*Locustella luscinioides*). It is bigger (5½ ins. long) than the grasshopper warbler, with a uniform brown back and unstreaked underparts. The reeling song is louder than that of the grasshopper warbler, the notes more distinct, and the spells of singing usually shorter. Savi's warbler bred in East Anglia over 100 years ago and has nested in small numbers in Kent at least since 1960 and in Suffolk probably since 1969.

1 GRASSHOPPER WARBLER   2 AQUATIC WARBLER

3 SEDGE WARBLER

4 MOUSTACHED WARBLER   5 SAVI'S WARBLER

WARBLERS. 2

1 REED WARBLER (*Acrocephalus scirpaceus*). This is the commonest of the unstreaked 'reed' warblers, about 5 ins. long, a uniform olive-brown above, and with pale underparts becoming buff on the flanks; the legs are usually dark brown. Juveniles look more rufous. The crown of the head appears to rise rather steeply from the bill, giving a high-foreheaded effect, particularly when the feathers are raised during singing.

It is a rather local summer visitor, most numerous in south-eastern England, but also in areas with extensive reed-beds, in Cornwall, South Wales and up to the northern English counties. It is only an occasional visitor elsewhere, though there is one breeding record from Ireland. Reeds are its particular habitat, and it is seldom seen away from them except on passage; but it does nest in bushes or other tall water plants when the reeds are late. Reed warblers are usually first identified by their songs, and then may be seen flitting through the tall dead reeds, gripping different stems with each foot, but seldom rising to the top. The song, based on a repetition of the phrase *chirr chirr chirr, chirruck chirruck chirruck* is less boisterous and harsh than that of the sedge warbler (p. 146), and there is no song flight. Its general habits and food are similar to those of the sedge warbler, but the nest is a beautifully woven basket supported by three or four reeds and made of their flower heads, grasses, and other plants, with a finer lining. The three to five whitish eggs, well marked with green, violet and brown, are incubated by both sexes for only 11 days; both also feed the young, which leave the nest in 10 to 14 days, often before they can fly. There are second broods in the south. This is one of the cuckoo's favourite fosterers (p. 116), in spite of its small nest.

. . . **4 5 6 7 8** 9 10 . .

2 MARSH WARBLER (*Acrocephalus palustris*). It is very difficult to distinguish from the reed warbler, except by its pale pink legs, though the plumage is usually less rufous-tinted and more grey-brown. The juveniles cannot be distinguished, except in the hand. The absence of the high forehead effect in the adult may be some guide.

This is one of the rarest of the breeding warblers, confined to the valley of the Severn and to the 'moors' of Somerset, with occasional nesting in some southern counties. Elsewhere it is only a rare visitor on passage. Its habitat is specialised: withy (willow) beds with nettles, meadow-sweet, mugwort, and willowherb, though it has nested in cornfields.

The marsh warbler is more active and easier to observe than the reed warbler and sings more in the open. The song is the best of the group to be heard in Britain, more musical than the sedge warbler, more varied than the reed warbler, with many mimicries recalling particularly the greenfinch's *jee* and the song thrush's repetitions; it has a scolding call-note something like that of the sedge warbler. The male uses song with movements of the wing and tail when courting the female. Marsh warblers eat berries as well as insects. The nest, more loosely built than a reed warbler's, is slung from several stems, of which one is dead, by characteristic 'basket handles'. The four or five white eggs, with comparatively few rich dark markings, are incubated by both sexes for about 11 to 12 days, and both feed the young, which leave the nest after 10 to 14 days.

. . . . **5 6 7** 8 9 (10) . .

3 GREAT REED WARBLER (*Acrocephalus arundinaceus*). This big warbler from Europe, 7½ ins. long, looks like a slim thrush, with a pronounced high crowned effect; it is uniformly dark brown above and pale below, and has a straight and powerful bill. After about ten scattered records in spring and autumn, it has been occurring annually, especially in Kent where the powerful song has been heard and breeding suspected. The nest, though slung on reeds like that of the common reed warbler, is made of wet material; in other respects breeding habits are similar.

PADDYFIELD WARBLER (*Acrocephalus agricola*) is a rarity from south Russia and Asia, very like a reed warbler but it looks paler in the field and has a more pronounced stripe over the eye. It has occurred twice on Fair Isle, in 1925 and 1953, both in autumn.

BLYTH'S REED WARBLER (*Acrocephalus dumetorum*) now breeds occasionally as near as Finland and has occurred in Britain in autumn about ten times, half of them on Fair Isle. It cannot be told from the marsh warbler except in the hand, but its beautiful song, full of expert mimicry, can be distinguished with experience.

FAN-TAILED WARBLER (*Cisticola juncidis*). There is one record, from Co. Cork in April 1962, of this very small (about 4 ins.) species which also breeds in southern Europe. It has dark brown upperparts with a reddish brown rump; the whitish throat and underparts are tinted buff on breast and flanks. There are black and white tips to the outer feathers of the short fan-tail.

1 REED WARBLER and nest   2 MARSH WARBLER and nest
3 GREAT REED WARBLER

1 BLACKCAP (*Sylvia atricapilla*). The only common black-capped warbler is about 5½ ins. long. The male (1b) is sometimes confused with the marsh tit (p. 129), although their shapes are quite different. The female (1a) has a red-brown cap, and the young birds look like adult females but with darker breasts, the males having darker crowns.

The blackcap is a summer visitor, passage migrant, and winter visitor in small numbers. It breeds throughout southern Britain, spreading into the Scottish Highlands, and from its Leinster stronghold in Ireland. The increasing number of winter records suggest an immigration, and the evidence of a ringed bird from Europe supports this theory. These winter birds are usually seen in gardens as visitors to bird-tables. The breeding habitat is woodland or woodland edge, with brambles, nettles, and bushes.

Cock blackcaps can be seen fairly easily when they arrive before most of the leaves are out and begin to sing their sweet, powerful, rather jerky song, which has earned them the name of the northern nightingale. Some are excellent mimics. Females are not nearly so easy to see and, as the foliage thickens, the hard alarm note *tack tack* becomes the chief evidence that blackcaps are about. When berries ripen in early autumn, especially on elders, they are easier to see again, but like other warblers, they feed mainly on insects. The male has various display actions, showing off the black cap and working the wings and tail, and there are gatherings of males while the females are sitting. The nest is a neat cup of dead grass stems with a finer lining, slung by basket handles among brambles and nettles or in a bush; there are usually cobwebs along the rim. Four to six eggs, marbled with brown or red, are incubated by both sexes in turn for 1½ to 2 weeks, and both feed the young, which soon bulge out of the nest and may leave after only a week if disturbed. There is sometimes a second brood.

*1 2 3 **4 5 6 7** 8 9 10 11 12*

2 GARDEN WARBLER (*Sylvia borin*). A typical 'little brown bird' whose most distinctive character is its lack of any outstanding features. It is 5½ ins. long and rather like a marsh warbler (p. 149), except that it has grey-brown legs. Male, female, and juvenile are all more or less alike.

As a summer visitor it is more widely distributed than the blackcap, nesting into the central Highlands of Scotland and found locally in several Irish counties. It is regular on passage elsewhere, including the Northern Islands. Its habitats, though similar to the blackcap's, also includes young fir plantations, and areas away from tall trees.

Arriving later than the blackcap, the garden warbler begins to sing after the other has mated and become quieter; the two songs are hard to tell apart, but the garden warbler has a more even and continuous warble, which ends less abruptly. Later in the season, these differences are less marked. There is a hard *tack tack* call and a churr like that of the whitethroat (p. 152). In general habits it resembles the blackcap, but the nest is a rather larger, less neat structure, placed in a bush or tangle and not slung. The four to six eggs are generally but not always paler than blackcap's with light brown marbling. Both sexes incubate them for 11 to 12 days and feed the young, which fledge in about 10 days. There is occasionally a second brood.

*. . (3) **4 5 6 7** 8 9 10 (11) .*

3 BARRED WARBLER (*Sylvia nisoria*). Although only half an inch longer, it looks a considerably bigger bird than the blackcap and garden warbler, with its long, white-edged tail. Most of those seen in Britain are juveniles, more or less grey-brown all over, though paler below, and with brown eyes (3a); the pale yellow eye of the adult is conspicuous. The female is browner than the male (3b) with less marked barring on the underparts.

The barred warbler is a regular autumn visitor down the east coast, dozens being recorded in some seasons, but there are very few records in spring or from the west. It nests as near as Germany and Denmark. Barred warblers in Britain are not usually easy to see for they spend their time in thick coastal cover. They fly heavily when flushed and soon drop out of sight again. They feed on insects and small crustaceans while on passage, and occasionally give their loud tacking call.

ORPHEAN WARBLER (*Sylvia hortensis*). A south European species, like the barred warbler in size, and also with white outer tail feathers, but the male has a dark grey cap reaching below the red eye and a white throat. The female's cap is less dark and the juvenile has a shorter tail than the juvenile barred warbler. There are only three British records, from Yorkshire (1848), Dorset (1955) and Cornwall (1967).

SARDINIAN WARBLER (*Sylvia melanocephala*). The male of this south European warbler has an extensive black cap and white throat and is nearly an inch shorter than the orphean warbler. The female's cap is less distinct and the juveniles are duller. There are three records: Lundy (1955), Fair Isle (1967) and Pembrokeshire (1968).

1a BLACKCAP, F.

1b BLACKCAP, M.

2 GARDEN WARBLER

3a BARRED WARBLER, Juv.

3b BARRED WARBLER, Ad.

1 WHITETHROAT (*Sylvia communis*). The male (1a), 5½ ins. long, is a grey-capped, white-throated, brown-backed warbler with white outer feathers to his grey tail; the female (1b) is brown-capped, and so are the juveniles and the male in autumn. The male in particular shows a high forehead effect when he raises his crown feathers.

The whitethroat is a very widely distributed summer visitor, nesting even on many of the island groups and in the glens of the Scottish Highlands. It is a bird of low scrub, particularly brambles and nettles, but is also found in open woodland. It is a common passage migrant along the east and south coasts.

Soon after arrival, male whitethroats perch on roadside wires or dance in the air, uttering their *wichity wichity* song; they are typical birds of the summer hedgerow, and are less secretive than many warblers, though they can slip through cover quietly and often seem to disappear after flitting on ahead and diving into a bramble bush, only the harsh *churr* call betraying their presence. Like blackcaps, they are fond of berries and fruit and they have similar excited displays, raising the head feathers, flicking their tails and wings. The nest is like that of the garden warbler (p. 150), but often lined with black hairs; the male builds several trial nests before the female chooses one. The four to six eggs are a dirty yellow-green with dark spots; both sexes sit on them for about 12 days and feed the young, which fledge in 10 or more days. There is sometimes a second brood.

. . (3) *4* **5 6** *7 8 9 10* (*11*) .

2 LESSER WHITETHROAT (*Sylvia curruca*). In spite of its name, it is only slightly smaller than the common whitethroat, from which it is distinguished by its generally greyer upperparts, shorter tail, and dark area behind the eye (the ear coverts). Both sexes look alike; the juveniles are rather browner.

A much more local summer visitor than the common whitethroat, mainly to the south and east, it is scarce or absent in south-west and northern England, and west Wales, has bred a few times in Scotland, and is a rare visitor to Ireland. It is regular on passage along the east coast. Its favourite breeding habitat is a lane with tall hedges over which brambles and briars grow.

The lesser whitethroat's typical song, unlike that of other warblers, is a loud rattle which breaks off suddenly; but there is a quieter warble as well. The call and alarm notes are the usual warbler *churr* and *tack tack*. It spends more time high in trees than the common whitethroat, singing and searching for insects; and it is fond of fruit in late summer, when it moves away from the breeding area and begins to sing again. The male displays his plumage when courting and pursues the female with a special fluttering flight. The nest is like a small blackcap's,

very neat and with a lining of hairs or rootlets; it i[s] often very deep in a creeper over a hedge, well insid[e] a bramble clump, or in the fork of a small bush[.] The four to six eggs are white, with yellow and dar[k] spots; both sexes incubate them for 10 to 11 day[s] and feed the young for the same period. There i[s] occasionally a second brood.

. . . . *4* **5 6** *7* **8 9** *10* (*11*) .

3 SUBALPINE WARBLER (*Sylvia cantillans*). Th[e] male (3b) of this southern European species, less tha[n] 5 ins. long, has a grey head and back and pinky-re[d] throat and breast, the two colours being divided by [a] white moustachial stripe; females (3a) and juvenile[s] are much browner. Most of the forty or so Britis[h] records since 1950 are from coastal points in late spring and autumn.

4 DARTFORD WARBLER (*Sylvia undata*). An al[-] most black-looking little bird, less than 5 ins. lon[g.] Its upperparts are dark brown, and its throat an[d] breast dull red. The male's head is grey (4a), and hi[s] breast a deeper tint than the female's (4b). Both sexe[s] have a reddish eye, with a red rim; the long graduate[d] tail is dark, with a white border, and there are white spots on the throat in autumn.

This is the only resident British warbler, and it i[s] confined to a few southern counties from Devon t[o] Sussex and Surrey, where it inhabits heaths with gors[e] and tall heather and moves about very little. Stra[y] birds have occurred further north and two in Ireland, one in 1968.

The quiet churring call can be distinguished fro[m] that of the whitethroat, which often shares the sam[e] habitat, and with patience a bird may be seen flitting between bushes or perched for a moment on a spray of gorse. On fine spring days, males may sing in the open and perform their dancing display flight[;] their song is simpler and more musical than that of the whitethroat. Their food consists mainly of insects an[d] spiders, and consequently in hard winters Dartfor[d] warblers suffer seriously. The small nest is compactly built of grasses and lined with fine stems, rootlets, and hair. The usual clutch is three or four whitish eggs with brown and grey spots; the female does most of the incubation, which lasts for about 12 days. Both parents feed the young, which fly after about 13 days. There are regularly two broods.

1 2 3 **4 5** *6 7 8 9* **10** *11 12*

SPECTACLED WARBLER (*Sylvia conspicillata*). This species, which breeds in southern Europe, has occurred twice, in Yorkshire (1968) and Cornwall (1969). Rather smaller than a whitethroat, it has a darker head and its white throat contrasts with the pinkish breast; the juvenile looks browner, especially on the head.

1a WHITETHROAT, M. 1b F.
3a SUBALPINE WARBLER, F.
3b SUBALPINE WARBLER, M.

2 LESSER WHITETHROAT
4a DARTFORD WARBLER, M.
4b DARTFORD WARBLER, F.

1 WILLOW WARBLER (*Phylloscopus trochilus*). The small 'leaf warblers' are very hard to separate on plumage alone. This species is 4¼ ins. long, and in spring (1a) is slightly greener above and yellower below than the chiffchaff, but becomes browner above as the feathers wear in summer; towards autumn the yellow on the underparts is more noticeable, and young birds (1b) may have quite bright breasts. The best distinction from the chiffchaff is the light brown colour of the legs.

The willow warbler is the most widespread of the leaf warblers, and is a summer visitor throughout the British Isles wherever there is even scattered tree-cover or scrub, though in parts of Ireland the chiff-chaff is more numerous. It is particularly common in the open birch and oak woodland of the north and west. On passage, when birds of the northern European race visit Britain, willow warblers may be seen in quite bare areas as well.

They arrive soon after chiffchaffs and sing their sweet phrase which rises and dies away in about 5 seconds. The call note, *hoo-it*, is usually softer and not so abrupt as that of the chiffchaff. Birds may utter it while searching leaves and twigs for small insects, or when alarmed. They occasionally come to the ground, chiefly in late summer when there are many juveniles about. Both sexes flutter or flap their wings in display. The female builds the domed nest low in grass, dead bracken, or other thick ground cover, where it is often very hard to see. It has a much bigger entrance than a wren's nest and is made of grasses and moss, thickly lined with feathers. The six or seven roundish white eggs are usually densely speckled with light red, but sometimes have fewer large dark-brown spots. The female incubates them for about 13 days, and both parents feed the young, which fly after about the same time. Family parties then roam the woodland and scrub, sometimes linking up with tit flocks.

. . (*3*) <u>4 5 6 7 8 9</u> *10* (*11*) .

2 CHIFFCHAFF (*Phylloscopus collybita*). About the same size as a willow warbler and usually browner, with black legs. Juveniles look much the same as adults, which are at their most yellow in autumn. The Siberian race (2a), which occurs on passage, is much whiter underneath, and Scandinavian birds are greyer above, but neither are at all easy to identify.

The chiffchaff is a summer visitor to most of Britain and Ireland, and a resident in small numbers in the south-west; many also pass through on migration. Its habitat is thick cover on the edge of woods; in the north it is often found among rhododendrons.

It is increasing in the Scottish Highlands but is still much less widely distributed than the willow warbler though commoner in parts of Ireland.

The chiffchaff's monotonous song, from which it gets its name, often announces the arrival of the first summer visitor when the trees are still bare; later in the season there may be a grating *churr* before the *chiff-chaff*. Its call note, though sharper, resembles that of the willow warbler, as do the chiffchaff's general habits and food. It flits among the leaves seldom flying long distances. In display the male uses a form of 'butterfly' flight. The female builds the nest which is rounder than a willow warbler's and made of larger grass stems and dead leaves, but also lined with feathers; it is generally a foot or more off the ground in brambles or other tangle. The usual clutch is six white eggs with dark brown spots. The female incubates them for about 13 days and does most of the care of the young, which fly after 2 weeks. There are sometimes two broods in the south.

(*1* *2*) <u>3 4 5 6 7</u> *8* <u>9</u> *10* (*11* *12*)

3 WOOD WARBLER (*Phylloscopus sibilatrix*). The biggest of the leaf warblers, 5 ins. long, and also the brightest in colour, it has a greenish back and rump, a pale yellow breast, and a white belly. The juveniles are duller, and so are the adults in autumn.

It is the most truly woodland British bird, and is found as a local summer visitor in the beech woods of south-east England. But its stronghold is in the scrub woods of the west and north, right into the Scottish Highlands; it breeds sporadically in Ireland. On spring and autumn passage it may be seen much more widely.

The arrival of the wood warbler coincides with the appearance of fresh greenery, with which it blends as it utters its two types of song. One is an explosive trill lasting about 3 seconds; the other is a drawn-out *piu piu piu*. The same bird may deliver both, and often sings in flight, fluttering down like a tree pipit (p. 162) or flapping slowly as part of its display. The male will also sing to warn off human intruders near the nest or territory. The call is a plaintive piping note rather like that of a bullfinch (p. 182). Wood warblers feed on small insects from the leaves. The female builds the domed nest on the ground, making it of dead stems, lined with finer stems and hairs, but not with feathers. She incubates the five or seven white eggs, thickly marked with very dark brown, which hatch after 13 days; then both sexes feed the young which fledge in about 12 days. After that parties roam the woodland until migration.

. . . <u>4 5 6</u> *7 8 9* (*10*) . .

1a WILLOW WARBLER, Ad.

1b WILLOW WARBLER, Juv.

2a CHIFFCHAFF, Siberian race
2b CHIFFCHAFF, Ad.
3   WOOD WARBLER

1 GREENISH WARBLER (*Phylloscopus trochiloides*). This rare visitor from northern Europe and Asia has a pale wing-bar and stripe over its eye; it is about 4½ ins. long, slightly smaller than the arctic warbler, from which it is distinguished by its darker legs. In autumn plumage when most likely to be seen in Britain, it may look greyish. Seventy-seven have now occurred, mainly in recent years and down the east coast; and one spent 2 months at a sewage farm near London early in 1962.

2 ARCTIC WARBLER (*Phylloscopus borealis*). A little larger than the greenish warbler, this leaf warbler from the far north shows a greenish tint on its upperparts, with very pale underparts and wing-bar. It has occurred some sixty times, mostly in autumn, on Fair Isle, which has a majority of the records, and down the east coast.

DUSKY WARBLER (*Phylloscopus fuscatus*). Thirteen of this species from Asia have occurred, twelve since 1961, and all but one in late autumn. The adults are brown above, with buff flanks and paler underparts; they show no yellow or green. Juveniles are greyer and show less of the brown tints. They are about 4 ins. long.

RADDE'S BUSH WARBLER (*Phylloscopus schwarzi*). Another Asiatic species, larger than the dusky warbler, it is more olive-brown above, and has a prominent stripe over its eye and a stronger bill and legs. The first British record was in 1898, and there have been nine since 1961, all but one from the east coast in October.

3 ICTERINE WARBLER (*Hippolais icterina*). This and the melodious warbler are very difficult to tell apart, except by their songs which are unlikely to be heard in Britain. Both these *Hippolais* warblers have a 'high forehead', like the reed warbler (p. 148), and are generally olive-brown above and yellowish below, rather like leaf warblers; but they are bigger. The icterine warbler is about 5½ ins. long. It has a longer, more pointed wing than the melodious warbler, and the adult in spring (3a) shows a pale patch on the closed wing, as does the juvenile in autumn (3b), which is the most likely plumage to be seen in Britain. By autumn the adult's feathers have become rubbed and this pale patch is lost; the melodious warbler seldom shows it. The legs of the icterine are bluish, and paler at the sides.

It is a scarce visitor on passage, mostly reported in autumn but sometimes in spring. It breeds as near as Holland, and a pair attempted to nest in Wiltshire in 1907. Icterine warblers are hard to see, for they keep well in the cover of the leaves where they search for insects; they also eat berries. They have a loud *tack* call resembling that of the blackcap (p. 150).

4 MELODIOUS WARBLER (*Hippolais polyglotta*). Slightly smaller than the icterine warbler, this species has shorter, rounder wings and does not usually show a pale patch on them when they are closed. Its legs are bluish-grey. It is a rare autumn visitor down both sides of Britain, though it nests in northern France.

OLIVACEOUS WARBLER (*Hippolais pallida*). About the same size as the melodious warbler but greyer above, buffish below, and with a rounder head, it has a pale stripe over its eye and a strong, rather flat bill. Olivaceous warblers have occurred ten times mostly in the southern half of Britain since 1951; their nearest breeding area is in south-west France.

BOOTED WARBLER (*Hippolais caligata*). This is the smallest member of the *Hippolais* genus ever to be seen in Britain (4½ ins. long), though not so small as the smallest leaf warbler (*Phylloscopus*). It is similar in appearance to the olivaceous warbler, but its outer tail feathers look white. Four of the five records are from Fair Isle between 1936 and 1968.

5 BONELLI'S WARBLER (*Phylloscopus bonelli*). A brownish leaf warbler with very pale underparts, and a yellowish rump, which distinguishes it from chiffchaffs and willow warblers (p. 155) but is not easy to see. Its legs are brown, and it is about 4½ ins. long. It has a plaintive call-note and a short trilling song like the start of the wood warbler's trill (p. 154). About 30 have occurred in Britain mainly in autumn, all of them since 1948; it breeds as near as Belgium.

1 GREENISH WARBLER, autumn   2 ARCTIC WARBLER
3a ICTERINE WARBLER, Ad.   4 MELODIOUS WARBLER
5 BONELLI'S WARBLER   3b ICTERINE WARBLER, Juv.

WARBLERS AND KINGLETS

1 YELLOW-BROWED WARBLER (*Phylloscopus inornatus*). The best known of the rare leaf warblers is this very small species, only 4 ins. long, which is distinguished by its contrasting green upper and whitish underparts, by the conspicuous stripe over its eye and, above all, by a double wing-bar, which goldcrests also have. It is a regular autumn visitor from Asia in small numbers, chiefly along the east coast, but sometimes reported in the west. It is seldom seen inland and is most likely to be found in shrubs along the shore of eastern counties in September or October.

PALLAS'S LEAF WARBLER (*Phylloscopus proregulus*). A tiny leaf warbler, only $3\frac{1}{2}$ ins. long, which has visited the east of England from Asia in autumn forty-three times, nearly all of them in recent years. Like the yellow-browed warbler, it has a pale double wing-bar, but is distinguished by its light yellow rump and a stripe along the middle of the crown.

2 GOLDCREST (*Regulus regulus*). Well-known as the smallest British bird, $3\frac{1}{2}$ ins. long, the goldcrest belongs to the kinglet family, and is closely related to the warblers. Its crest distinguishes it from the yellow-browed warbler, and its face pattern from the firecrest. The goldcrest has a rather pale area round its prominent dark eye, and black stripes on either side of the gold crown, which is yellow in the female (2b). The juvenile (2c) has no crest or stripes on its head; it gets them by a moult in its first winter.

The goldcrest is a resident throughout the British Isles wherever there are coniferous woods, although it is also found in small numbers in broadleaved woodland. It has increased in some areas due to recent afforestation, and in some plantations is one of the commonest birds to be seen. But many die in hard winters when their normal insect food is not available. In autumn single birds or small parties wander about, often with tit flocks, and birds on passage hunt quite open country.

Although the goldcrest's high-pitched 'needling' call and screepy song are easy to recognise, it may be hard to catch sight of the singer as it works its way through the dense branches of a yew or other conifer. Usually the tiny bird shows up at the end of a twig and then vanishes again or flits off on rounded transparent wings. It feeds on minute insects and spiders. The male uses his crest both in courtship and when threatening other males. The nest, unique in Britain, is a rounded hammock of moss and cobwebs, lined with feathers and slung by three or four handles from near the end of a fir bough, or sometimes from ivy leaves or a spray of gorse. The clutch of seven or more tiny pale-buff eggs have zones of darker markings; the female incubates them for about 16 days, a long time for so small a bird; then both parents feed them until they fly in about $2\frac{1}{2}$ weeks. There are two broods in a season. Some British goldcrests move south in autumn, and many migrants from Europe, usually only passing through, are reported in some years.

*1 2 3 **4 5 6 7** 8 *9 10 11* 12*

3 FIRECREST (*Regulus ignicapillus*). This visitor from Europe, the same size as a goldcrest, is brighter green above and paler below. It is mainly distinguished by the prominent white stripe over its eye, the black stripe through the eye, and the fainter white one below. The juvenile also shows these markings, though, like the juvenile goldcrest, it lacks the orange-red crest with its black edge.

Firecrests are regular autumn visitors to the east and south coasts, and a few stay the winter and are recorded from inland counties; but they are very rare in the west, north, and in Ireland. Firecrests are now known to have bred in the New Forest at least since 1961 and are apparently increasing. They have also been discovered nesting in Buckinghamshire.

Firecrests behave much like goldcrests, but visiting birds in Britain occur in open country away from woods and in general they are not so attached to conifers. Their call note is lower-pitched than that of the goldcrest, and the song can also be told apart with practice.

2b GOLDCREST, F.
2a GOLDCREST, M.
1   YELLOW-BROWED WARBLER

3 FIRECREST
2c GOLDCREST, Juv.

FLYCATCHERS

1 PIED FLYCATCHER (*Ficedula hypoleuca*). About 5 ins. long and much rounder headed than a spotted flycatcher, it is distinguished by its white wing-bars. Males in summer (1c) vary considerably in the amount of black, grey, or brown in the upperparts, though even quite mottled birds look blackish at a distance; but the primary flight feathers are always dark brown. The white patch on the forehead is often divided into two spots, like false eyes. The female (1a) is less variable; her wing-bar is smaller, and her underparts are very pale brown rather than white. Males on autumn migration (1b) are almost impossible to tell from females when their moult is complete, and some retain the brown winter plumage over the breeding period. Juveniles, apart from creamy white wing-bars, are like juvenile spotted flycatchers.

Pied flycatchers breed in western and northern Britain, very locally in the Scottish Highlands as far as Wester Ross, but do not breed in Ireland. But on passage they may appear all over the country and in some autumns are common down the east coast.

The simple song, *tchee tchee tchee cher cher*, once learned, is unmistakable and is often the first sign of the pied flycatcher's presence, though the flashing black and white males soon make themselves conspicuous when they are chasing each other or newly arrived females. They display near suitable nest holes and often control several, one of which the mate chooses. They feed on insects caught in the air and off the foliage, and collect much nest material off the ground. They use holes in trees and walls and nest-boxes for nesting, making a foundation of dead leaves, honeysuckle fibres, moss, and bark, and lining it with fine grass. The female lays five to eight pale greenish-blue eggs and incubates them for about 13 days. Both parents feed the young, which fly at about 16 days. Occasional second broods are hatched in early seasons. The families then disappear, but may be found high in the woodland canopy for some weeks before departing.

. . . **4 5 6 7** *8 9 10 (11)* .

2 COLLARED FLYCATCHER (*Ficedula albicollis*). The female of this very rare central-European species is almost exactly like the female pied flycatcher (1a), but the male in spring has a white collar, an almost white rump, and usually a much bigger white patch on the forehead than a pied flycatcher; even in the brown autumn plumage it has a whiter rump. There have been only six British records, five males in spring and one bird in autumn.

3 RED-BREASTED FLYCATCHER (*Ficedula parva*). This small flycatcher is 4½ ins. long and distinguished in all plumages by the white patches on either side of the tail. Males in full plumage with the orange throat (3b) are seldom seen in Britain usually white-throated immature birds occur, and these resemble females (3a). The juveniles are scaly looking. They are most often recorded in autumn in small numbers of passage migrants all down the east coast from Shetland southwards, and sometimes in the west and south as well. They can be recognised by their habit of flirting their distinctive black and white tails, which they often cock up like a wren. They feed mainly by taking insects on the wing. Their nearest breeding areas are in Denmark and Germany.

4 SPOTTED FLYCATCHER (*Muscicapa striata*). This is the most common member of the family grey-brown above with spots on the head, almost white below with faint streaks on the breast, and 5½ ins. long. The sexes are alike; juveniles (4a) look more spotted owing to their pale feathers with dark edges.

One of the last summer visitors to arrive, the spotted flycatcher is generally distributed throughout Britain and Ireland, except northern Scotland and its islands; it also occurs on passage. Its original habitat was probably open glades or valleys in woodland; but it is now found in gardens and parks, along road sides, and on the edges of woods.

It has a dull plumage and a simple, squeaky song, but it attracts attention by its sallies into the air after flying insects, returning to the same perch on a post or bare branch, where it sits upright with its rather long tail held downward, a characteristic position. The call is a thin *zee*, to which a loud *tuck tuck* of alarm is added. Its display includes flying chases as well as tail movements with the head and bill pointed upwards, and it lifts its wings alternately when it is excited. Spotted flycatchers build nests of moss and cobwebs, with a lining of fine grass and hairs, and place them on ledges of some kind on a building, wall, rock face, or tree; they often use old nests of other birds. The four to five eggs are usually pale blue with many reddish markings, but spotless clutches occur. Both sexes share the incubation for 12 to 14 days and then feed the young, which fly after the same period. There are sometimes two broods. After nesting, family parties move about and may be seen perched on fence wires as the young birds learn to feed themselves; at this time they occasionally land on the ground.

. . . *4* **5 6** *7 8 9 10* . .

1a PIED FLYCATCHER, F.   1b M., autumn   1c M., spring
4a SPOTTED FLYCATCHER, Juv.   4b Ad.   2 COLLARED FLYCATCHER, M., spring
3a RED-BREASTED FLYCATCHER, F.   3b M.

1 TREE PIPIT (*Anthus trivialis*). This typical pipit is about 6 ins. long, very like the meadow pipit in appearance but generally a brighter brown above and below and with paler legs. The sexes are alike and juveniles resemble adults but are more buff with darker streaks.

The tree pipit is a summer visitor, locally common throughout Britain to northern Scotland but not found in Ireland or most of the island groups, except rather rarely on passage. It inhabits rough ground of various types, provided there are scattered trees or other tall perches, but the disappearance of this sort of habitat in south-east England is causing the tree pipits also to disappear, and they are now probably commonest in very open scrub of birch, with bracken, tussocky grass, and heather below, country which is found along the valleys and glens of the west and north.

The 'paper-dart' flight of the singing male tree pipit, his song rising to a final *see-er*, *see-ir*, *see-ir* as he glides downwards, identifies this species in spring because the meadow and rock pipits do not normally take off from perches for their songs. But he may also utter a short form of song without flying. The call note is a penetrating *see*, which is also distinctive. Tree pipits may be watched walking about rather slowly, snapping at insects, then stopping to stand more upright than meadow pipits. They have a slow display flight. The nest is of grass and is on the ground, often very well-hidden under a tussock. The five or six eggs show an exceptional variety, with red, purple, greenish, brown, and grey streaks or marbling. The female incubates for about 13 to 14 days; then both parents feed the young, which fledge in about 12 days. There are occasionally two broods. Cuckoos quite often lay in tree pipits' nests, but probably mistaking the nest for that of a meadow pipit.

. . (3) <u>4 5 6 7 8 9</u> (10 11) .

2 MEADOW PIPIT (*Anthus pratensis*). This is the commonest 'little brown bird' of rough ground in the British Isles. It is about 5¾ ins. long, rather dark olive-brown above with black streaks, pale below with well-separated streaks or spots, and with darker legs than those of most tree pipits. But the plumage is variable, and some adult birds in spring, as well as the juveniles (2b), look as bright as tree pipits.

One of the most widely distributed passerines (perching birds), it is both a resident and summer visitor, found on commons and waste ground near cities and on the most remote islands. But the meadow pipit does not breed on cultivated land in the south though it may spend the winter there. Its great strong hold is the moorland, though most birds leave the hills in autumn and many emigrate; there are also passage migrants from the far north and winter visitors.

The meadow pipit's song is delivered in the air after it has risen rapidly from the ground; on a sunny day the moorland seems alive with little birds rising and falling. But they also sing from perches. The call note is a shrill *sipp* which is repeated excitedly when the bird is alarmed. They hunt on the ground like tree pipits and their display is similar. The nest, usually well-hidden, may be in a tuft on flat ground or in a bank; the clutch, usually of five dark-brown eggs, is incubated by the female for 13 to 14 days; both parents feed the young, which take about the same time to fledge. There are regularly two broods. Meadow pipits are the cuckoo's favourite fosterers in open country. Loose flocks form after breeding, when the birds leave for lower ground or farmland.

1 2 3 <u>4 5 6 7</u> 8 9 10 11 12

3 ROCK PIPIT (*Anthus spinoletta petrosus*). Two races of this species are illustrated: the dark grey-brown rock pipit (sub-species *petrosus*) with pale grey outer tail feathers, and the water pipit (*A. spinoletta spinoletta*) which is shown on p. 165. The sexes of the rock pipit are alike, and juveniles are very like adults but with more dark streaks in their plumage.

Rock pipits breed round most of the rocky coasts of the British Isles and are found in winter on flatter shores. Birds from Scandinavia appear inland on passage in marshy areas and round reservoirs.

The song is like that of the meadow pipit but more powerful; a bird will fly up to 10 or 15 ft. and sail down, singing as it glides, to land on a stone or bank. Their sharp call note can be distinguished from that of meadow pipits with practice. They live almost entirely from the low tide zone to just above it, feeding especially on small creatures in the rotten seaweed at the high tide mark. But they also search the vegetation on slopes near the shore, overlapping with meadow pipits. The male's song flight is his principal display. The nest is often built in a rock crevice or perhaps in a grassy bank like a meadow pipit's; but the four to five eggs are larger and usually greyer. The female incubates them for about 2 weeks and both parents feed the young for about the same period. There are two broods in the season.

1 2 3 <u>4 5 6</u> 7 8 9 10 11 12

2a MEADOW PIPIT, Ad. 2b Juv.

1 TREE PIPIT

3 ROCK PIPIT

1 RED-THROATED PIPIT (*Anthus cervinus*). A northern European pipit 5¾ ins. long, which resembles the tree rather than the meadow pipit (p. 163), but is distinguished by its reddish throat and breast (1a) in spring and summer, and at other times by its strongly marked rump area. The call note is also distinctive and is described as a musical *chup*. About seventy have occurred in Britain, mostly on Fair Isle and the east coast in autumn; over thirty have been reported in recent years.

2 WATER PIPIT (*Anthus spinoletta spinoletta*). This is the European race of the rock pipit shown on p. 163. It breeds in the mountains, not along the coast as its relative does. It has a stripe over the eye, white outer tail feathers and in spring (2a) a pinkish breast. The American race, which has also occurred in autumn in Scotland and Ireland, has buffish underparts.

Water pipits, like Scandinavian rock pipits, are usually seen inland by sheets of water, by marshes, and at sewage farms, and appear to be winter visitors. They look at this season rather like big meadow pipits, among parties of which they may be found, feeding on small animals along the shore or in wet ground.

3 RICHARD'S PIPIT (*Anthus richardi*). A big pipit, 7 ins. long and rather dark above, with streaks on its buff lower breast. It has pale stripes above the eye and along the chin. Its single call note is rather harsh and loud. Richard's pipits are irregular visitors in autumn, winter, and spring, mainly to south and east England; in recent years up to 150 have been reported. Their breeding area is in Asia. They may sometimes be seen among parties of other pipits on passage.

4 TAWNY PIPIT (*Anthus campestris*). A big, sandy pipit, 6½ ins. long. Adults can be distinguished from Richard's pipit by their generally lighter colouring and by the fewer and fainter streaks on both upper and underparts. The juveniles are more streaked. Although they nest just across the English Channel, tawny pipits are rare visitors, mainly to the south and east of England in autumn. Up to 27 are recorded in some years. There is a supposed breeding record in 1905 in Sussex, but there have been no reliable reports since, although the bird gave its name to a famous film.

PECHORA PIPIT (*Anthus gustavi*). A little smaller than the tree pipit (p. 163) which it closely resembles, this species from north-east Europe has occurred sixteen times on Fair Isle in autumn, and once in Yorkshire (1966). It has two pale stripes down the back, a strongly marked rump, and pale buff outer tail feathers. The distinctive call note, heard from birds on Fair Isle, is described as a hard *pwit*. Pechora pipits on the island are difficult to flush.

OLIVE-BACKED PIPIT (*Anthus hodgsoni*). Individuals of this Asiatic species (sometimes called the Indian tree pipit) were recorded on Fair Isle in 1964 and 1965. It is smaller than the European tree pipit, more olive-brown above; streaking on the breast is more marked, but is less obvious on the back.

1a RED-THROATED PIPIT, M., spring   1b M., autumn
    2a WATER PIPIT, summer   2b winter
3 RICHARD'S PIPIT   4 TAWNY PIPIT

1 WHITE WAGTAIL (*Motacilla alba alba*). This is the same species as, but a distinct Continental race of, the pied wagtail. Adult white wagtails have pale grey backs and rumps, making a clear contrast with the black neck. The female is a duller grey, and may be confused with female pied wagtails in their first winter, though these usually have black rumps. Young grey-backed male pied wagtails (shown in background, top right) may in the autumn be confused with old male white wagtails, though females and first year birds of the white race are at that time grey from the back, over the crown, to the bill (shown in background, top left). The first plumage of the juveniles is the same for both races.

White wagtails are common visitors on passage in spring and autumn all over the country, and pairs sometimes breed in Britain or individuals interbreed with the resident pied wagtails. They are similar in behaviour and feeding and nesting habits, and are usually to be seen on cultivated land and grassland.

2 PIED WAGTAIL (*Motacilla alba yarrellii*). The commonest resident British wagtail is about 7 ins. long, nearly half of which is tail. The male's apparently black back and rump is, in winter, mixed with grey, and his black throat becomes whitish, though the upper breast remains black. The female (2c) is similar but with a rather greyer back, shading to black at the rump, and she has less black on her head and breast.

Pied wagtails are resident or summer visitors throughout the British Isles, though not in some of the island groups. They also breed in northern France. Called 'water wagtails', and certainly to be found at all times along streams and rivers and round lakes and reservoirs, they are not so closely associated with water as the grey wagtail, but inhabit farms, villages, big gardens in the country, and country roads with stone walls. Outside the breeding season they are found on cultivated land and grassland.

A pied wagtail pattering across the lawn, now pausing to pick something out of the grass, now darting up to take an insect on the wing, then, uttering its loud *chissick* call, flying off in big bounds to try its luck elsewhere, is a typical sight on a garden lawn in the country. After breeding, probably on a creeper-clad wall, the whole family may be watched learning to feed themselves on the grass. Their food is mainly insects, but they take very small fish and some seeds and will come to bird-tables in hard weather. Outside the breeding season they roost in numbers, usually in vegetation, but sometimes in or on buildings. A famous tree roost in central Dublin has contained several thousand birds at a time. The display is elaborate, the male showing off his plumage

by stretching his wings and tail, lifting his bill, circling round the female, and using his *chissick* call. His rather sweet warbling song is not often heard. The nest is built in a cavity of some kind, or well hidden amongst ivy and other creepers, quite often in the old nest of another bird. It is made of grasses and lined with fur and hair. The five or six white eggs with grey markings are incubated mainly by the female for 13 to 14 days, and both parents feed the young, which fledge in about the same period. When the female starts to sit on her second clutch, the male looks after the first brood. Sometimes there may be a third brood.

1 2 3 4 5 6 7 8 9 10 11 12

3 GREY WAGTAIL (*Motacilla cinerea*). The pale yellow on the underparts of this graceful wagtail, which is about 7 ins. long including the very long tail, makes it easy to confuse with the yellow wagtail (p. 169); but its distinctive feature is its blue-grey upperparts. The male has a black throat in summer and a pale stripe over the eye; the female has little or no black. In autumn and winter both sexes have pale buff throats. The juveniles, which are similar but with dark marks on the throat, can be confused with young pied wagtails, but they always show some pale yellow on the underparts.

The grey wagtail is a resident or summer visitor to most of Britain and Ireland, moving from its more northerly haunts after breeding. It is a bird of fast-flowing water, and may be found by isolated weirs on slow rivers; it may also nest by ponds or even some way from water. In autumn and winter it is also found in towns, even in central London. It suffered very much in the cold winter of 1962-3 when many streams were frozen for a long period.

It is most usual to see a grey wagtail standing on a stone in mid-stream, bobbing its tail up and down before flying up to take an insect. Its call is rather like the *chissick* of the pied wagtail, but can be told apart with practice; it sings more often, generally a single phrase, but sometimes a musical warble like that of the pied wagtail. There is a 'butterfly' display flight and the male also shows off his plumage. Grey wagtails feed mainly on insects and small water creatures. They usually build their nest near water in a steep bank or hole in a wall or bridge, and make it of twigs, grasses, and moss, lined with hair. The female, with some help from the male, incubates the five or six rather dirty-looking pale brown eggs for 13 to 14 days; but both parents feed the brood, which fledges in 12 to 13 days. There is sometimes a second brood.

1 2 3 4 5 6 7 8 9 10 11 12

1a WHITE WAGTAIL, 1st autumn   1   M., summer   2   PIED WAGTAIL, M., 1st autumn
2a PIED WAGTAIL, Juv.   2c   F., summer   2b   M., summer
3a GREY WAGTAIL, F., summer   3b   M., summer, and young

1 YELLOW WAGTAIL (*Motacilla flava flavissima*). In fact, all the birds on this page, except the last described, belong to the species *Motacilla flava*, but there are a number of different races. The yellow wagtail, shown in the middle of the plate opposite, is the typical British race, though several of the others do occur in Britain.

The yellow wagtail is 6½ ins. long, and the male bird is the only one of the races seen in Britain to have a yellow head in its spring plumage (1a). The rest of the plumage — the green back and blackish wings and tail with white outer feathers — is much the same for all the races. The female (1b), the juvenile (1c), and the male in autumn are duller, browner above and paler below, with a pale stripe over the eye. The juvenile has dark markings on the throat.

The breeding distribution of the yellow wagtail in Britain is now more or less confined to England and Wales, with one or two pockets in southern Scotland, a few pairs in Co. Wicklow and occasional nests in Northern Ireland. Some also nest in northern France. On passage, birds are seen more widely. Their habitat is open ground of some kind, from coastal dunes and golf links to cultivated fields, riverside meadows, gravel pits, heaths, and rough grazing on the edge of the moors to nearly 2,000 ft.

The penetrating *tsip* call announces the yellow wagtail as it flies over in typical 'bounds'; then it lands close to the water and flirts its tail to show the brilliant spring plumage. Yellow wagtails often hunt insects disturbed by grazing cattle, and they perch on trees and bushes more freely than other wagtails. Their food is similar. They have a simple song which may be uttered in flight, perhaps combined with display actions. The nest, a grass cup lined with hair, is placed on the ground, sometimes well-hidden, sometimes quite open with just a sheltering tuft or plant. The five or six eggs are like those of the grey wagtail, but more uniformly marked with yellow brown. The female does most of the incubation, for 12 to 13 days, and both parents feed the young, which leave the nest from 10 days onwards. There may be a second brood in the south.

. . 3 4 **5 6** 7 8 9 10 (11)

2 BLUE-HEADED WAGTAIL (*Motacilla flava flava*). This race regularly breeds across the Channel and is a common passage visitor to Britain. Pairs occasionally nest in Britain, or males may mate with female yellow wagtails. The male in spring (2a) has a beautiful grey-blue head with a pale stripe over the eye. The female (2b) and the male in autumn are rather less bright but are usually recognisable, especially by their pale chins.

SYKES'S WAGTAIL (*Motacilla flava beema*). From time to time birds which look like this Siberian race appear in England and even nest. The male has a pale grey head and a white stripe over the eye. In fact, ringing them has proved that they do not come from Asia but are independent mutant forms — that is, variants which have arisen from the British yellow wagtail.

3 GREY-HEADED WAGTAIL (*Moticilla flava thunbergi*). This is the north European race which is occasionally seen in Britain on passage. It is recognised by its blue-grey head, darker than that of the blue-headed wagtail, and the fact that it has no pale stripe over the eye. This distinguishes both male and female, but not the juvenile.

One or two birds of the Ashy-headed and Black-headed races from south and south-east Europe have been seen in Britain, but they may be mutants in the British stock, like the Sykes's wagtail type.

CITRINE WAGTAIL (*Motacilla citreola*). This Russian wagtail is a separate species, which resembles a white wagtail in its general appearance, except that the male in breeding plumage has a bright yellow head and underparts, and both the grey-headed female and the juvenile show some yellow on their heads and breasts. Two immature birds on Fair Isle in the autumn of 1954 were the first British records; since then there have been thirteen more, all in autumn and one in 1970.

2a BLUE-HEADED WAGTAIL, M., spring 2b F.
1a YELLOW WAGTAIL, M., spring 1b F.
3 GREY-HEADED WAGTAIL, M.   1c YELLOW WAGTAIL, Juv.

SHRIKES

1 **RED-BACKED SHRIKE** (*Lanius cristatus*). The male shrike, which is 6¾ ins. long, is an unmistakable bird; but the female, who usually has crescent markings over her brown and buff plumage pattern, might be confused with a thrush until her head and beak are seen. Females showing a dull version of the male dress are also not uncommon. The juvenile is much more 'scaly' and generally a richer brown than the young woodchat, which is sometimes seen in Britain in autumn. Four of the pale Asiatic race known as the red-tailed or Isabelline shrike have occurred as wanderers, one in spring and three in autumn.

Red-backed shrikes are rapidly decreasing summer visitors, now more or less confined to south and east England, having lost their foothold west of the Severn; they are still found on the heaths of Hampshire and East Anglia where there are scattered bushes of thorn, brambles, and briars. Their decrease is probably due in part to cold wet weather in summer, which stops the insects on which they feed from flying. Birds on passage occur much more widely, even in the Scottish Highlands.

Though at times he is secretive, the male shrike often proclaims his presence from the topmost spray of a bush, flicking his long tail side to side or up and down, and dancing into the air after insects or gliding to another perch with spread wings and tail. As well as large insects, the shrike takes lizards, young birds, and small mammals, sometimes sticking them on thorns in the shrike's 'larder', from which habit he has been called the butcher-bird. The 'larder' is usually some way from the nest and hard to find. The red-backed shrike has a remarkable song, a mixture of chattering, warbling, and the notes of other birds. He also has a variety of harsh call and alarm notes, and sometimes, when alarmed, he may 'freeze', pointing at the intruder. The male's display shows off his rosy breast and black and white tail. The nest, like a small blackbird's without the mud lining and often ornamented with wool, is placed in a young tree, bush, or trailing brambles from ground level to 20 feet high; the eggs are pale buff with a zone of brown markings, though a red type is quite common. The hen incubates the clutch of four to six for at least 2 weeks, and then both birds share duties until the young fly from 12 days onwards.

. . . *4* **5 6** *7 8 9 (10 11)* .

2 **WOODCHAT SHRIKE** (*Lanius senator*). Perhaps the most colourful of the European shrikes, the female being hardly less bright than the male. The juvenile (2a) is a scaly brown, very much like the young red-backed shrike, but greyer, and showing a small whitish patch on the closed wing. This shrike is a rare visitor, on spring and autumn passage to southern Britain; there are very few records from elsewhere. It is most likely to be seen in gardens and orchards rather than on the bushy heaths favoured by the red-backed shrike.

3 **LESSER GREY SHRIKE** (*Lanius minor*). This rare visitor is about 8 ins. long and is distinguished by the black 'mask' meeting over the beak, though this is less obvious in the female. Juveniles are brownish and rather 'scaly' but by the first winter they show a white patch on the closed wing, and soon look like the adults. In flight, the white patch looks shorter and deeper than that of the great grey shrike. Over seventy have occurred in Britain, both in spring and autumn. The nearest breeding area is central France.

4 **GREAT GREY SHRIKE** (*Lanius excubitor*). This rare and handsome winter visitor is 9½ ins. long; it can be distinguished from the lesser grey shrike not only by size but by the extension of the grey crown right to the beak. Females are a little duller than males and have faint markings on the breast, which are more pronounced in the first winter plumage (4a); juveniles are brownish-grey above.

The great grey shrike arrives in autumn usually in small numbers along the east coast, and some move inland to spend the winter in various parts of the country; a few more come on passage in spring.

Perched on top of a thorn bush, this big grey and white bird is conspicuous from some distance. It may then glide down and reappear some minutes later on another bush. It spends a good deal of time on the ground, searching for small mammals and insects, but its principal prey in Britain is probably small birds, which it has often been seen to chase and kill. It seldom utters its harsh call in Britain.

1 2 3 4 5 (6 7) . . *10 11 12*

1a RED-BACKED SHRIKE, F. 1b M.
2a WOODCHAT SHRIKE, Juv. 2b M.
3a LESSER GREY SHRIKE, Ad.
4a GREAT GREY SHRIKE, 1st winter
3b LESSER GREY SHRIKE, 1st winter
4b GREAT GREY SHRIKE, Ad.

1 GOLDEN ORIOLE (*Oriolus oriolus*). Although green woodpeckers (p. 115) are sometimes reported as orioles, in fact the male (1b) is unmistakable with its black and golden-yellow plumage and reddish bill. The female (1a) is much duller, with a streaked breast, and the juvenile resembles her. They are about 9½ ins. long.

The golden oriole is a rare spring visitor mainly to the south and south-east of England, though birds occasionally appear even in the northern Isles of Scotland. It has been said that shooting prevented it becoming a regular breeding bird, but more likely the British climate is the barrier. It has nested in several counties, principally in Kent, most recently in Shropshire (1964) and Suffolk (1967).

In spite of its brilliant colour, the oriole is hard to see because of its skulking habits; it is more easy to hear for it utters a noisy cat-like cry possible to confuse with a jay's call, and also various screeches and growls. The song after which it is named, is a beautiful fluting *orr-i-ole*. The food consists of insects in spring and fruit in summer. Golden oriole's display, which may be seen in England, includes dashing flights among the trees. The nest is a basket of bark fibres and grasses woven to a forked horizontal branch, often in oakwoods and orchards, and the three to five eggs, like white song thrush's eggs with black spots, are incubated by both sexes for about 2 weeks. Both also feed the young for the same period before fledging.

. . . *4 5 6 7 8 9* . . .

2 STARLING (*Sturnus vulgaris*). This most familiar bird of town or country, about 8½ ins. long, has a stout body, short tail, rather long blunt bill, and broad pointed wings. There are a great variety of plumages which are confusing, especially when the brown juveniles are moulting into the first-winter spotted dress and still have their brown heads (2c). In summer the adults are less spotted than in winter. when the female looks more variegated than the male owing to her broader feathers; his are noticeably more pointed. The spots on first-winter birds are more conspicuous than on adults, but the feathers wear away to give the more uniform and darker spring plumage. The bill which is dull in winter, becomes yellow in spring, the male's having a blue-grey and the female's a pinkish base. The female often has a white ring to the dark brown eyes. It is not unusual to see starlings with deformed bills, sometimes one mandible being much longer than the other.

Except in some western districts and islands of Scotland, Wales, and Ireland, starlings are widespread and abundant on cultivated land of all kinds, grass pastures, shores, and in towns and villages. The starlings of Shetland are considered to be a separate race. Except in remote habitats, starlings are usually resident, though their numbers are increased in winter by a huge immigration from eastern Europe.

Starlings hunt for grubs in the lawn or other grass land, running actively over the ground and probing with mandibles held apart. They often visit bird-tables from which they drive away other birds, and they feed on rubbish dumps, in seaweed at the high-tide line and in trees which are infested with caterpillars. The also hawk after flying ants in the air, almost as grace fully as swallows. They are useful to the farmer because they destroy wireworms in freshly ploughed fields. Normally their flight is noisy, bustling, and direct. After rapid wing-beats, they close their wings and drop for a moment; they also plane and glide especially during the remarkable flights made by flocks before they settle to roost. Roosts in London and other big cities are well-known because of attempts to get rid of them, but country roosts usually in thickets and bushes, are much bigger, some being estimated to contain over a million birds Starlings fly up to 30 miles to roost. Winter visitor are usually found in the country, and the city gatherings are mainly residents.

The starling's usual call is a harsh *churr*, and the song is a mixture of whistles, clicks, *chissicks*, and notes taken from other birds; it is a very good mimic and can take in even experienced observers. Flocks at roost keep up a continual 'murmuration', and the nestlings a loud begging chorus. When singing starlings often shiver and droop their wings; this may be part of the display, which also includes chases in the air and along branches. The nest is a simple mass of straws and grasses with a cup, placed in holes of all sizes: under the eaves of houses, in chimneys, walls hollow trees, and nestboxes; in the north and west starlings build in rock crevices, and they sometimes take over old woodpecker holes and drive out smaller birds. The usual clutch is four to six blue eggs, which both sexes incubate for about 13 days. The female incubates at night, and she does most of the care of the brood, which fly after about 3 weeks. There are sometimes second broods, and occasional winter nests in towns are reported. Starlings, more than most birds have the habit of laying odd eggs on the ground Noisy parties of juveniles form at the end of May.

1 2 3 4 5 6 7 8 9 10 11 12

3 ROSY STARLING (*Sturnus roseus*). About the same size as the common starling, this visitor from eastern Europe can be easily recognised in a reasonable light by its pink body contrasting with the black tail wings, and crested head. The juveniles (3b) are hard to tell from juvenile common starlings but are paler.

The rosy starling usually visits Britain in summer but without showing a distinct pattern of passage it occurs mainly down the east coast and in the Northern Isles of Scotland, but there are records from south-west England. In general habits it resembles the common starling, with which it often associates Some birds reported have probably escaped from captivity.

1a GOLDEN ORIOLE F. 1b M.   2a STARLING, M., summer
3a ROSY STARLING, Ad. 3b Juv.   2b STARLING, Juv.
2c STARLING, Juv., moulting   2d STARLING, F., autumn

1 WAXWING (*Bombycilla garrulus*). If the crested silhouette of this starling-sized bird (about 7 ins. long) can be seen, it can hardly be confused with any other British bird; also the plumage in reasonable light is quite distinctive, with its 'wax' spots on the wing and yellow band at the tip of the dark tail. The female usually lacks the red on the wing and has less of a crest, but both sexes at all times of year have a rich chestnut-brown under the tail.

The waxwing is an 'irruptive' visitor to Britain in winter, that is, there are sometimes only a few, but sometimes hundreds may appear, first on the east coast and then spreading right across to Ireland and the Scottish Isles. A few remain until spring, but they have not been known to breed. Berry-laden hedges and bushes are the places to look for them; they show no fear of man, and will come confidently to take cotoneaster berries from the walls of houses.

After feeding, parties may sit still for a long time, before flying off with strong starling-like flight. They swarm agilely over bushes, gobbling the berries, but seldom come to the ground except to drink. In winter they are rather silent birds, but a thin *sirrr* call and a piping note may be heard.

1   2   3   4   (5)   10   11   12

2 HAWFINCH (*Coccothraustes coccothraustes*). This is the largest British finch, 6½ ins. long. It is much the same size and build as a waxwing, and also as a cross-bill (p. 181), but in most positions its powerful head and almost top-heavy bill contrasted with the short tail are distinctive. Males are usually brighter tinted than females, but in winter they are not easy to tell apart. The juvenile has no black on the throat and its underparts are barred brown.

Hawfinches are local residents with their stronghold in the south and east of England. They are very scarce in the west and in Scotland, but are found as far north as Perthshire, though very rarely further north or in Ireland. Their habitat is broad-leaved woodland, including orchards, large gardens, and sometimes bushy commons.

Like some other birds of striking appearance, for most of the year hawfinches tend to hide and are hard to see; but for a period in early spring they perch high in trees. They fly between woods at a considerable height, but can be picked up from their call-note *tzik* rather like the call of a great spotted woodpecker. The song is simple and rather variable. Outside the breeding season they form flocks or parties and feed much on the ground on fallen seeds; they also take them off trees. Their powerful bills enable them to crack olive stones with ease. The winter flocks break up with fighting, which leads to courtship. The male shows off his plumage to the female, and then chases her through the trees; he also has a special courtship flight. The nest, often in a horizontal branch and built in a variety of trees, is a light structure of twigs lined with moss, lichen, rootlets, and grass. The four to six greenish eggs with dark scrawls are incubated by the female for about 12 days, and then both parents feed the young which fly after 12 to 13 days.

1   2   3   4   5   6   7   8   9   10   11   12

ROSE-BREASTED GROSBEAK (*Pheucticus ludovicianus*). A male of this magnificent big North American finch was seen in County Antrim in November 1957; a second was reported from Ireland in 1962, followed by records from Scilly (1966) and Pembrokeshire (1967). It is 8 ins. long, with mainly black upperparts and white underparts, against which its rosy breast stands out. The female is quite different, dark brown above with a pale stripe over the eye and light underparts, streaked and spotted.

EVENING GROSBEAK (*Hesperiphona vespertina*). This large (7¼ ins.) North American finch joins the British list on the strength of a male seen on St. Kilda in March 1969. The plumage is a mixture of greenish-brown, yellow and black with white wing-bars; the male has a yellow forehead, the female has white on the black tail. The colour of the huge pale bill varies.

1a WAXWING. Ad.   1b WAXWING. 1st winter
2a HAWFINCH, M.   2b HAWFINCH, F.

1 SISKIN (*Carduelis spinus*). This small green finch, under 5 ins. long, has a fairly distinctive male plumage (1a) with its black cap and bib, yellowish rump, and generally bright tints. Females (1b) and juveniles (1c) are duller, with a general greenish-grey appearance and streaked underparts; in poor light they are difficult to tell from redpolls, which have the same fork-tailed silhouette and pale wing-bars.

Siskins are increasing residents; they have spread into the north of England from the Scottish Highlands, and other groups are established in North Wales, Devon, and elsewhere. They have been increasing in Ireland also for many years and are now widespread. In addition, siskins are winter visitors in varying numbers to the rest of Britain. When breeding they are birds of coniferous woodland, and their spread has been helped by recent afforestation; but in winter they are usually found along streams and by lakes where alders grow.

As with many finches, the call-note, a loud, musical *tzing*, is distinctive and often the best way of picking up a flying bird or party. When they land, they may twitter musically as they swarm over an alder, prizing the seeds from the cones; but more often they feed silently, only calling as they prepare to leave. They feed on many other seeds, quite frequently on grass seeds. At the end of the winter, flocks may sit in the trees and utter a fuller song, which is perfected when the males perform their exaggerated flights over the future breeding area. The male also displays to the female and chases her. The small mossy nest, with a foundation of twigs and a soft lining, is usually placed well out on a horizontal branch of a tall conifer, or near the leading shoot. The four or five eggs are like small greenfinch eggs; the female incubates them for about 12 days, then both parents feed the brood from the throat until they fly in about 14 days. There are generally two broods.

1   2   3   4   5   6   7   8   9   10   11   12

CITRIL FINCH (*Serinus citrinella*). The same size as a siskin this little finch from the mountain forests of Europe looks like a miniature greenfinch without the bright yellow patches. Only one has ever been recorded in Britain — in Norfolk in January 1904.

2 SERIN (*Serinus canarius*). The wild form of the domestic canary is only 4½ ins. long; the plumage of both sexes is a yellow-green streaked with brown, and with a pale yellow rump which shows in flight. The

male (2a) can be told by the yellow on his head; the female (2b) is very like a female siskin but with no yellow on the tail and a noticeably short, stumpy bill. Juveniles do not have the yellow rump.

After increasing occurrences, serins were found nesting in Dorset in 1967 and breeding has continued in south-coast counties. But the serin has been very seldom recorded further west and north, though a male sang in County Cork, Ireland, in May 1947. On the Continent, the serin is found much round houses and gardens, feeding on seeds of all kinds. Its general behaviour is like that of the other small finches.

3 GREENFINCH (*Chloris chloris*). Although not as massive as a hawfinch, the greenfinch, nearly 6 ins. long, has a stout body, big head, and a powerful bill. Females (3b) are duller than the green males (3c) and the juveniles (3a) are quite brown and streaked and can be confused with juvenile crossbills (p. 181), but in all plumages the bright yellow on tail and wings is distinctive.

Because it haunts rather tall bush-cover, the greenfinch is very much a bird of cultivated land with hedges, gardens, and occasional scrub patches; in the barer and remoter parts of the British Isles it is found only round villages and houses. In the central highlands of Scotland it breeds in pine trees, which may be an original habitat. Some British birds emigrate, though most are resident, while many passage migrants and winter visitors arrive from Europe in autumn.

Greenfinches are colourful members of the winter flocks of finches and sparrows in the hedgerows, where they are particularly fond of rose hips, and they visit farmyards after dropped grain and weed seeds. They fly up with a musical twitter when disturbed. In spring the drawn-out call *jeee* and the floating 'butterfly' flight of the male as he sings are characteristic. Greenfinches often nest in small groups, appearing suddenly in April and beginning to build; but another year they may go elsewhere. This erratic behaviour is typical of many finches. The nest is a solid structure of moss, twigs, and wool, lined with soft material; the four to six whitish eggs are marked with light chestnut and are incubated by the female for about 2 weeks. Both parents feed the young by regurgitating food from the throat; they fly after 13 to 15 days. Two broods are normal. Family parties are prominent in late summer and link up to form flocks, sometimes of many hundreds of birds, on weedy fields or waste ground.

1   2   3   4   5   6   7   8   9   10   11   12

1a SISKIN, M. 1b F.
1c SISKIN, Juv.
    3a GREENFINCH, Juv. 3b F. 3c M.

2a SERIN, M. 2b F.

1 LINNET (*Carduelis cannabina*). In any plumage, this very common small finch, 5¼ ins. long, can be distinguished from the twite by its more distinct pale wing-bar and from redpolls by its lack of black bib, as well as by the wing-bar. Linnets are residents throughout the British Isles, though they are replaced by twites in the Highlands and Islands of Scotland and the remoter areas of Ireland. They are equally at home in gardens, hedgerows, heaths, and coastal dunes, and they flock in winter on stubbles and ground rich in weed seeds.

Whereas siskins and redpolls often associate, linnets keep to their own kind, rising from the ground in a cloud with soft twittering calls. The male has a most musical and sustained song, and used to be a popular cage-bird. His display includes dropping of the wings and spreading of the tail. Linnets feed on a variety of seeds and take insects to their young. Like greenfinches, they often nest in a group, building substantial foundations of grasses and moss, lined with wool, fur, or hair, in a variety of sites: bushes, creepers, banks, and grass-tufts. The five or six pale blue eggs with brown markings are incubated mainly by the female for about 11 days; both parents feed the young in the nest for a further 11 days. There are two, often three, broods.

1 2 3 4 5 6 7 8 9 10 11 12

2 TWITE (*Carduelis flavirostris*). Another small fork-tailed finch, about 5¼ ins. long, which can be confused with female and juvenile linnets. But in winter twites have yellow bills and more streaky upperparts, and the males have pinkish rumps. In summer their bills are greyish like the linnet's, but the white mark on the wing is less obvious.

Twites are resident but local on the moors of northern England. They are rare in southern Scotland, commoner in parts of the West Highlands, and numerous on some of the Hebrides. They are widely distributed in Ireland, particularly in the west. Winter visitors from Scandinavia come to the east coast of Britain and some inland places, for example Cannock Chase in Staffordshire. Though typically moorland birds, twites breed and feed on crofts and along the coastal zone in the Hebrides.

Twites live in flocks or parties most of the year, and often nest in groups. They feed on various seeds, being fond of the heads of thrift by the shore; they take some insects. The call-note is more metallic and drawn-out than the linnet's and the song is less musical. In display the male shows off his pink rump. The nest, built in heather on a bank, in low bushes, walls, even under a ploughed furrow, is lined with wool or fur. Five to six eggs, resembling those of other small finches, are incubated by the female for about 12 days; both parents feed the young on regurgitated food until after they fly at about 2 weeks. There are often two broods.

1 2 3 4 5 6 7 8 9 10 11 12

3 LESSER REDPOLL (*Carduelis flammea*). Several races of this small finch (about 5 ins. long) occur in the British Isles and can with practice be told apart. The 'lesser' redpoll (3a, b) the native race and the smallest, has dark rather reddish-brown upperparts, a pale buff double wing-bar, and streaked underparts. The male in spring (3b) may be bright pink on the breast. The black chin patch of the adults is faint in the juvenile, which has a shorter forked tail than twites and linnets, and lacks the yellow of young siskins.

The mealy redpoll (3d) is, as its name suggests, a paler form, slightly larger, and with white wing-bars. The Greenland redpoll (3c) is very like the mealy but larger and darker.

The lesser redpoll is a resident, widely distributed in the British Isles and now commonest in the west and north, especially in North Wales, the Scottish Highlands, and Ireland; in southern and eastern England it is a very local breeding species, but more numerous in winter, when there are many visitors, among them a few mealy redpolls from northern Europe. Greenland redpolls are fairly regular on passage, and a pair, apparently of this race, bred in Scotland recently. Redpolls breed in scrub of birch, sallows, alders, hawthorn, and in gardens and parks with bushes; in winter they feed on birches, alders, and weeds, often with siskins and blue tits.

Redpolls have a particularly bounding flight and can be recognised high overhead by their metallic call, rendered *chuch-uch-uch-uch*; they also have an anxious but musical single note. The song, often delivered in flight, is an extension of the call-note; and males have a special display flight of 'butterfly' type, when they perform aerobatics. They feed on seeds of many kinds, behaving like siskins (p. 176); they also take insects in summer. The nest has a rather untidy appearance, with twigs sticking through the moss, but the soft cup lining is beautifully neat. The female incubates the clutch of five to six eggs, which are pale blue with dark markings, for about 11 days; both parents feed the young, which may fly in 11 or more days; there is sometimes a second brood.

1 2 3 4 5 6 7 8 9 10 11 12

4 ARCTIC REDPOLL (*Carduelis hornemanni*). Also called Hornemann's redpoll, this form is not always considered a separate species from the lesser redpoll group. It is as big as a mealy redpoll but even paler, with a white unmarked rump and white underparts. Arctic redpolls are rare visitors to the east coast, most often to Fair Island. In habits they resemble other redpolls.

4   ARCTIC REDPOLL, M.   3c GREENLAND REDPOLL   3d MEALY REDPOLL
3a LESSER REDPOLL, F.   3b M.
1b LINNET, M., summer   1a F., summer   2b TWITE, M., autumn   2a F., autumn

FINCHES. 3 (CROSSBILLS)

1 COMMON CROSSBILL (*Loxia curvirostra*). This stoutly-built fork-tailed finch, about 6½ ins. long, has the mandibles of its powerful bill crossed when adult. Its plumage shows great variation, from the brick-red, dark-winged adult males (1a) to the young orange-red males (1c), the yellow-green females (1b), and the greenish-grey streaked juveniles, which at first do not have the crossed bill and can be mistaken for greenfinches except that they lack the bright yellow on wings and tail. In their slightly topheavy appearance, crossbills resemble hawfinches (p. 175). It is impossible to distinguish for certain the common crossbill from the parrot or Scottish crossbill (2) without handling it, though individuals of the rarer species have much stronger bills.

The common crossbill is an invader from the Continent which establishes more or less permanent breeding colonies in parts of southern Britain. Its stronghold is East Anglia, but groups have remained in Surrey, Hants, Northumberland, and several other counties for years, after one of the big invasions which occur from time to time — in 1953, 1956, 1958 and 1962, for example. Earlier invasions left breeding groups in Ireland for many years. Invasions usually begin after breeding on the Continent in late June, and parties reach the furthest islands of Britain. Their usual habitat is conifer forest, and they can most often be seen where there are clumps of mature trees.

Like the smaller finches, crossbills go about in parties, landing on the top of a conifer and attacking the cones busily like so many small parrots, wrenching the scales open to get at the seeds. They often feed silently, but sometimes 'talk' continually: *tchook tchook tchook*. When they take off, this changes at once to a more musical *plink plink plink*, by which they can easily be recognised. The song, delivered from the top of a tree, is a rather jerky sequence of notes, but there is a rarer warbling form. As well as from cones, crossbills when on an invasion will take seeds from berries and fruit and from low-growing plants; they also eat some insects. Males break away from the group into their display flight, rather similar to that of greenfinches (p. 176). They chase the females and then court them, until the pairs are formed and the flock breaks up. Crossbills nest very early in the year; they build, usually well out on a horizontal branch, a mossy nest on a foundation of twigs and line it with fur and feathers. The four or five

eggs, which are just like greenfinches' eggs, are incubated by the female for 12 or 13 days; the male feeds her on the nest, then both feed the young with regurgitated food, the male at first supplying the female. The young do not fledge for nearly 3 weeks; then family parties unite and may roam widely.

1   **2**   **3**   **4**   **5**   6   7   8   9   10   11   12

2 PARROT (SCOTTISH) CROSSBILL (*Loxia pytyopsittacus scotica*). The crossbills which form an isolated population in the old pine forests of Strathspey in Inverness-shire are regarded by some authorities as a race of the Continental parrot crossbill, which may have bred in Surrey in 1963. Scottish birds resemble the common crossbill in general appearance but their bills are between those of the common crossbills and those of the Continental parrot crossbills in size.

The Scottish crossbill is a fairly stationary resident; from its stronghold in Strathspey it has spread to neighbouring counties where there are suitable old woods of pine, which is its favourite conifer. A few birds of the Continental race occur in years where there are invasions of common crossbills. The Scottish crossbill resembles the common crossbill in habits and nesting.

1   **2**   **3**   **4**   **5**   6   7   8   9   10   11   12

3 TWO-BARRED CROSSBILL (*Loxia leucoptera*). This northern European species, particularly associated with larch forests, occurs in Britain from time to time in invasion years. The double white wing-bar is distinctive in all plumages, and the call note is also different from that of the common species, which otherwise resembles it in its general habits.

PINE GROSBEAK (*Pinicola enucleator*). About 8 ins. long, this big finch is rather like a crossbill, though without the crossed mandibles. The male has a pinkish-red head and breast, while the female and juvenile are a dull orange in all plumages; they have two thin white wing-bars. There are at least 7 accepted British records between 1890 and 1959, the last in Kent. The nearest breeding area is in northern Scandinavia.

The more often seen scarlet grosbeak is shown on p. 191, where it is contrasted with sparrows which, in its autumn plumage, it closely resembles.

1a COMMON CROSSBILL, M. 1b F.   2a SCOTTISH CROSSBILL, Juv. F. 2b Ad. M.
  1c COMMON CROSSBILL, Imm. M. 3a TWO-BARRED CROSSBILL, M.
     3b TWO-BARRED CROSSBILL, F.

1 BULLFINCH (*Pyrrhula pyrrhula*). Its big stubby bill and clear-cut plumage pattern make the bullfinch (5¾ ins. long) easy to recognise, just a glimpse of the black tail, grey back, and square-looking white rump as the bird flits away along a hedge is enough. The brown-headed juveniles (1c), though not quite so distinctive, have the black tail and white rump.

Bullfinches are well-distributed residents throughout woodland and scrub country in the British Isles, though they are not found in some of the island groups. They are probably most numerous in the south, where they have increased in recent years and are a menace to fruit-growers. Consequently, they are no longer protected in fruit-growing areas. Their favourite habitat is a thicket of hawthorn, blackthorn, or other closely-growing bushes, but they are also found in gardens, in tall hedges, and in coniferous and broadleaved woodland. At times parties go out on open moorland after heather and other seeds. The brighter-coloured northern race from north-eastern Europe is a visitor in varying numbers in autumn and winter; at home it is a forest bird.

Bullfinches are seen in pairs at all times of year, though where they are abundant they form parties and small flocks. They used to be considered shy, but now they come more into the open, perching on telegraph wires and feeding on the ground on the seeds of low-growing plants. They attack seeds, fruit, and buds of many kinds — a small party may completely strip a sizeable tree of blossom. But they also take many diseased buds and feed their young largely on insects.

The piping call may be a single *tew*, a double *tew tew*, or a triple *tew cher tew*, of which the young have a louder version. Bullfinches have no full song, but birds sometimes warble sweetly. The male displays his pink breast to the female and, like other finches, spreads his wings and tail. The nest is light but strong, built on a foundation of twigs and rootlets with a cup of finer rootlets and hair. The four to six eggs are a deeper blue and have larger markings, often zoned, than those of other finches. The female undertakes most of the 12 to 14 day incubation, but both parents feed the young on regurgitated food, the male supplying the female, who passes it on. There is regularly a second brood.

1 2 3 **4 5 6 7** *8 9 10 11 12*

2 GOLDFINCH (*Carduelis carduelis*). About 5¼ ins. long, the same size as their close relatives the redpolls, twites, and linnets (p. 179), goldfinches are distinguished by their black wings with 'gold' bands and white spots, black, white-tipped tails and red, white, and black heads. Juveniles (2b) lack the bright coloured head, but in other respects are easily recognisable.

Goldfinches have increased over the past 50 years, perhaps because the law now prohibits trapping birds for caging. They are breeding residents all over England, Wales, and Ireland, and as far as the southern Highlands of Scotland, though in upland and moorland country they are mainly confined to the neighbourhood of houses and gardens. Even in the south they prefer the surroundings of man and are often common in towns with avenues of elms and horse-chestnuts, and in orchards. In winter they haunt waste ground where there are seed-bearing weeds, especially thistles and other members of the daisy family (Composites). They sometimes visit alders with siskins and redpolls. Some British goldfinches emigrate in winter, but as far as we know few birds from Europe visit Britain.

A 'charm' of goldfinches working a patch of thistles in seed is a lovely sight. When busy feeding, the birds often allow a close approach, and then all take wing with their musical calls, circle round, and may return if the observer stays still. They also take insects in summer like many finches, but do not often land on the ground. Their bounding flight seems even more erratic than that of redpolls and siskins. As with linnets, it was largely their attractive tinkling song which made them popular as cage birds. The male displays his golden wing to the female, and when paired they fly off together to the nest site, which is often at the end of a branch or spray, well hidden by the leaves and usually more than 10 feet from the ground. The nest, built of rootlets, wool, moss, and vegetable fluff, is one of the daintiest of any finch, yet often lasts through the winter. The five or six eggs are of the usual finch type, but more pointed than some. The female incubates them for 12 to 13 days, then both parents feed the young with regurgitated food. They fledge in about 2 weeks, and there is usually a second, sometimes a third brood. The birds usually desert the breeding area until the next spring.

1 **2** *3* **4 5 6 7** *8 9 10 11 12*

1a BULLFINCH, F.   1b M.   1c Juv.
2a GOLDFINCH, Ads.
2b GOLDFINCH, Juv.

1 CHAFFINCH (*Fringilla coelebs*). One of the commonest British land-birds, the chaffinch, 6 ins. long, shows a fine variety of colours. No other common small bird has so much white on the wing — a big shoulder patch and a wing-bar, and the white outer tail feathers show clearly when the bird takes flight. The male's bright plumage is somewhat obscured in winter (1b), especially on the head; but the brown margins to the feathers wear off to give the full tints in spring (1c). Juveniles resemble females (1a) but with duller rumps, but the young males soon begin to show a recognisably different plumage. Male Scandinavian chaffinches have pinker rather than brick red breasts, while those from western Europe are more wine-red. But British birds themselves vary so much that it is not easy to tell the races apart.

The chaffinch, originally a woodland bird, is a breeding resident or summer visitor throughout the British Isles wherever there are trees and shrubs; in winter it feeds with other finches and sparrows in the fields, deserting its remoter breeding areas. Passage migrants and winter visitors arrive in large numbers from northern and eastern Europe from September onwards, and in very hard weather many move towards the south-west.

The song of a male chaffinch from the bare bough of an oak tree in February is one of the first signs of spring returning to the woodland; it is quite a short burst, but powerful, with a final *cheweeou*, and the bird quivers as he delivers it. Soon he is chasing a female, flashing white among the tree trunks. As nesting approaches, the anxious *pink* call is heard more often, but chaffinches have many other calls, and their song varies in different districts. For most of the year chaffinches feed on grain and seeds, working over the ground in mixed flocks, running and hopping. If alarmed, they all fly up to the nearest tree or hedge, but soon flutter down again to resume feeding. They come to bird-tables, especially in areas where sparrows are scarce, and in spring and summer they take a great many insects and feed their young on them. The nest is famous for its neatness, a rather deep, beautifully moulded cup of moss and lichen, adorned with cobwebs, bark fibres, paper and even tinfoil, and lined with hair; it may blend with the fork of a tree or be quite obvious in a bare hedge or bramble bush. The four or five eggs are usually brown or blue, with round dark brown spots and scrawls; pure blue eggs occur. The female incubates for about 12 days, then both parents feed the young, which fly in about 2 weeks if not disturbed. Though most finches have at least two broods, the chaffinch only has one. The rather poor singing heard again in autumn is partly at any rate from young males.

*1 2 3 **4 5 6** 7 8 **9 10 11** 12*

2 BRAMBLING (*Fringilla montifringilla*). Bramblings replace chaffinches in northern Europe. They are about the same size and shape and alike in colouring, but when bramblings fly up among a flock of chaffinches, their narrow white rumps distinguish them. Both sexes have prominent orange shoulder patches and not very distinct white wing-bars. The male in winter (2a) looks more like the female (2c), but in spring he has a 'plummy' black head (2b) and sometimes shows this plumage in Britain.

The number of bramblings which winter or pass through Britain varies a great deal; they are usually most numerous in eastern counties, but bad weather may drive them westward. In autumn and winter they are found in flocks with chaffinches in farmland or under beech trees when the mast (nuts) is plentiful; but on passage in spring they may appear in the birch and conifer woods which are their breeding habitat in Scandinavia. In bad seasons or in mid-winter they are found on the fields and round stackyards where these still exist. Their general behaviour is like that of chaffinches, but they have quite a different call, more metallic and often rendered *scape*. The full song is musical and fluting, but usually only a greenfinch-like *jeee* and a brief rattle are heard in Britain. There is only one certain nesting record, from Sutherland in 1920, though others have been reported, and singing males are quite often heard.

1a CHAFFINCH, F.
1b CHAFFINCH, M., winter   1c M., spring
2b BRAMBLING, M., spring   2a M., winter   2c F., winter

BUNTINGS. 1

1 YELLOWHAMMER (*Emberiza citrinella*). This well-known bunting is 6½ ins. long. The plumage on the head and breast varies, some females in summer having as much yellow as the duller males, while others show none and are like female cirl buntings, except for the chestnut rump. Juveniles are like very dark females. But yellowhammers in all plumages have chestnut rumps and white outer tail feathers. There is an eastern race, the pine bunting, which is often regarded as a separate species, *Emberiza leucocephala*. Both sexes have distinctive chestnut and white head markings. It has been recorded once in Shetland and twice in Orkney.

Yellowhammers are widely distributed residents in the British Isles, nesting as far north as Orkney; they also occur in winter on some islands where they do not breed. In the south they are associated with hedgerows in farmland and with heaths and commons, but in the north they are found in open woodland, often where there are boggy patches. In winter, yellowhammers often join with finches and sparrows in flocks on the fields and round farms, but they seldom come near large towns.

The yellowhammer's 'pebbly' call, *tshripp*, is distinctive, and the famous 'little bit of bread and no cheese' song is one of the most persistent along hedges in high summer. Males from the winter flocks start taking up their song posts early in spring. They feed principally on seed and grain, but take a number of insects and other small animals in summer. The male's display includes a special flight and chases. The solid nest of grasses lined with hair is built from ground level to a few feet up in banks or bushes; the three to five white or pinkish, heavily scribbled eggs are brooded mainly by the female for about 13 days, but both parents feed the young. They fly after 12 to 13 days, and there is a second, sometimes a third, brood.

1 2 3 4 5 6 7 8 9 10 11 12

2 CIRL BUNTING (*Emberiza cirlus*). Very slightly smaller and neater looking than the yellowhammer, the cirl bunting can be distinguished by the dull brown rump, and by the colours of the male's head and breast (2a). The females (2b) and juveniles can be told from sparrows by their white outer tail-feathers and from pipits by their stouter bills.

Cirl buntings are local residents in southern England as far north as the Chiltern and Malvern Hills, but are not now found in Wales and only occasionally elsewhere. Their habitat is sheltered tree and bush-clad slopes of downs and low hills, and they may be seen near yew trees or in gardens with *Macrocarpa* cypresses. Parties wander in autumn, but there is no real migration.

The male cirl's rattle, which he delivers from an elm or other hedgerow tree, is quite distinct from the yellowhammer's full song but may be confused with a short version of it, or with the song of the lesser whitethroat (p. 152), often found in the same habitat. In general habits cirls resemble and associate with yellowhammers, though also found in parties of their own. There is no striking display. The mossy nest is more like a greenfinch's than a yellowhammer's, and is usually fairly high in a hedge or bush, or in a yew or cypress tree; otherwise its breeding habits are the same as the yellowhammer's.

1 2 3 4 5 6 7 8 9 10 11 12

BLACK-HEADED (*E. melanocephala*) AND RED-HEADED (*E. bruniceps*) BUNTINGS. The former can be regarded as the western and the latter the eastern race of the same species, only the male plumages differing. The black-headed male in summer has a black cap and cheeks, a yellow collar and breast, and a chestnut back; the red-headed male has a bright chestnut head and upper breast. Females, juveniles, and winter males are rather sparrow-like. In no plumage have they any white on the tail. The black-headed bunting, which breeds in Italy, has been seen in Britain about twenty-five times, sixteen since 1958. But some were almost certainly escapes; for this reason the redheaded bunting is no longer accepted as a British bird.

3 YELLOW-BREASTED BUNTING (*Emberiza aureola*). A rare bunting which breeds as near as Finland and has occurred over thirty times in Britain, mainly along the east coast. The male in summer is quite distinctive; the much duller female is yellow below, and has a white wing-bar and some white on the tail. Her striped head is conspicuous. Juveniles, which are the most likely to be seen in Britain, resemble females.

4 ORTOLAN (*Emberiza hortulana*). This bunting, about the size of a yellowhammer, has a distinctive male plumage (4b), and the female (4a) is only a little duller. The juveniles also show the pinkish bill and legs, buffish underparts, and the narrow pale rim which makes the black eye so conspicuous. Ortolans are regular passage migrants in very small numbers, mostly in the Northern Isles of Scotland.

ROCK BUNTING (*Emberiza cia*). A southern European bunting with a black-striped grey head and a chestnut rump alike the yellowhammer; juveniles of both species are very alike. There are six British records. the latest from Caernarvon in 1967. Some were possibly escaped cage-birds.

1a YELLOWHAMMER, M. 1b F.   2a CIRL BUNTING, M. 2b F.

3 YELLOW-BREASTED BUNTING, F., autumn

4a ORTOLAN, F., 1st autumn   4b ORTOLAN, M., summer

1 REED BUNTING (*Emberiza schoeniclus*). The male, rather smaller than a yellowhammer (6 ins. long), has a distinctive black head and throat with a white collar in spring and summer (1b). The female (1a) has a chestnut crown and cheek, with a pale stripe over the eye and a dark 'moustachial' stripe. Both become much duller in winter. Juveniles are like dull females.

A widely distributed resident or summer visitor, the reed bunting's principal habitat is wet ground, not necessarily with reeds, in river valleys, and round lakes and ponds; and it is found increasingly in dry areas. Reed buntings visit farmland in the winter, often joining other seed-eating birds. Some emigrate, and there are winter visitors from Europe.

The reed bunting appears more restless than the yellowhammer (p. 187), constantly flicking its tail as it clings to a reed with feet wide apart. The call-note is a drawn-out *seee*, and the song a short, variable phrase, *chi chi chi chitty*. The display starts with the male chasing the female, to whom he later shows off his plumage. They feed on seeds and grain for most of the year, with insects in summer. The nest, often very well-hidden in a tussock, is of grasses, lined with hair. and the four to six eggs are dull brown with dark spots and scrawls. The female does most of the incubating for nearly 2 weeks, and both parents feed the young, which may leave the nest after 10 days. There are regularly two broods.

*1 2 3 **4 5 6 7 8** 9 10 11 12***

RUSTIC BUNTING (*Emberiza rustica*). A rare northern visitor which breeds in Sweden. Both sexes look rather like reed buntings, but have white underparts with a chestnut breast-band and streaks, and the male in summer has a pale eye-stripe. There are about sixty British records, nearly all from the northern isles of Scotland and the east coast in autumn.

2 LITTLE BUNTING (*Emberiza pusilla*). This small bunting (about 5¼ ins.) bears a general resemblance to the reed bunting. The black stripes on the reddish crown help to identify the male, but this is not an easy species to distinguish except by size. It is a fairly regular visitor to the east coast and northern isles of Scotland on autumn passage from its northern breeding areas. It is a shy and difficult bird to see but has a distinctive call note, a high, quiet *pwick*.

CRETZSCHMAR'S BUNTING (*Emberiza caesia*). An individual of this south-east European species was recorded on Fair Isle in June 1967. It resembles the ortolan (p. 186) but the male has a blue-grey head and rusty brown throat; the female has no yellow on the throat and is generally duller.

3 LAPLAND BUNTING (*Calcarius lapponicus*). Another far northern species with a distinctive male plumage in spring (3a), though much duller in autumn (3b). Females and juveniles look like dark reed buntings, but have shorter tails, showing less white, yellow bills, and no prominent markings on the face.

Lapland buntings are regular visitors on autumn passage in varying numbers, and some spend the winter, usually on the east coast; spring visitors are rare. They are most easily recognised by their call-notes, a short rattle and a musical falling *teeew*. They feed on the seeds of plants either along the shore or in fields near it, and often allow a close approach.

4 SNOW BUNTING (*Plectrophenax nivalis*). This large stoutly-built bunting, 6½ ins. long, has a variety of plumages. In autumn and winter both sexes are buffish brown birds with white underparts and white on tail and wings, the male having the most white (4a). In the breeding plumage, shown opposite in top right-hand corner, he has a white head, shoulders and underparts, and the female also shows much more white than in winter.

Snow buntings are regular autumn and winter visitors, chiefly to the north and east of Britain, though odd birds occur more widely, usually on the coast or high hills. A party of stout brown birds run busily about the high-tide line, pecking at seed-heads, then suddenly turn into snowflakes as they fly away with pleasant twittering calls, circle round and come back to feed again, the birds behind flying over those in front as they work over the ground. The few breeding pairs in the Cairngorm Hills of Scotland have an elaborate display, including a song-flight. The nest is well hidden in loose rocks or boulders and is made of grasses, with a fine lining. Four to six whitish, boldly marked eggs are incubated by the female for about 11 days; both parents feed the young, largely on insects; they fly in under 2 weeks.

*1 2 3 4 **(5 6 7** 8) 9 10 11 12***

RUFOUS-SIDED TOWHEE (*Pipilo erythrophthalmus*). One of this distinctive North American species occurred on Lundy in June 1966. The male (7¼ ins.) has mainly black breast and upperparts (brown in the female) with chestnut flanks, white underparts and large white spots on the long black tail.

AMERICAN 'SPARROWS'. Four species, closely related to the buntings and about the same size, have occurred in Britain. The adult **WHITE-THROATED SPARROW** (*Zonotrichia albicollis*) has a distinctive black and white head pattern. One was shot on the Scottish Flannan Isles in 1909; there have been eight records since, one by Southampton Water in 1961. A male **SONG-SPARROW** (*Melospiza melodia*) appeared and sang on Fair Isle in the spring of 1959. There have been records since from Yorkshire and Caernarvon. It has bright-brown upperparts and a big dark spot in the centre of the breast. A single **FOX SPARROW** (*Passerella iliaca*), a larger bird with a reddish tail and heavily marked breast, was reported on the Copeland Islands near Belfast in 1961. A single **SLATE-COLOURED JUNCO** (*Junco hyemalis*), dark above and with white underparts, was found in Ireland in 1905. There have been five more recent records.

4a SNOW BUNTING. M., winter   4b F., winter   4c M., summer
3a LAPLAND BUNTING. M., spring   3b autumn   1c REED BUNTING. M., winter
2   LITTLE BUNTING   1a REED BUNTING. F.   1b M., spring

CORN BUNTING, GROSBEAK, SPARROWS

1   CORN BUNTING (*Emberiza calandra*). The largest British bunting, 7 ins. long, lacks the white outer tail-feathers which most buntings have (*see* pp. 187, 189), and so can possibly be confused with female house sparrows. The brown tail also distinguishes it from the skylark (p. 123), a bird otherwise of similar plumage in the same habitats. Corn buntings are stout-looking brown birds with no striking features; the sexes are alike, and the juveniles rather paler.

Corn buntings are now very local in Ireland and the Scottish Highlands and Islands, and almost extinct in Wales. But down the east side of Britain and in parts of the south they are still common over large areas of open agricultural land. They are generally resident, but there are some winter movements and passage migration.

The male, sitting dumpily on a bush, post, or telegraph wire, repeats his simple jangling song, like a bunch of little keys rattling; then he takes off in heavy, whirring flight, calling a loud *tshripp*, and following the female who has just left her nest in the thick crop below. They feed together on seeds on the ground, and he accompanies her back to the nest. After breeding, corn buntings join in parties and roam about a good feeding area. Males sometimes return to their territories even in winter and sing. The nest, usually well-hidden on the flat or in a bank, is a loosely-built cup of grasses with a hair lining. The female incubates the four to six very variable, boldly-marked eggs for 12 to 13 days, and she also mainly cares for the young, which may leave the nest after 10 days. There may be two broods, and in some districts a male may have several mates.

1   2   3   4   5   6   7   8   9   10   11   12

2   SCARLET GROSBEAK (*Carpodacus erythrinus*). This medium-sized finch, about 5¾ ins. long, in the plumage most often seen in Britain can easily be confused with a female house sparrow or a corn bunting. It is less bulky than either and shows a whitish double wing-bar in flight. It also has a stouter bill. The rosy-tinted male in spring is hardly ever seen in Britain, as the bird is almost entirely an autumn passage visitor, mainly to the northern isles of Scotland, where it occurs on open, cultivated land, feeding on seeds or grain and perching on fence wires.

3   HOUSE SPARROW (*Passer domesticus*). This best known of city birds is just under 6 ins. long. Males in clean plumage can be confused with tree sparrows, but they are larger, their crowns are grey instead of chestnut, and their cheeks less white. The male's black bib is smaller in winter and on young birds. In the country the female (3c) can be distinguished from the smaller buntings by the lack of white on her tail and a fairly distinct pale stripe over the eye. Juveniles (3b) at first resemble females.

House sparrows are to be found wherever man has settled, except for some remote islands and upland farms. Though they usually breed near houses, they sometimes form colonies at a distance in hedges, trees, or rocks, but close to agricultural land. Some migrate along the east coast and to and from the continent. Sparrows will eat almost anything, even attacking flowers to get at the sweet nectaries. Their cheeky stance and hopping action are well-known; also their chirps and *jiddicks* which the male may repeat as a song. 'Sparrows weddings', the pursuit of a single female by several males, are probably a form of courtship. Their untidy feather-lined nests are built in trees, bushes, holes or ledges on buildings, house martins' nests, and many other places. The female incubates the three to six eggs, white with grey or brown streaks, for about 2 weeks, and both parents feed the young, which fly in about 15 days. There may be three broods in a year, and breeding may occur out of season, but sparrows have the habit, unique among British birds, of occupying 'winter nests' for protection, and not for nesting.

1   2   3   4   5   6   7   8   9   10   11   12

TREE SPARROW (*Passer montanus*). Rather smaller (5½ ins. long) and much slimmer than the house sparrow, the tree sparrow can be identified by its completely chestnut crown and clean white cheeks indistinctly marked with black; both sexes and juveniles are alike.

Tree sparrows are residents, and are increasing in the east and south of England, but are local or rare in Scotland, Wales, and Ireland. They breed in old trees and buildings near arable farmland, and in winter they flock about the fields and hedges, often joining finches and buntings. Some migrate along the east coast in autumn and spring. They resemble house sparrows in general habits, but have a distinct call, much more metallic and finch-like, and a better developed chirping song. They feed chiefly on grain and seeds and do not usually come to bird tables. Tree sparrows nest in colonies or scattered groups, nearly always building in a hole where little more than a lining of feathers is needed. Both parents incubate the four to six eggs, which are smaller than house sparrows' eggs and marked with dark brown. When the young hatch in 12 to 14 days, both parents feed them until they fledge in a further 12 to 14 days. There are regularly two, sometimes three broods.

1   2   3   4   5   6   7   8   9   10   11   12

SPANISH SPARROW (*Passer hispaniolensis*). One of this southern European species, which hybridises freely with the house sparrow, was recorded on Lundy in June 1966. The male has a chestnut-red crown and much more black on the throat and elsewhere than the house sparrow, but females and juveniles cannot be told apart from house sparrows in the field.

1	CORN BUNTING	4	TREE SPARROW
3a	HOUSE SPARROW, M.	2	SCARLET GROSBEAK, F., autumn
3c	HOUSE SPARROW, F.	3b	HOUSE SPARROW, Juv.

NORTH AMERICAN PASSERINE FAMILIES

Fourteen members of families which have no Old World representatives are recognised as British birds on the strength of one or two occurrences, nearly all in recent years.

1 YELLOWTHROAT (*Geothlypis trichas*). In autumn plumage, this is a brown-backed round-tailed bird, about 5 ins. long, with a yellow throat and breast; the male has traces of his summer black mask. An immature male occurred on Lundy in autumn 1954. In America it is found mainly in damp areas with thick cover, from which it sings its simple song: *wichity wichity wichity witch.*

2 BLACK AND WHITE WARBLER (*Mniotilta varia*). One of these New World warblers was found dead in Shetland in October 1936. It was the first of this family to be recorded in Britain. It is about 5½ ins. long and looks and behaves like a black-and-white striped treecreeper (p. 133), but it builds its nest on the ground, like a European wood warbler (p. 154).

3 NORTHERN WATERTHRUSH (*Seiurus noveboracensis*). This species belongs to a group of American warblers which look like pipits or small thrushes, having brown upperparts and light underparts with broken black streaks. The northern waterthrush is about 6 ins. long and has a prominent pale buff stripe over its eye. One occurred on St. Agnes, Isles of Scilly, where it spent much of its time on the shore, in the autumn of 1958, and a second in October 1968.

4 MYRTLE WARBLER (*Dendroica coronata*). The adults of this species, about 5½ ins. long, have yellow patches on their rumps, the sides of their breasts, and their crowns. Immature birds, which are most likely to be seen in Britain, usually show these marks too, but they are brown on the head and upper back, and grey streaked with black on their wings and tails, and have pale underparts. There are three records, from Devon (1955 and 1960), and Scilly (1968).

YELLOW WARBLER (*Dendroica petechia*). One record, Bardsey, Caernarvonshire, August 1964. All plumages of this 4 in. warbler are predominantly yellow with brown stripes on the breast, but the adult male is much the brightest. Yellow spots on the dark tail are also distinctive.

BLACKPOLL WARBLER (*Dendroica striata*). Two recorded, October 1968, in Scilly and on Bardsey. The male (4½ ins.) is somewhat like a black-headed tit but with white cheeks and streaked upperparts. The female and all autumn plumages lack the black crown and are distinguished by white wing-bars and undertail coverts; the legs are buffish yellow.

PARULA WARBLER (*Parula americana*). Three autumn records, Scilly 1966, Cornwall 1967, Dorset 1968. Both sexes (3¾ ins.) have mainly blue upperparts, a double white wing-bar, and yellow throat; the juvenile is brown above with yellow throat and breast.

AMERICAN REDSTART (*Setophaga ruticilla*). Two

October records, from Cornwall (1967) and Co. Cork (1968). This is no relation to the European redstart but a 4½ ins. long North American warbler. The adult male in spring is a mixture of black and orange with white underparts, but the female and juvenile are brown above, with yellow patches on wings and tail.

5 RED-EYED VIREO (*Vireo olivaceus*). About 6½ ins. long this common vireo looks like a big, heavy, leaf warbler (p. 155) with a white stripe over its eye. But in habits vireos are more like Old World flycatchers; this one has a monotonous song which lasts through the hottest days of summer. A bird was found on the Tuskar Rock, County Wexford, Ireland, in October 1951. There are five records since.

BROWN THRASHER (*Toxostoma rufum*). A single bird, the first of this American family in Britain, lived in Dorset in winter 1966-67. Somewhat like an elongated thrush, 10 ins. long, it has rich brown upperparts, a speckled breast and a thin, slightly curved bill.

6 BOBOLINK (*Dolichonyx oryzivorus*). The summer plumage of the male (8 ins. long) is exceptional among song-birds in being black below and light-coloured above, with a very pale-brown nape to its neck, and large white wing-bars and rump patch; the end of the tail is black, and the rest of the upperparts are striped light and dark. The smaller female is 'sparrow-coloured', but with rather striking light and dark streaks over her head. The male in autumn resembles her. The only British records are of birds on St. Agnes, Isles of Scilly, September 1962, and October 1968.

7 BALTIMORE ORIOLE (*Icterus galbula*). The black and orange male of this colourful bird is about 7½ ins. long. Females are brown rather than black above and paler below, and the immature birds, the most likely to wander to Europe, resemble them and also show two white wing-bars. One appeared on Lundy in October 1958, and there was a male at Beachy Head, October 1962. There are nine records since.

SUMMER TANAGER (*Piranga rubra*). This representative of a finch-like American family has occurred once, on Bardsey, North Wales, in September 1957. It was an immature male, yellowish-orange with darker upperparts. The female resembles the immature bird, but the male in full plumage is bright scarlet all over. It is about 7½ ins. long.

8 SCARLET TANAGER (*Piranga olivacea*). The male in spring is scarlet-red with black wings and tail, about 7½ ins. long. He moults in autumn to resemble the green and yellow female and he sings his simple phrase high in a tree. The first British record, from the Copeland Islands, N. Ireland, in October 1963, was rejected but a fresh one is under consideration.

1 YELLOWTHROAT, M.
3 NORTHERN WATERTHRUSH
7 BALTIMORE ORIOLE, M. (head)
8 SCARLET TANAGER, M., summer

2 BLACK AND WHITE WARBLER, M.
4 MYRTLE WARBLER, F.
5 RED-EYED VIREO
6 BOBOLINK, M., F. (head)

SPECIAL FEATURES OF THE BIRD'S ANATOMY

Birds have travelled a long way from the reptile ancestor of 150 million years ago. The scales which cover their feet and toes are the most obvious link with the past, and feathers are supposed to have developed from scales; but no link between the two structures has yet been discovered in any fossil species. The evolution of birds has given them a shape adapted to their particular needs: to stand on their hind-limbs and to use their fore-limbs for flying. At one moment their legs are carrying their whole weight; at the next it may be transferred to their wings. The body, therefore, is shorter than that of a reptile or mammal walking on all-fours so that the centre of gravity is brought close both to legs and wings. The special demands of flight have caused the skeleton to become both much more rigid and relatively much lighter than that of an animal tied to the earth.

Many bones which are separate in other vertebrates are fused in the bird's skeleton. In the lower part of the spine the vertebrae are joined, and so are the bones of the hip-girdle which form a light but very strong plate. This rests on the thigh-bones and supports the weight of the bird when it is on the ground. Similarly, the vertebrae in the breast region are fused, and the breast-bone (sternum) which connects the ribs in front has developed into a deep, keeled plate, which both protects the lungs and provides an area to which the powerful muscles that work the wings are attached. Flightless birds, such as ostriches, do not have the keel, but penguins do, because they use their flipper-like wings so much when swimming.

Since their fore-limbs have become wings, birds are dependent on their bills to do the work of the mammal's paws. For this purpose they have long, supple necks enabling the bill to reach every part of the body. The number of neck vertebrae varies from eleven to twenty-five, whereas the mammal has seven.

The bird's head has also been modified. The eyes have developed at the expense of the organs of smell because sight is vital to an animal flying mainly by day. Birds which hunt their prey, such as owls (3), hawks, herons, and gannets, can focus both eyes in front, as humans can; birds which are hunted have eyes on opposite sides of the head to cover as large a field of vision as possible (2). Birds need a large brain to control their sensitive nervous system, and this is housed in a very light skull behind the eye-sockets (8). In front, instead of the reptile's jaws, they have a horny and very light bill. This has taken on a remarkable variety of shapes according to the feeding methods of different groups. Birds' tongues are also variable; the long tongues of some woodpeckers actually originate in bones coiled round their skulls and anchored to a nostril. Modern birds have no teeth; instead, they break up their food in the gizzard, which has powerful muscle walls. Seed-eating birds swallow grit which helps crush the husks and other hard matter.

Like reptiles and most mammals, birds stand on their toes, which number two to four, never five (5). The shank or tarsus, though it does the job of the human leg, is, in fact, the equivalent of the human foot. But some water-birds which cannot walk well, such as divers and petrels, rest on their tarsi. The bird's ankle has been simplified to give a strong single-action joint for walking, hopping, running, and flying take-offs, and the short thigh-bone (femur) is hidden in the body. The feet may either be scaled or feathered (1) and the toes end in claws, which are similar structures to human finger-nails. Like their bills, birds' feet are variously adapted to suit different habits.

The shoulder-girdle, which forms a base for the wings, is very strong, but the three bones forming it are not fused; in front is the wish-bone or furcula, probably the best-known bone in the bird's skeleton. The wing (4) fits into the shoulder-girdle at a ball-and-socket joint, and the upper arm (humerus) is short and strong because important muscles used in flight are attached to it. One of the bones of the forearm, the ulna, is the base for the secondary flight feathers, while a combination of two fingers supports the primaries. These together are the main flight feathers. In between ulna and 'hand' is the angle or carpal joint of the wing corresponding to the human wrist. The third surviving finger is the bone of the alula, which acts like an aeroplane's 'slot' in the main wing. The larger bones of the wing are hollow and connected to the lungs from which they are filled with air, as are other bones in the skeleton. But not all birds have air-filled bones in spite of their great advantage in flight.

The adaptation of the bird's body to its way of life is remarkable; the feathers which cover it are unique. They are of five types and all have quills bedded in the skin layer which nourishes them. When growth is complete, the quill is sealed off, so that the feather, though it is manipulated by muscles in the skin, is itself a 'dead' structure. The simplest feathers make up the down or under-plumage; each has a quill and a fluffy head of narrow branches called barbs, which themselves have tiny branches called barbules. The duck family has an especially thick coat of down. Herons and other birds which have no preen-glands (see below) have modified feathers called powder-down. These grow continuously, the barbs breaking off into fragments which help keep the plumage well-groomed and water-resistant.

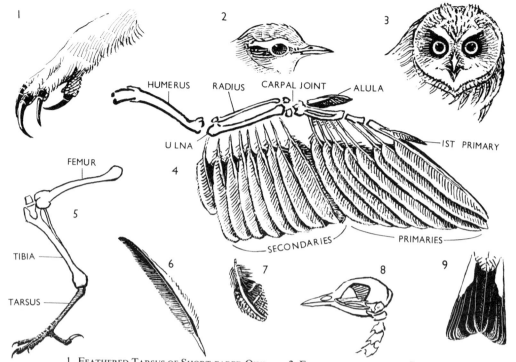

1 Feathered Tarsus of Short-eared Owl   2 Eye on side of head of Passerine
3 Eyes of Predator placed frontally   4 Under side of wing of Passerine with covert feathers removed
5 Leg bones and scaled tarsus of Passerine   6 Primary wing feather of Passerine
7 Median wing-covert feather of Game Bird   8 Skull of Passerine
9 Tail feathers (rectrices) of Passerine

Vane or contour feathers (6) are the most highly developed and give each species its characteristic appearance. A central shaft continues from the quill, and rows of barbs on either side form the two-webbed vane. The barbules of these barbs, unlike those in the down, interlock to give a smooth, uniform surface. If the web is disturbed, the bird has only to pass it through the bill for the barbules to link up again — even clumsy human fingers can achieve the same result. Contour feathers vary greatly in length and stiffness, from the remiges, or main flight feathers (4), and rectrices or tail feathers (9), to the soft feathers covering the body (7). The other types of feathers are the semi-plumes, between the contour and the down in appearance, and the curious filo-plumes which stand up like hairs from the skin of a plucked bird.

Only a few rather primitive groups grow feathers all over their bodies; all British species grow their plumage in about eight definite tracts, leaving large parts of the skin bare. Among these bare areas are the brood patches which cover the eggs and small young. Birds change their feathers usually by regular moults. Adults often change into their winter plumage after breeding, and assume their spring dress again early in the following year. Young birds may have a succession of moults, into juvenile, first winter, and immature phases; some larger birds, such as gulls and hawks, may not get full adult plumage for five years.

The number of a bird's feathers varies from under 1,000 on a humming-bird in spring to over 25,000 on a swan in winter, and may make up between 15% and 20% of its total weight. Birds have more feathers in winter than in summer; they were probably evolved as a protective cover rather than to help in flight.

Feathers get their colours either from pigment cells within or from the way light is reflected off their surface. Pigment cells are of two types, providing dark and light colours, while a blue effect, for example, is produced by reflection. Feathers full of pigment wear better than others, and that is probably why many sea-birds have black tips to their wings. Feathers may change colour by abrasion, which is the rubbing off of the ends by use; some changes from winter to spring plumage come about like this and not by a moult. Feathers also bleach, which is how the delicate pink breast tints of some gulls and terns are lost. Changes in diet, secretions from glands (hormones), and increasing age may also influence plumage colour when new feathers are growing. Most birds keep their feathers in order by preening with the bill, which is first rubbed in the preen-gland just above the tail. This helps to keep the plumage waterproof, but the presence of tiny pockets of air among the feathers is also important. Birds have no sweat glands; sweat would destroy the set of the plumage.

195

FLIGHT

Some of the features of their anatomy which make the flight of birds possible have been described on pages 194–5. In addition, birds have large hearts (the heart of a sparrow is relatively four times as big as a man's) and a most efficient breathing system which helps to cool their high-temperatured bodies. The wing action involved in a long flight is the most sustained effort by any group of voluntary muscles in any higher animal and is excelled only by the automatic action of the heart which keeps pumping blood to them. A party of terns beating slowly over the Atlantic Ocean shows not only the strength of the migratory drive but the perfect adaptation which enables a few ounces of flesh, bones, and feathers to obey it successfully.

There are two main types of flight: gliding or soaring, and flapping. Gliding is probably the earliest and the easiest form, the secret of which has to some extent even been mastered by man. First, the body must be streamlined; that is, rounded in front and narrowing more or less to a point behind; and then it must have blades or wings to support it. Although flight is possible on flat wings, it is much better if they are streamlined too, and better still if the underside is concave (curved inwards) and the upper surface convex (curved outwards). When the wing moves forward, there is greater pressure on the concave underside than on the convex upper surface and this creates a lifting force under it strong enough to overcome the drag, which is the resistance of the air to the movement of the wing. By tilting the wing upward, the lift is increased, but if tilted too far, the air flowing over it will become turbulent, and the glider, whether machine or bird, 'stalls' and begins to fall.

Many birds use gliding as a sort of free-wheeling after bursts of flapping (4). When it is used to gain height, it becomes soaring flight, of which there are again two main types. Soaring over land makes use of various up-currents of air and is the type most often seen, especially with large birds of prey (7), crows, and herons. These birds have broad wings and can separate the primary flight feathers so that each becomes a miniature wing or slot, able to adjust itself to changes in the currents. The tail plays an important part too, acting like a rudder and moving through as much as a right angle while the wings remain more or less still. Overland soaring is relatively effortless for the breast muscles, the sinews and tendons taking much of the strain.

The other type of soaring is over the sea, used by birds, especially albatrosses, with long, narrow wings. They exploit the air currents which move at different speeds over the water. They glide down from a faster to a slower current, then turn to rise against the wind, rather as a cyclist uses his momentum at the end of free-wheel downhill to take him up part of the next slope. Gulls (5), with not so highly specialised wings, can do this quite successfully for a time, but eventually have to resort to flapping to gain height.

Flapping flight, of which the starling (2) is a typical exponent, is much more complicated, and its mechanics were little understood until the development of high-speed photography. The same principles of stream-lining as in gliding govern success, but flapping demands very strong breast muscles; in some pigeons (1) these total nearly half the whole weight of the bird. These muscles make their main drive on the downward and forward beat; the upward and backward beat is like the oarsman's recovery, a split second of relaxation when the wing bends and the flight feathers let the air through. But big birds cannot afford to waste the up-beat or they would lose too much momentum, so their primaries, which are the principal driving or propelling feathers, have to do some work then as well. The secondaries are the lifting feathers, and are less important: a bird can still fly with many of them missing. Some big birds, such as game-birds, are 'sprinters' and become exhausted quite quickly. On the other hand, flapping flight is the usual method of many long-distance migrants, from the tiny warblers to the ducks, geese, and swans.

Birds inherit the ability to fly at birth; indeed, some juveniles can, if necessary, fly a distance of several miles straight from the nest. The rate of flapping varies from two or three times a second (ducks, doves) to thirty times a second (titmice); differences in rate can be used to help identification; for example, between the great and lesser black-backed gulls. There is no evidence that birds ever flap their wings alternately in flight, though they can certainly raise them independently in display or when stretching and preening.

Birds show a number of different adaptations in the shape of their wings to meet different needs and different combinations of flight. In the same order there are wrens with round wings, suitable for short flights in thick vegetation, but capable of migration as well, and narrow-pointed-winged swallows, with superb powers of manoeuvre when chasing insects in the air. Some birds glide only when coming to rest; some flap upwards then glide downwards in what is called undulating flight (3). Woodpeckers (9) actually close their wings and move in great 'bounds'. A very few, in particular kestrels (8), have the ability to hover with wings beating rapidly over a very small range; little owls and some passerines (6) can do this for short periods, and buzzards seem to hold themselves motionless against up-currents. Heavy-bodied birds have difficulty in taking

1 WOODPIGEON 2 STARLING: DIRECT FLAPPING FLIGHT
3 BULLFINCH: UNDULATING FLIGHT
4a, b FULMAR: GLIDING FLIGHT, USE OF LEGS AND TAIL
5 BLACK-HEADED GULL: TACKING IN A WIND
6a, b SPOTTED FLYCATCHER: DARTING AND MOMENTARY HOVER
7 BUZZARD: SOARING
8a, b KESTREL: HOVER AND POUNCE
9 WOODPECKER: BOUNDING FLIGHT
10 COOT: TAKING OFF FROM WATER

 off (10) and landing; all have to 'brake', that is, lose their forward momentum in some way when coming to rest. Some tilt their wings up, flapping vigorously, until they stall; some thrust head and legs forward; some run along the ground like a man jumping off a bus, or splash over the water like a sea-plane.

Since flight gives birds so many advantages, it seems surprising that five out of the twenty-seven orders of modern birds, and many individual species, especially in the rail family, are flightless. The only flightless British bird was the extinct great auk. It is now believed that the ancestors of the ostriches, the largest living birds, were able to fly millions of years ago, while penguins have exchanged flight for the ability to drive themselves through the water with their fore-limbs. It is probable that flight was evolved largely as a safety device, and birds which have lost the power of flight more recently have been able to survive because they have no natural enemies where they live. Unfortunately, the birds which gave it up could not foresee that man would arrive on their island sanctuaries with his dogs, cats, and rats, and several of them have now been exterminated.

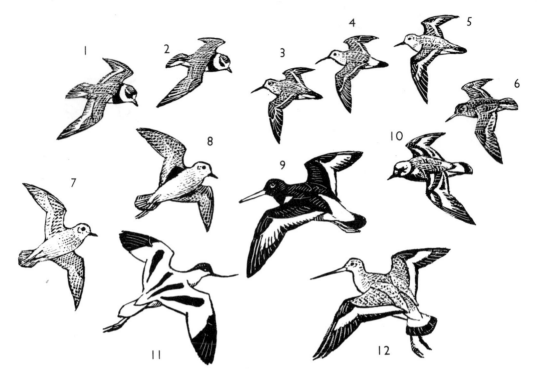

WADERS IN FLIGHT (pp. 60 - 82)

1 RINGED PLOVER   2 LITTLE RINGED PLOVER   3 DUNLIN, autumn   4 CURLEW SANDPIPER, autumn
5 SANDERLING, autumn   6 PURPLE SANDPIPER   7 GOLDEN PLOVER   8 GREY PLOVER   9 OYSTERCATCHE
10 TURNSTONE   11 AVOCET   12 BLACK-TAILED GODWIT

DABBLING DUCKS IN FLIGHT (pp. 16 - 19)

1 PINTAIL, M., F.   2 WIGEON, M., F.   3 GARGANEY, M., F.   4 TEAL, M., F.   5 GADWALL, M.,
6 MALLARD, M., F.   7 SHOVELER, M., F.

OTHER DUCKS IN FLIGHT (pp. 22 - 29)

Goldeneye, M., F.   2 Pochard, M., F.   3 Long-tailed Duck, M., F., winter   4 Tufted Duck, M., F.
Scaup, M., F.   6 Common Scoter, M., F.   7 Velvet Scoter, M., F.   8 Eider, M., F.   9 Goosander, M., F.
10 Red-breasted Merganser, M., F.   11 Smew, M., F.

BEHAVIOUR AND BREEDING

Birds spend most of their time searching for and eating food, looking after their plumage, resting, and sleeping. But this regular routine is interrupted by the need to avoid enemies and chase away rivals, and by the big annual events in their lives: breeding and migration. To meet these different situations, each species of bird shows appropriate behaviour which has been evolved over millions of years and which is instinctive, that is to say, the individual is born with the ability to respond in a certain way, just as it is born with a certain shape of bill and pattern of plumage. Instinctive behaviour enables the bird to deal with normal situations and to survive; but if something out of the usual happens, the bird does not know what to do.

A fairly simple example is that of a male song-bird which in spring establishes a territory, an area of which he is the master. Here he sings, both to warn other males of his species to keep away and to attract a mate. Normally, after a few days, a female enters his territory, and her arrival releases in the male the right behaviour with which to court her and so lead to successful breeding. But if, for some reason, no female appears, the male will continue singing for weeks and perhaps months. At best, this means that he does not breed in that season; at worst, his continual singing attracts a bird of prey and that is the end of him. It does not occur to an instinct-governed bird to go somewhere else and set up a territory where there are more females.

But birds do also show intelligence, and some families, as well as some individuals, are more clever than others. They can learn both by experience and, less often, by what is called insight. Most human learning is by experience or 'trial and error', but the great advances in knowledge are made by insight, which is the ability to size up all the factors in a situation and come to the right answer. On the whole, the more intelligent bird families are those with the less specialised bodies, beaks, and limbs. Most of the birds which have learned to live successfully close to man — the crow family, starlings, sparrows, and gulls — are 'all-rounders'. The common tits, though fairly specialised, are also intelligent and able to solve simple problems such as opening matchboxes to pick out a nut.

Instinct, however, rules the bird over most of its life, each fresh situation calling from it a response proved by the long processes of natural selection to be the right one. The study of behaviour is concerned with working out the sequences of movements employed in various activities and in trying to discover how they have been evolved from other movements, and how they are related to the movements performed by birds of the same genus or family. For example, a chaffinch preening its feathers seems at first just to be running its bill aimlessly through them; but close observation shows that certain regular motions are used in a certain order. A similar routine is followed by the chaffinch's closest relative, the brambling, but the methods used by other finches will be slightly different. Birds show their evolutionary relationships by their behaviour as well as by their anatomy.

The most remarkable forms of behaviour are the displays which have been developed to frighten or lure away enemies (6), defeat rivals (2), or court a mate. In general, displays involve repeated and exaggerated actions differing from the routine movements of feeding, preening, walking, and flying. Two great crested grebes (4) are swimming quietly on a lake; suddenly they move together, stretch their necks, extend their ruffs, and facing each other, begin to waggle their heads, with bills almost touching. Almost as quickly the display dies down, and the birds relax until something starts them off again. But what special function such ritual behaviour must be fulfilling is not always clear. For years it was thought that the robin's spreading of its red breast to threaten a rival (5) was part of its courtship—an excusable mistake because male and female robins are frequently aggressive towards each other in the early stages of their association. In fact the grebes' head-waggling may include elements both of aggression and mutual attraction.

The movements used in displays are often related to prominent parts of the birds' plumage, as in the case of the grebes' crests or ruffs, which were probably evolved with the display, since, in general, birds with better ruffs would be more successful in getting mates. But another grebe display, in which both birds pick up pieces of weed and present them to each other, seems to have its origin in the routine of nest-building. Other actions may come from feeding, preening, or even sleeping. Some of these are seen in 'displacement activities;' for example, if an enemy is near a wader's nest, to which its instinct urges it to return, it may stand some way off and put its bill under its wing as though it were going to sleep, or it may make quick pecking movement as though trying to feed.

If a male bird in spring is successful in his various displays, he will acquire both a territory and a mate, and the climax of the 'breeding cycle' approaches. One or other of the pair selects a nest-site, usually but not always inside the territory, and they begin to build, again following instinctive sequences of behaviour. Each species produces a characteristic nest which can often be identified without seeing birds or eggs.

1 HEN HARRIERS: MALE ABOUT TO 'PASS' PREY TO FEMALE
2 BLACKCOCK 'LEK'
3 PIED WAGTAIL (FOSTER PARENT) FEEDING YOUNG CUCKOO
4 GREAT CRESTED GREBES: PART OF COURTSHIP DISPLAY
5 ROBINS: LOWER BIRD THREAT POSTURING AT UPPER BIRD
6 GOLDEN PLOVER FEIGNING INJURY: 'DISTRACTION DISPLAY'
7 WOODPIGEON FEEDING YOUNG (SQUAB)

Nests and eggs vary enormously even among the 190 species which nest in Britain and details are given in the main text. The eggs are laid after a remarkable journey through the female's body. Although birds are born with two ovaries, normally only the left one develops and becomes bigger during the breeding season as a number of eggs equal to the bird's usual clutch begin to grow. As each egg is laid, the yolk of the next one leaves the ovary and enters a long tube called the oviduct, where it receives its 'white' (albumen), a membrane to surround it, a shell over that, and finally the pigments or colours. An egg's time in the 'production line' varies between one or two days. Laying a large clutch of eggs is a great effort for the hen bird; they may total more than her own weight. Females, of course, can lay without fertilisation by the male, as most domestic hens do, but wild birds usually do not begin the sequence of activities leading to egg-laying until they are paired.

Some birds begin to incubate before the clutch is complete; others only pay a brief visit to the nest to lay, generally early in the morning. The incubation period, though it may vary according to weather conditions or to incidental disturbances, is more or less fixed for each species. So is the fledging period, the time taken for the young to attain their juvenile plumage and fly. Passerine birds and many others spend this time helpless in the nest; ducklings, young waders, game-birds, and rails can run or swim as soon as they are hatched and leave the nest almost at once. The parents of helpless young use various methods to feed them: food may come from the male by way of the hen (1), it may be prepared in the parents' crop (7), or fed direct — even when the recipient is a fosterling (3).

MIGRATION, NUMBERS, AND AGE

The descriptions in the main text include a sentence on the status of each species, whether it is a resident, summer visitor, winter visitor, or passage migrant. Some birds come into all these categories, and so migration poses a complex problem for the ornithologist.

It might be said that the winter movement of a robin into the garden from the wood where it has nested is as much a migration as the flight of the arctic tern which almost spans the globe from north to south. Also, the movements of tropical birds are governed not by the seasons of the year but by periods of rain and drought. The invasions or 'irruptions' of birds like crossbills and waxwings are not true migrations, because only a few birds appear to make a return journey, unlike the coming of the swallows to breed in Britain each spring and their return to Africa in autumn.

Other animals carry out migrations; but, because of their size and powers of flight, the twice-yearly mass movement of birds has attracted most attention since man first began to record facts about nature. At first it seemed that many birds just disappeared, and it was even thought that they changed into similar-looking species (cuckoos into sparrowhawks, for example), that they flew to the moon, or, with more reason, that they went into hibernation, as some other animals do in northern countries. It had been long recognised that migration was the way that cranes, storks, and other large birds avoided the northern winter, and it gradually became understood that even the smallest summer visitors used the same method. Then, when the hibernation of birds had become a joke, it was found that at least one kind of American nightjar can, in fact, become torpid in winter like a hibernating snake. Several other species are now known to have this ability.

Once it was accepted that large-scale migration of birds did take place, several questions had to be faced. Why should birds migrate and how did the habit start? How do migrating birds find their way and at what height, speed, and for how long do they fly? The answers to the first two questions are still largely guess-work, though it is clear that migrants are obeying a powerful inherited instinct which drives them forward, and, therefore, that migration probably has great survival value. The arctic during its short summer is an ideal place to raise young, with plenty of food and long hours of daylight in which to collect it; but if the millions of ducks, waders, and others did not leave the arctic regions after breeding they would certainly die. So the object of migration is, broadly, to find the most favourable living place at each season. It need not worry us that many birds leave the north long before winter, because by natural selection those which migrated first would tend to have an advantage, and those that delayed might perish.

One view is that migration originated in the Ice Ages when birds and animals of all kinds were forced to abandon most of the north temperate zone, and that they have only been able to reoccupy it for part of the year. The fact that some British birds are both residents and summer visitors may give a clue to the way that migration originated as the northern climate gradually got worse. In a long series of cold winters the residents would be wiped out, but the species would survive because of the summer visitors.

The problem of bird navigation can be tested by experiments and observations, and good progress has been made in recent years. It seems practically certain that day-migrants steer by the sun, as human navigators do, and at least possible that night-migrants use the moon and the stars in the same way. This ability must be another inherited instinct, because parties of juveniles can migrate without adults to guide them, even though many fall by the wayside each autumn. Once they have done the journey, birds probably remember landmarks extremely accurately, which is why the same swallow returns to nest in the same shed year after year.

Some birds show remarkable homing powers. Manx shearwaters released well beyond their known range have returned safely to their breeding islands. The homing ability of racing pigeons is not really outstanding, since they are carefully trained by being released at increasing distances from their lofts, so that they can make use of known landmarks.

The use of radar screens to track migrants has shown that many small birds travel at heights up to 5,000 feet and sometimes as high as 20,000 feet; radar also shows the enormous volume of migration on favourable nights, when there is no evidence of it from the ground. A good night for migration is one with a clear sky and a following wind; a wind of 30 m.p.h. will give a small bird a ground speed of 60 to 70 m.p.h., and enable it to cover 400 or 500 miles in a few hours, far enough to carry it over the North sea, for example. Stronger winds from the west, sweeping them off course on migration, could account for the occasional small birds that cross the Atlantic from America. The process does not work the other way; no small European birds have reached the North American continent.

When migrating normally, birds move on a broad front over open country, but concentrate when the geography demands it — at mountain passes in the Alps or Pyrenees, for example, or for short sea-crossings such as the Straits of Gibraltar. These flight lines can be observed from the ground. When the weather is unfavourable, migrants land wherever they can, and that is why islands and headlands attract both rare birds, and bird watchers. Nearly all the British bird observatories shown on the map are in such spots. At them the main object is to catch birds and mark them with individually numbered rings round their legs. Ringing has provided all our information on the distances birds travel, and some idea of their routes. For example, extensive marking of pied flycatchers all over Europe shows, from recoveries of ringed birds, that the whole population tends to concentrate in its autumn migration on the Gibraltar crossing, although it would seem more natural for east European birds to make for Africa via Italy or the eastern Mediterranean.

Ringing also helps in the study of bird numbers. If sufficient individuals in a population — for example, the pink-footed geese that winter in Scotland — can be ringed, the recaptures in the next season will give some idea of the number which have survived. If the ringing programme is kept up for several years, then the probable size of the total population can be arrived at, and also an indication of whether the species is increasing or decreasing. Direct counting of the flocks is used as a check.

It is essential for the conservation of bird life to have an accurate estimate of the numbers of rare species or of those which are shot for sport; and the study of populations has great scientific interest. Why should some species increase and others decrease? What factors regulate these changes? If food supply is the final control, is it possible that birds and other animals can limit their own numbers before they exhaust it? These are some of the problems which fascinate ecologists, who are the biologists concerned with the relation of a plant or animal to its whole environment.

The survival of ringed birds also provides most of our knowledge about the age birds can attain in the wild. Their expectation of life is usually far shorter than their possible life span. A robin can live for 10 or 12 years, but the recovery of ringed birds which have

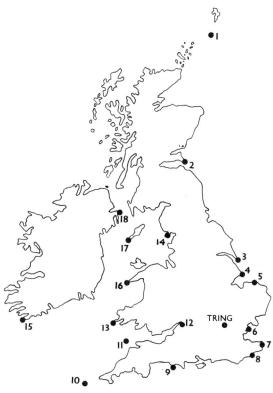

BIRD OBSERVATORIES IN THE
BRITISH ISLES, 1972

1 Fair Isle 2 Isle of May 3 Spurn Point 4 Gibraltar Point 5 Cley 6 Bradwell 7 Sandwich Bay 8 Dungeness 9 Portland 10 St. Agnes 11 Lundy 12 New Grounds, Slimbridge 13 Skokholm 14 Walney 15 Cape Clear 16 Bardsey 17 Calf of Man 18 Copeland

The office of the British Trust for Ornithology at Tring in Hertfordshire is the headquarters of the bird-ringing scheme for Great Britain and Ireland. The B.T.O. also provides a link between the observatories, which are all independent organisations; they welcome visitors who are willing to help in their work.

died suggests that, if they survive their first winter, their further expectation is about a year. Fifty-two female pied flycatchers were ringed in Gloucestershire one summer; twenty-six were recovered alive the next year, ten in the second year, five in the third, two in the fourth, and none in the fifth. This showed that the expectation of life does not change much from year to year.

Small passerine birds, living active lives among many enemies, are likely to have a poor survival rate, and expectation of life in general increases with size, except for birds which are shot by man either for sport or as pests. The longest-lived group are the sea-birds. If the dangerous first winter can be passed successfully, they have few enemies, plenty of food, and are perfectly adapted to what seems to us a cruel environment.

SUGGESTIONS FOR FURTHER READING

Field Guides

BENSON, S. V., *The Observer's Book of British Birds*. 1960. Warne.

BRUUN, BERTEL & SINGER, ARTHUR, *The Hamlyn Guide to Birds of Britain and Europe*. 1970, reprinted 1971. Hamlyn.

CAMPBELL, BRUCE & FERGUSON-LEEᶜ, JAMES, *A Field Guide to Birds' Nests*. 1972. Constable.

FITTER, R. S. R., *Collins Guide to Bird-Watching*. 2nd edition, 1970. Collins.

FITTER, R. S. R. & RICHARDSON, R. A., *Pocket Guide to British Birds* Revised 1966, reprinted 1968. Collins.

FITTER, R. S. R. & CHARTERIS, GUY, *Collins Pocket Guide to Nests and Eggs*. Revised 1968, reprinted 1969. Collins.

GOODERS, JOHN, *Where to Watch Birds*. 1967, reprinted 1968. Deutsch.

GOODERS, JOHN, *Where to Watch Birds in Britain and Europe*. 1970. Deutsch.

HEINZEL, H., FITTER, R. S. R. & PARSLOW, JOHN, *The Birds of Britain and Europe with North Africa and the Middle East*. 1972. Collins.

PETERSON, ROGER, MOUNTFORT, G. & HOLLOM, P. A. D., *A Field Guide to the Birds of Britain and Europe*. Revised 1965, reprinted 1969. Collins.

SCOTT, P., *A Coloured Key to the Wildfowl of the World*. Revised 1968. Royal Publications Ltd.

READE, WINWOOD & HOSKING, ERIC, *Nesting Birds: Eggs and Fledglings*. Revised 1968. Blandford.

General Reading and Reference

BANNERMAN, D. A., *The Birds of the British Isles*, 12 vols. 1953–1963. Oliver & Boyd.

BRITISH ORNITHOLOGISTS' UNION, *The Status of Birds in Britain and Ireland*. 1971. B.O.U.

COWARD, T. A., revised BARNES, J. A. G., *Birds of the British Isles and their Eggs*. 1969. Warne.

FISHER, JAMES & PETERSON, ROGER TORY, *The World of Birds*. 1964. Macdonald.

LACK, DAVID, *The Life of the Robin*. 4th edition. 1965. Witherby.

LACK, DAVID, *Natural Regulation of Animal Numbers*. Re-issued 1967. O.U.P.

LACK, DAVID, *Population Studies of Birds*. 1966. O.U.P.

LOCKLEY, R. M., *The Book of Bird-Watching*. 1968. Arthur Barker.

MATTHEWS, G. V. T., *Bird Navigation*. 2nd edition, 1968. C.U.P.

THOMSON, SIR A. LANDSBOROUGH, *A New Dictionary of Birds*. 1964. Nelson.

TINBERGEN, NIKO. *The Herring Gull's World*. Reprinted 1965. Collins.

TINBERGEN, NIKO & FALKUS, HUGH, *Signals for Survival*. 1970. O.U.P.

WELTY, C. J., *The Life of Birds*. 1964. Constable.

WITHERBY, H. F., JOURDAIN, F. C. R., TICEHURST, N. F. & TUCKER, B. W., *The Handbook of British Birds*, 5 vols. 1937–1941. Witherby.

YAPP, W. B., *The Life and Organisation of Birds*. 1970. Edward Arnold.

The journal *British Birds* is published monthly by H. F. & G. Witherby, Ltd., 15 Nicholas Lane, London E.C.4.

SOCIETIES

There are four national ornithological bodies, all with their own journals, reports, and other publications:

The British Ornithologists' Union, c/o Zoological Society of London, Regent's Park, London N.W.1.

The British Trust for Ornithology, Beech Grove, Tring, Hertfordshire.

The Royal Society for the Protection of Birds, The Lodge, Sandy, Bedfordshire.

The Wildfowl Trust, Slimbridge, Gloucestershire.

The last two have junior sections; the B.T.O. reduces younger member's subscriptions. There are also:

The Scottish Ornithologists' Club, 21 Regent Terrace, Edinburgh 7.

Irish Wildbird Conservancy, c/o Royal Irish Academy, 19 Dawson Street, Dublin.

INDEX

The numbers in heavy type refer to pictures